Dred Scott v. Sandford

A Brief History with Documents

SECOND EDITION

Paul Finkelman

University of Saskatchewan College of Law

bedford/st.martin's
Macmillan Learning
Boston | New York

For Bedford/St. Martin's

Vice President, Editorial, Macmillan Learning Humanities: Edwin Hill
Publisher for History: Michael Rosenberg
Senior Executive Editor for History: William J. Lombardo
Director of Development for History: Jane Knetzger
Developmental Editor: Alexandra DeConti
Marketing Manager: Melissa Famiglietti
Production Editor: Lidia MacDonald-Carr
Production Coordinator: Carolyn Quimby
Director of Rights and Permissions: Hilary Newman
Permissions Assistant: Michael McCarty
Permissions Manager: Kalina Ingham
Cover Design: William Boardman
Cover Photo: Dred Scott, ca. 1857 (oil on canvas) / © Collection of the New-York
    Historical Society, USA/Bridgeman Images.
Project Management: Books By Design, Inc.
Cartographer: Mapping Specialists, Ltd.
Composition: Achorn International, Inc.
Printing and Binding: RR Donnelley and Sons

For information, write: Bedford/St. Martin's, 75 Arlington Street, Boston, MA 02116
    (617-399-4000)

ISBN 978-1-319-04898-3

Acknowledgments

*Acknowledgments and copyrights appear on the same page as the text and art selections they
cover; these acknowledgments and copyrights constitute an extension of the copyright page.*

Foreword

The Bedford Series in History and Culture is designed so that readers can study the past as historians do.

The historian's first task is finding the evidence. Documents, letters, memoirs, interviews, pictures, movies, novels, or poems can provide facts and clues. Then the historian questions and compares the sources. There is more to do than in a courtroom, for hearsay evidence is welcome, and the historian is usually looking for answers beyond act and motive. Different views of an event may be as important as a single verdict. How a story is told may yield as much information as what it says.

Along the way the historian seeks help from other historians and perhaps from specialists in other disciplines. Finally, it is time to write, to decide on an interpretation and how to arrange the evidence for readers.

Each book in this series contains an important historical document or group of documents, each document a witness from the past and open to interpretation in different ways. The documents are combined with some element of historical narrative—an introduction or a biographical essay, for example—that provides students with an analysis of the primary source material and important background information about the world in which it was produced.

Each book in the series focuses on a specific topic within a specific historical period. Each provides a basis for lively thought and discussion about several aspects of the topic and the historian's role. Each is short enough (and inexpensive enough) to be a reasonable one-week assignment in a college course. Whether as classroom or personal reading, each book in the series provides firsthand experience of the challenge—and fun—of discovering, recreating, and interpreting the past.

Lynn Hunt
David W. Blight
Bonnie G. Smith

Preface

In 1846 Dred Scott sued for his freedom in a St. Louis court. Scott argued that for more than two years he and his wife had lived in the federal territories north of Missouri. Congress had prohibited slavery in those territories in the Compromise of 1820, also called the Missouri Compromise. Before that, Scott had lived for more than two years in Illinois, where slavery was prohibited by the state constitution. Thus, having lived in free jurisdictions, Scott argued that he became free, and once free, he was always free.

Scott had no reason to believe that his would be an extraordinary or even famous case. Courts in Missouri, Kentucky, Louisiana, and even Mississippi had freed scores of slaves who had lived in free states or free territories. In the previous quarter century, about a hundred slaves had gained their freedom in the St. Louis courts based on similar sojourns in free jurisdictions. Scott's lawyers were confident that Scott and his family would soon have their freedom. And so they did. In 1850 a court in St. Louis declared the Scotts free.

The case should have ended there. History, legal precedent, and existing public policy were on Scott's side. But by 1850 nothing about slavery and its relation to American law and politics was settled. In 1852 the Missouri Supreme Court overturned the decision freeing Dred Scott.

Once again, the case should have ended, but another twist kept it going. Although a slave with no financial resources of his own, Scott's white friends hired a new lawyer, who brought Scott's case before the U.S. Circuit Court in Missouri. In 1854 that court deferred to the Missouri Supreme Court, and Scott remained a slave.

And once again Scott's case should have ended. But by this time debates over slavery in the territories were at the center of American politics. Montgomery Blair, a Washington lawyer opposed to the spread of slavery into the territories, took the case to the U.S. Supreme Court for free.

Thus Scott's personal quest for freedom evolved into an issue of national importance. In 1854 the Kansas-Nebraska Act repealed part of the Missouri Compromise, allowing settlers in much of the Great Plains territories to decide for themselves if they wanted slavery. This program, known as *popular sovereignty,* soon led to a mini-civil war in Kansas, as northern and southern settlers battled to control the territory. Meanwhile, hostile reaction to the Kansas-Nebraska Act led to the creation of the Republican Party, which was dedicated to preventing slavery in the West.

It was in this context that the Supreme Court heard the case. In a ruling that stunned much of the nation, Chief Justice Roger B. Taney declared that the Missouri Compromise was unconstitutional, that Congress had no power to prohibit slavery in the territories or to emancipate slaves brought into those territories, and that African Americans, even if free, could never be considered citizens of the United States. In words that shocked many Americans, Taney wrote that in 1787, when the Constitution was written, blacks "had for more than a century before been regarded as beings of an inferior order, and altogether unfit to associate with the white race, either in social or political relations; and so far inferior, that they had no rights which the white man was bound to respect; and that the negro might justly and lawfully be reduced to slavery." While talking about conditions in 1787, Taney was in fact asserting his view of how the Constitution should be interpreted in 1857.

No other Supreme Court decision has had the political impact of *Dred Scott.* Most northerners found the decision shocking and immoral. Leaders of the new Republican Party attacked it with great effect, which helped Lincoln win the presidential election in 1860. That led to secession and civil war, the Emancipation Proclamation, and to what Abraham Lincoln would call "a new birth of freedom." Three by-products of that war—the Thirteenth, Fourteenth, and Fifteenth Amendments to the Constitution—reversed Taney's decision by ending slavery, making African Americans full citizens, and prohibiting racial discrimination in voting.

This book examines this momentous decision and the reaction to it. I first published this book two decades ago. Since then, there has been significant new scholarship on *Dred Scott* and on many issues and individuals related to the case. This edition takes this new scholarship into account. Part One reflects new understandings of the case and discusses recently discovered evidence about Dred Scott, his wife Harriet, his owners, his lawyers, and the history of freedom suits in Missouri. Part Two begins with an edited version of the massive official report of the *Dred Scott* case. There are excerpts from the opinions of every justice; in fact, it was the first time every justice wrote an opinion in a case. I have reduced the nearly three hundred pages of the case to a readable length and have divided them with subtitles and enhanced them with footnotes. Thus an intimidating set of opinions can now be easily read and understood. The documents also include excerpts from the Lincoln-Douglas Debates, speeches by Frederick Douglass and Charles Sumner, and a sampling of editorials supporting and opposing the result of the case. In this edition I have added President James Buchanan's inaugural address and the post–Civil War amendments, which collectively reversed the major holdings in *Dred Scott*. This new edition also contains new questions for consideration, an updated bibliography, and an expanded chronology of events related to *Dred Scott*.

ACKNOWLEDGMENTS

The first edition of this book grew out of conversations with Chuck Christensen, then the publisher at Bedford Books. I also worked with Niels Aaboe and Katherine Kurzman. For this new edition I am indebted to Senior Executive Editor William Lombardo and Developmental Editor Lexi DeConti at Bedford/St. Martin's. I would also like to thank Publisher Michael Rosenberg, Director of Development Jane Knetzger, Marketing Manager Melissa Famiglietti, Production Editor Lidia MacDonald-Carr, Cover Designer William Boardman, and Production Coordinator Nancy Benjamin of Books By Design. This is my second book with Nancy, who is the best of the best in this business. It is a delight to work with her.

Over the years many colleagues, friends, and students have read parts of this book, helped with the research, or provided important insights into the subjects discussed here. For this edition and my first edition I owe a special debt to Stanley N. Katz, who has mentored me throughout my career and who first introduced me to the problems raised by *Dred Scott*. I also thank the late John Hope Franklin, Don E. Fehrenbacher, and Walter Ehrlich as well as Peter Wallenstein, Seymour Drescher, James Oakes, David Blight, David Brion Davis, Natalie Duck, Susan Huffman, Jean Tanaka, Stephen A. Siegel, Robert Kenzer, Tim Huebner, Eric Foner, James Oakes, Lea VanderVelde, Sanford Levinson, Jack Balkin, David Thomas Konig, Christopher Alan Bracey, and Charles Ogletree.

All scholars rely on librarians, and I could not have so easily completed this edition without the help of Bob Emery at the Albany Law School Library and Greg Wurzer and Jennifer Murray at the University of Saskatchewan Law Library.

Everyone who works on *Dred Scott* is indebted to Dr. Robert Moore, the historian at the Old Court House in St. Louis, where Dred Scott first filed his suit for freedom. Dr. Moore and the staff at the Court House have combed local and national records to fill in important details about Scott's life and the case. Bob has generously shared this work with me. I finished this book while holding the Ariel F. Sallows Visiting Chair in Human Rights at the University of Saskatchewan College of Law. I thank the law school for its hospitality and for providing such a wonderful environment to consider past human rights violations, such as American slavery. Finally, once again this book is dedicated to Isaac Chaim Finkelman, who arrived as I was putting the finishing touches on the first edition of this book and who is now finishing college as the second edition comes out, and to the memory of his namesakes, his immigrant great grandfathers.

Paul Finkelman

Contents

Maps and Illustrations

PART ONE

Introduction:
The *Dred Scott* Case, Slavery,
and the Politics of Law

On April 6, 1846, Dred Scott, a slave living in St. Louis, sued in a Missouri state court to prove that he, his wife, Harriet, and their two daughters, Eliza and Lizzie, were legally free. Eleven years later, the U.S. Supreme Court, by a vote of 7–2, rejected Scott's claim. Writing for the Court, Chief Justice Roger Brooke Taney reached two major conclusions. First, he held that blacks, even if free, could never be considered citizens of the United States, and thus in this particular case Scott did not have a right to sue in the federal courts. Second, Taney held that Congress lacked the power to prohibit slavery in any federal territories, and so the Missouri Compromise, which banned slavery in the vast territories north and west of the state of Missouri, was unconstitutional. By implication this meant that the congressional ban on slavery in the Oregon Territory was also unconstitutional. This result also could have meant that it would be unconstitutional for a territorial legislature to ban slavery before statehood. This was particularly important because of the ongoing struggle in the Kansas Territory, where southern and northern settlers were battling each other over whether Kansas would become a slave state or a free state. This decision affected Dred Scott personally, of course, but because Chief Justice Taney addressed issues beyond the scope of Scott's immediate claim, the case had an enormous effect on the politics of the nation.

The story of Dred Scott is really three stories. The first is the story of a slave struggling to gain his freedom through the state courts, the U.S. Circuit Court, and eventually the U.S. Supreme Court. Scott lost that suit. In the end, he gained his freedom through other means, when the son of his former owner purchased and freed Scott and his family.

The second story is about the Supreme Court, its role in interpreting the Constitution and federal law, and the limits of its power to resolve political problems. In *Dred Scott*, Chief Justice Taney tried to settle, with one sweeping decision, the volatile problem of slavery in the territories. He also tried to relegate American blacks, even if free, to a permanent state of inferiority. Taney ultimately failed in both attempts. His decision led to a temporary diminution of the prestige and influence of the Supreme Court. More permanently, the case was a catalyst for a fundamental alteration of the Constitution through the Thirteenth, Fourteenth, and Fifteenth Amendments, forever changing the nature of American law and race relations. The Thirteenth Amendment ended slavery. The Fourteenth Amendment made all people born in the United States—including former slaves—citizens of the United States and guaranteed them equal rights under the law. And the Fifteenth Amendment prohibited discrimination in voting on the basis of race. In the aftermath of *Dred Scott* and the Civil War, the United States witnessed what Abraham Lincoln called "a new birth of freedom" for African Americans.

The third story concerns the politics of slavery and the coming of the Civil War. The Supreme Court decision sparked enormous political reaction, particularly in the North. It partially destroyed any chance of agreement between the North and the South over slavery in the territories. It would be an exaggeration to say that the *Dred Scott* decision *caused* the Civil War. But in complicated ways it certainly pushed the nation far closer to that war. The decision played a decisive role in the emergence of Abraham Lincoln as the Republican Party's presidential candidate in 1860 and his election later that year. That in turn set the stage for secession and civil war.

AN OVERVIEW OF THE *DRED SCOTT* CASE

The case began simply enough. Dred Scott wanted to be free. Unlike most slaves, however, Scott had a plausible legal claim to his freedom. For many years Scott had been the slave of Dr. John Emerson, an army surgeon who had taken him to live at Fort Armstrong in the free state of

Figure 1. *Dred and Harriet Scott*
In 1850 Dred and Harriet Scott initially won their freedom when a jury in St. Louis declared that their residence in the area that later became Minnesota had emancipated them. But the litigation dragged on for seven more years, and they ended up being the plaintiffs in the most important Supreme Court case between 1820 and 1954. They eventually gained their freedom in 1857, when Taylor Blow, the son of Scott's former owner, purchased and emancipated them.
Library of Congress Prints and Photographs Division, Washington, D.C.

Illinois and later to Fort Snelling, in what is today St. Paul, Minnesota. At that time, present-day Minnesota was part of the Wisconsin Territory. In 1846 Scott filed suit in a Missouri court to gain freedom for himself, for his wife, Harriet, and for their two children (Figure 1). Scott argued that living in those free jurisdictions had made him and his family free and that, once free, they remained free, even after returning to Missouri.[1]

In 1847, when the case went to trial, Scott lost on technical grounds. In 1848 the Missouri Supreme Court granted Scott the right to a new trial, and in January 1850 Scott and his family won their freedom in a St. Louis court, when a jury of twelve white men concluded that Scott's residence in a free state and a free territory had made him free. However, in 1852 the Missouri Supreme Court reversed this result.

In 1854 Scott turned to the federal courts and renewed his quest for freedom in the U.S. Circuit Court in Missouri. There Judge Robert W.

Wells upheld Scott's right to sue in a federal court but, after a trial, rejected his claim to freedom. Scott remained a slave. Scott then appealed to the U.S. Supreme Court. In 1857 the Court, in a 7–2 decision, held that Scott was still a slave. In his "Opinion of the Court," Chief Justice Taney declared (1) that no black person could ever be a citizen of the United States, and thus blacks could not sue in federal courts, and (2) that Congress did not have the power to prohibit slavery in the federal territories, and thus the Missouri Compromise of 1820 was unconstitutional, as were all other restrictions on slavery in the territories. These two dramatic and controversial rulings placed the decision at the center of American politics and law for the next decade and a half.

A BAD DECISION

Perhaps no legal case in American history is as famous—or as infamous—as *Dred Scott v. Sandford*.[2] Few cases were as politically divisive when they were decided; few have taken on such symbolic meaning. The case dramatically affected the politics of the immediate pre–Civil War years. During and after the war, the case continued to have an impact on American law and politics. *Dred Scott* came to symbolize the high point of racism in American law, but it also helped lead to the adoption of the Fourteenth Amendment, which became the fountainhead of racial equality in the twentieth century and remains central to much of American constitutional law today.

In the modern era, *Dred Scott* has also taken on the appearance of the ultimate "bad decision." Professor Alexander Bickel of Yale Law School called it a "ghastly error." Similarly, Charles Evans Hughes, who later became chief justice himself, argued that *Dred Scott* was one of the few "notable instances" in which "the Court has suffered severely from self-inflicted wounds."[3] This sort of analysis is not limited to legal scholars. In 2004, during a presidential debate, President George W. Bush (who was seeking reelection) was asked to identify a "bad" Supreme Court decision, and he responded by naming *Dred Scott*, although it was not clear he really understood what the case was about.[4]

Conservative jurists and legal scholars cite *Dred Scott* as the Court's most notorious decision. For example, Justice Felix Frankfurter believed that courts should "refrain . . . from avoidable constitutional pronouncements" and thought "the Court's failure in *Dred Scott v. Sandford*" was one of those "rare occasions when the Court, forgetting 'the fallibility of the human judgment,' has departed from its own practice."[5] Similarly, in

1992 Justice Antonin Scalia complained that a Supreme Court decision from which he was dissenting was no more legitimate than *Dred Scott*.[6]
More progressive jurists have also used *Dred Scott* as a symbol of mistakes made by the Court. When the Supreme Court voted 8–1 to uphold racial segregation in *Plessy v. Ferguson* (1896), Justice John Marshall Harlan, the lone dissenter, compared the Court's decision to *Dred Scott*: "In my opinion, the judgment this day rendered will, in time, prove to be quite as pernicious as the decision made by this tribunal in the *Dred Scott* case."[7] A half century later Justice Hugo Black dissented from a majority opinion, in which North Carolina was allowed to deny full faith and credit to a Nevada court decree in a divorce case. Black noted that the underlying basis for the North Carolina decision (and implicitly the Supreme Court's decision upholding that result) was "the assumption that divorces are an unmitigated evil, and that the law can and should force unwilling persons to live with each other." Black analogized this Court's attempt to solve the issue of divorce to the Taney Court's attempt to solve the problem of slavery. Thus Black wrote: "[T]oday's decision will no more aid in the solution of the problem than the *Dred Scott* decision aided in settling controversies over slavery."[8]

For more than a century, members of the Court have considered *Dred Scott* to be the ultimate bad decision, and they cite it, almost always in dissent, not for authority, but as a way of attacking those with whom they disagree on the Court.[9] For example, while serving on the same Court, both the liberal justice William Brennan and the conservative justice Antonin Scalia accused majorities of acting like the *Dred Scott* Court. While dissenting in *McCleskey v. Kemp*, a death penalty case, Brennan quoted *Dred Scott* to illustrate the way racism has long been a factor in American law. Brennan noted that the justices had only recently "sought to free ourselves from the burden of this history."[10] Similarly, in his dissent in *Planned Parenthood of Southeastern Pennsylvania v. Casey*, an abortion rights case, Justice Scalia complained that the Court's decision was not based on "reasoned judgment" but only on "personal predilection," and then he quoted Justice Benjamin R. Curtis's dissent in *Dred Scott* to support his position.[11]

More recently justices have also used *Dred Scott* when they have opposed judicial negation of state or federal laws, even when the particular justice might be sympathetic to a different outcome. Thus, in a concurring opinion upholding a state ban on assisted suicide in *Washington v. Glucksberg*, Justice David Souter dragged *Dred Scott* out of the jurisprudential closet in which it is usually kept to argue that the Court should be cautious about second-guessing a legislature:

Dred Scott was textually based on a Due Process Clause (in the Fifth Amendment, applicable to the National Government), and it was in reliance on that Clause's protection of property that the Court invalidated the Missouri Compromise. This substantive protection of an owner's property in a slave taken to the territories was traced to the absence of any enumerated power to affect that property granted to the Congress by Article I of the Constitution, the implication being that the Government had no legitimate interest that could support the earlier congressional compromise. The ensuing judgment of history needs no recounting here.[12]

Thus, for Souter, striking down the Washington State law would have been the equivalent of overturning the Missouri Compromise. This seems to be a highly exaggerated analysis. In *Dred Scott* the Court struck down a major piece of federal legislation that had regulated settlement of the western territories for more than a quarter of a century, at a time when western expansion and settlement were a central aspect of American political, economic, and social life. At issue in *Glucksberg* was a recently passed statute on a relatively minor issue that affected few people. Nevertheless, Souter used *Dred Scott* to underscore his opposition to unnecessary judicial interference with legislative enactments.

Judges who cite *Dred Scott* today often see the decision as the product of an overly ideological and reactionary judge—Chief Justice Taney—who willingly overturned settled law in order to shape public policy to his own views. The decision is further condemned as a striking example of poor scholarship and weak legal reasoning. The decision was so "bad" that even judges and legal theorists with diametrically opposed views on how to interpret the Constitution agree with this conclusion. Thus originalists argue that Taney reached an erroneous decision because he failed to follow the intent of the framers; opponents of originalism point out—correctly, I think—that this is perhaps the most originalist opinion in the Court's history.[13]

A COMPLEX AND CONFUSED CASE

Despite its reputation as a "bad" decision, *Dred Scott* is one of the most significant cases in American constitutional history. A simple description of the case as found in the official reports of the U.S. Supreme Court suggests its importance and complexity. Each of the nine justices on the Court wrote an opinion in the case, the only time before the Civil War that this occurred. The opinions range in length from Justice Robert C. Grier's half-page concurrence to Justice Benjamin R. Curtis's seventy-page dissent. Chief Justice Taney's "Opinion of the Court" is fifty-four pages long. The nine opinions, along with a handful of pages summarizing the lawyers' arguments, consume 260 pages of *United States Reports*.

In *Dred Scott*, Chief Justice Taney declared unconstitutional that part of the Missouri Compromise which prohibited slavery in all of the federal territories north and west of the state of Missouri. This was only the second time the Supreme Court had declared a federal law unconstitutional. Moreover, it was the first case in which the Supreme Court held a major federal statute to be unconstitutional. The only other antebellum decision to strike down a federal law—*Marbury v. Madison* (1803)—held unconstitutional a minor provision of the Judiciary Act of 1789.[14]

The contrast between *Marbury* and *Dred Scott* is striking. *Marbury* began as a politically motivated case designed to embarrass President Thomas Jefferson, but in the end it produced very little political fallout. The case is remembered for its long-term impact on the development of American jurisprudence. In his opinion, Chief Justice John Marshall deftly established judicial review, the power of the Supreme Court to declare acts of Congress unconstitutional. The decision is still favorably cited today, as it has been ever since 1803. Indeed, by establishing judicial review of federal laws, it is arguably the most important case in Supreme Court history.

In contrast to *Marbury*, *Dred Scott* has virtually no precedential value; actions by Congress, the executive branch, and state governments during and after the Civil War, and later Supreme Court cases, effectively reversed most of Taney's decision. Justices rarely cite the case, except as an example of a "bad" decision.[15]

But if *Dred Scott* has been more or less a jurisprudential dead end, it had an enormous constitutional and political impact. It provoked more comment—and more heated debate—than any other Supreme Court decision in the four decades before the Civil War. It became a central political issue in the 1858 congressional elections and the 1860 presidential campaign. Privately produced pamphlet editions made the justices' opinions accessible to the public. Lincoln's Emancipation Proclamation and the Thirteenth, Fourteenth, and Fifteenth Amendments to the Constitution emphatically negated Taney's three most important conclusions: Congress could not ban slavery from the territories, blacks could never be citizens of the United States, and African Americans "had no rights which the white man was bound to respect."[16]

Moreover, unlike *Marbury*, *Dred Scott* at least initially had an enormous political impact. The case meant that slavery would be legal in all existing federal territories. Had it not been for the Civil War, *Dred Scott* would have dictated federal policy on slavery in the territories until the nation was able to end slavery or amend the Constitution. In 1857 neither seemed likely. Unlike *Marbury*, virtually everyone in the United States knew of *Dred Scott*, and most Americans had opinions—strong opinions—about it.

Why did the Supreme Court spend so much energy on this case? How did the Court rationalize its decision? Why did the Court reach such a controversial result? Why is the case still synonymous with bad—even evil—decision making?[17] Why was it so important to American politics? The answers to these questions begin with a discussion of the problem of slavery in the territories.

SLAVERY IN THE TERRITORIES

In 1787 the old Congress, operating under the Articles of Confederation, passed the Northwest Ordinance. This law prohibited "slavery and involuntary servitude" in all of the American territories north and west of the Ohio River—that is, the present states of Ohio, Indiana, Illinois, Michigan, and Wisconsin and the eastern portion of Minnesota. After the Constitution went into effect in 1788, the new Congress reaffirmed the Northwest Ordinance.[18]

In 1803 the United States purchased Louisiana—a vast territory stretching from the Mississippi River to the Rocky Mountains—from France. Most of this territory was north and west of the southernmost point on the Ohio River. In 1819, when Missouri asked to be admitted to the Union, Congress heatedly debated the status of slavery in the new state. Northerners argued that because most of Missouri was north and west of the Ohio River, it should enter the Union as a free state. Southerners argued that the Northwest Ordinance did not apply to the Louisiana Purchase; it applied only to those territories owned by the United States in 1787. They also argued that because the Ohio River ended when it flowed into the Mississippi, the Ordinance could apply only to land east of the Mississippi.

After much debate in both 1819 and 1820, Congress passed the Missouri Compromise. The compromise had three parts. First, Maine (which had been part of Massachusetts) entered the Union as a free state. Second, Missouri entered the Union as a slave state. Third, slavery was "forever prohibited" in all the federal territories north and west of Missouri. Section 8 of the law declared: "That in all that territory ceded by France to the United States, under the name of Louisiana, which lies

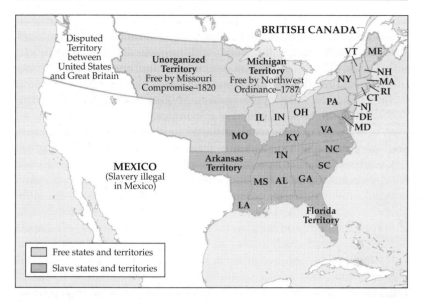

Map 1. *Free and Slave Areas in 1821*
When Congress debated the Missouri Compromise, everyone understood that Florida, like Arkansas, would eventually come into the Union as a slave state. In 1821 President Monroe appointed Andrew Jackson governor of Florida, which Spain had ceded to the United States under the Adams-Onis Treaty of 1819. On March 30, 1822, Congress created the Florida Territory, where slavery was legally permitted.

north of thirty-six degrees and thirty minutes north latitude (36°30′), not included within the limits of the state [of Missouri] . . . slavery and involuntary servitude . . . shall be, and is hereby, forever prohibited."[19] Dred Scott would later claim to be free because he lived in Illinois, which was made free by the Northwest Ordinance (and the Illinois Constitution), and in what is today Minnesota, which was made free by the Missouri Compromise (Map 1).

Many southerners were unhappy with the Missouri Compromise. Some believed it was a bad bargain, while others thought it was unconstitutional as well. Northerners, however, viewed the compromise as almost akin to the Constitution itself, as a fundamental part of the American compact. Many northerners also saw it as an almost sacred pledge to keep slavery out of most of the western territories.

For the next quarter century, the 1820 compromise helped defuse the issue of slavery in the territories. During this period only two new states, Arkansas (slave) and Michigan (free), entered the Union. The dynamics of slavery in the territories dramatically changed in 1845 and 1846, as Texas entered the Union and the United States went to war with Mexico. The likely outcome of the war—the acquisition of new territories—led northern congressmen to endorse a new prohibition on slavery in any territory acquired from Mexico. The prohibition, introduced into Congress as the Wilmot Proviso, ultimately failed. It did, however, raise sectional tensions. After the Mexican-American War, Congress seemed paralyzed by the question of slavery in the new western territories.

Congress broke through this deadlock with the Compromise of 1850, which was actually a series of separately passed laws dealing with slavery and other sectional problems. The compromise banned the public sale of slaves in the District of Columbia, which pleased the North. However, the compromise also included a new, and extremely harsh, fugitive slave law, which denied alleged slaves a jury trial or the right to testify on their own behalf while providing that the law be enforced by newly appointed federal commissioners as well as federal marshals and, if necessary, the military. The Fugitive Slave Law of 1850 pleased the South but led to significant resistance in the North. The compromise also brought California into the Union as a free state but allowed slavery in the rest of the territories acquired from Mexico, including those north of the 36°30′ line established by the Missouri Compromise (Map 2). This set the stage for six or more new slave states in the West, where slaves could have been used for mining, cattle ranching (as they had been in colonial South Carolina), and, with irrigation, growing cotton and other crops in much of the new southwest.[20]

Four years later, in 1854, Congress passed the Kansas-Nebraska Act, which repealed the slavery prohibition of the Missouri Compromise as it applied to the territories west of Missouri. Thus the ban on slavery that was originally part of the Missouri Compromise no longer applied to the territories that make up present-day Kansas, Nebraska, and all or part of the Dakotas, Montana, Colorado, and Wyoming. Congress did not actually establish slavery in these territories. Rather, it adopted the concept of popular sovereignty articulated by Senator Stephen A. Douglas of Illinois (Map 3). A Democratic presidential hopeful who would defeat Abraham Lincoln in the U.S. Senate race in 1858, Douglas believed that the settlers of a territory should decide for themselves whether to adopt slavery. Under popular sovereignty, settlers could bring their slaves into the territory. Northern opponents of popular sovereignty argued that the presence of slaves would drive out free labor. Hostility to this partial repeal of the Missouri Compromise led to the formation

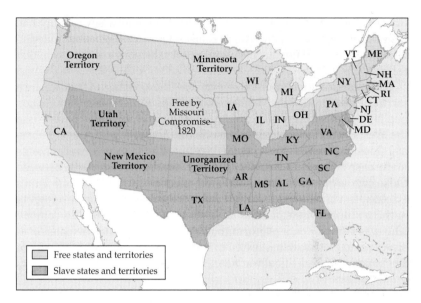

Map 2. *Free and Slave Areas in 1850*

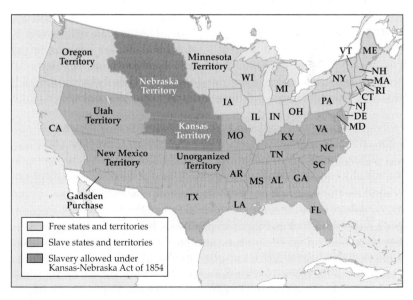

Map 3. *Free and Slave Areas in 1854*

11

of the Republican Party in the North. By 1856 popular sovereignty had degenerated into a mini-civil war in Kansas, known as "Bleeding Kansas," as southerners and northerners battled over the status of slavery in that territory.

It was in the context of these events—the opening of vast western territories to slavery, the violence of Bleeding Kansas, and the creation of a new political party dedicated to stopping the spread of slavery into the West—that the Supreme Court heard the *Dred Scott* case in February 1856. In May the Court decided it wanted to hear further arguments in the case and scheduled them for the following December. In between these two arguments the presidential election took place, and James Buchanan, running on a platform that endorsed popular sovereignty in the territories, defeated the Republican candidate, John C. Frémont, who was running on a platform that opposed any further expansion of slavery into the West. In March 1857, after the inauguration of President Buchanan, the Court finally announced its decision.

WHO WAS DRED SCOTT?

Dred Scott was born a slave in Virginia around 1800. In 1818 Scott's master, Peter Blow, moved from Southampton County, Virginia, to Alabama and then in 1830 relocated to St. Louis, Missouri. Blow took his property—Dred Scott—with him as he migrated west. Blow died in 1832, and by the late fall of 1833 Dr. John Emerson, a surgeon in the U.S. Army, had purchased Scott. From December 1, 1833, until May 4, 1836, Emerson served as the post physician at Fort Armstrong, which was located in Illinois near the modern city of Rock Island. Throughout this period Scott also lived at or near the fort.[21]

Illinois was a free state, and Scott might have claimed his freedom under its constitution. The two and a half years that Scott spent there were sufficient to emancipate him.[22] Dred Scott did not, however, claim his freedom during this period. Even if he had known of this right, it is unlikely that Scott could have found a lawyer to take his case. In the 1830s some Illinois attorneys were willing to fight for a slave's freedom even if the slave had no money to pay them, but such activist attorneys were not found in the remote area around Fort Armstrong. It is also possible that Dred Scott had no strong interest in seeking his freedom at that time, in that place. He may have found Dr. Emerson a tolerable master and felt that freedom on the Illinois frontier was not terribly advantageous. But most likely, Scott failed to assert a claim to freedom while in

Illinois because as an illiterate slave on an isolated army base he never learned that he could become free.

In 1836 the army evacuated Fort Armstrong, and Dr. Emerson, with Scott in tow, relocated to Fort Snelling, in what is today St. Paul, Minnesota. The Missouri Compromise "forever prohibited" slavery in this region. Thus, when Dr. Emerson and Dred Scott crossed the Mississippi River north of the state of Missouri, they entered territory where all slavery had been prohibited by an act of Congress.

Additionally, two weeks before Emerson and Scott departed for Fort Snelling, Congress passed the Wisconsin Enabling Act, creating the Wisconsin Territory.[23] This territory encompassed most of the present-day states of Wisconsin, Minnesota, and Iowa. The Missouri Compromise, with its ban on slavery, remained in effect, but the Wisconsin Enabling Act reinforced the ban, declaring that settlers in the territory would "enjoy" all "the rights, privileges, and advantages, granted and secured" under the Northwest Ordinance of 1787 and also "be subject to all the conditions and restrictions and prohibitions" of the ordinance. Article 6 of the Northwest Ordinance declared that "there shall be neither slavery nor involuntary servitude in the said Territory, otherwise than in the punishment of crimes, whereof the party shall have been duly convicted." The Wisconsin Enabling Act also applied all the laws of Michigan to the new territory until they were repealed or modified.[24] Michigan also prohibited slavery. Thus the Missouri Compromise, the Northwest Ordinance, and the laws of Michigan all prohibited slavery in the territory into which Dr. Emerson brought Dred Scott and kept him for a number of years.

Dr. Emerson was able to keep Dred Scott as his slave while at Fort Snelling because, apparently, no military or civilian official ever tried to enforce the federal laws prohibiting slavery. Because Scott was illiterate, he probably did not know that he had a legal claim to his freedom while at Fort Snelling. Additionally, given the relatively closed environment of an army post on a remote frontier, it is unlikely anyone was willing to aid him in gaining his freedom. Had Scott been in a free state in the East, where antislavery lawyers would have volunteered to take his case, he likely would have been declared free by a state judge.[25] But this was not the case in the Wisconsin Territory. Dred Scott remained at Fort Snelling from May 1836 until April 1838. During this period he met and married Harriet Robinson, a slave owned by Major Lawrence Taliaferro, the Indian agent stationed near Fort Snelling.[26] Taliaferro was also a justice of the peace, and in that capacity he performed a formal wedding ceremony for his slave and her new husband.

This civil marriage of the Scotts has misled some scholars in their understanding of the odyssey of Dred Scott. Throughout the slave states some masters provided ceremonies for slave marriages as a way of encouraging stability within slave families. Southern ministers persistently urged masters to let them perform weddings for slaves,[27] and many masters supported such weddings. But it is important to understand that American slaves could never be legally married, even with ceremonies performed by a minister or a judge.

Slave states never gave legal recognition to slave marriages for three important reasons. First, a legal recognition of slave marriages would have undermined the property interest of masters, perhaps limiting the right of the master to sell one of the partners. Second, a civil marriage is a contract, and no American state allowed slaves to make contracts or in any other way perform legally binding acts. Finally, recognition of slave marriages might have caused slaves to claim other rights. For example, under common law a husband or wife cannot be compelled to testify against his or her spouse in a prosecution; however, slave partners could be forced to testify against their spouses.[28]

Lawyers for Dred Scott later argued that his marriage to Harriet Robinson before a justice of the peace was proof that both Major Taliaferro and Dr. Emerson believed that both Dred and Harriet actually were free people. The fact that Taliaferro, acting in his official capacity as a justice of the peace, performed the marriage himself supports this analysis. However, after the marriage Taliaferro gave Harriet to Dr. Emerson, who continued to treat the couple as his slaves. This suggests that neither Taliaferro nor Emerson thought the Scotts were legally free. Rather, they believed, as many masters did, that a marriage ceremony was useful for the management of their slaves and helped masters gain the most value from their slaves.

No matter how we might interpret the meaning of the Scotts' marriage, the fact that the Scotts were living in a free jurisdiction with the knowledge and consent of their owners could have been used as proof that they were in fact free. But once again Dred Scott made no attempt to gain his freedom. This is further proof that at the time neither Dred nor Harriet believed they were free.

In October 1837 the army transferred Emerson to Jefferson Barracks in St. Louis. Because the trip down the Mississippi at that time of year was dangerous, Emerson left Dred and Harriet Scott at Fort Snelling, where he rented them to other people. This fact could have significantly buttressed their subsequent claims to freedom.

By leaving the Scotts at Fort Snelling and hiring them out at a profit, Emerson was in fact bringing the system of slavery itself into the Wisconsin Territory. Courts in a number of states often made a distinction between bringing a slave into a free jurisdiction and bringing slavery. The difference was simple. A master traveling from one slave state to another — say from Virginia to Missouri — might have to pass through a free state, like Illinois or Indiana. That brief transit through a free state did not bring the institution of slavery into the state and might not be seen as imposing slavery on the state. Thus, particularly in the Midwest, state judges often determined that the mere transit through a free state would not free a slave. However, all northern state supreme courts agreed that it was a violation of free-state law if a master allowed a slave to work in a free state, particularly if the master hired the slave out. The act of hiring out Dred Scott at Fort Snelling clearly brought the institution of slavery into the territory. Thus Scott had a claim to freedom that all northern state supreme courts, and a good many southern judges, would have upheld.[29]

Emerson might have claimed that he should be allowed to bring his slave into a free jurisdiction because as a military officer he had to provide his own domestic servants.[30] Or he might have claimed that while in military service in a free jurisdiction he was exempt from local laws prohibiting slavery. But once Emerson left Fort Snelling, he could surely claim no immunity from laws prohibiting slavery. Thus his hiring out of the Scotts was an unequivocal violation of the Missouri Compromise, the Northwest Ordinance, and the Wisconsin Enabling Act.

In November 1837 Dr. Emerson received new orders. The army sent him to Fort Jesup in Louisiana. There he met, courted, and quickly married Eliza Irene Sanford, who usually went by the name Irene. The ceremony took place on February 6, 1838. Emerson now wanted his slaves, and in April they joined him in Louisiana. When the Scotts arrived in Louisiana, they might have sued for their freedom in that state. For more than twenty years, Louisiana courts had upheld the freedom of slaves who had lived in free jurisdictions.[31] Had the Scotts claimed their freedom in Louisiana in 1838, it would have been an open-and-shut case. But once again they did not seek their freedom. It is likely that they simply had no knowledge that the Louisiana courts routinely freed slaves who had lived in free jurisdictions. But even if they had such knowledge, it is not clear that at this point in their lives they were ready to challenge their bondage.

The more interesting question is not why the Scotts failed to sue for their freedom but why they came to Louisiana at all. Dr. Emerson had left them in Minnesota, which was part of a free territory. They knew people there and probably could have found help if they had sued for their freedom or simply tried to escape from slavery. The trip down the

Mississippi River to Louisiana took them by numerous towns in Iowa and Illinois where they might have escaped. They could also have jumped ship in St. Louis and melted into that city's growing free black population. Instead, unaccompanied by their owner, or evidently any other person with authority over them, they traveled more than a thousand miles to reach Dr. Emerson. Given their subsequent attempts to become free after Emerson's death, we can only assume that at the time the Scotts found their bondage to be mild and their lives reasonably happy. Emerson had let them marry, had kept them together as a couple, and had apparently treated them well enough so that they did not seek their freedom from him. He may also have told them that eventually he would free them, and the Scotts perhaps not only believed him but also thought that gaining a legal manumission was worth the wait. So they journeyed to Louisiana.

Their sojourn in the Deep South was brief. Within five months the army transferred Emerson back to Fort Snelling, where he remained from October 1838 until May 1840. During this trip, on a Mississippi River steamboat north of the state of Missouri, Harriet Scott gave birth to her first child, whom she named Eliza after Dr. Emerson's bride. Thus Eliza Scott was born on a boat in the Mississippi River, surrounded on one side by the free state of Illinois and on the other side by what is today Iowa and at the time was the free territory of Wisconsin. Presumably she was born free.

In May 1840 the army ordered Dr. Emerson to Florida to serve in the Second Seminole War. On his way there he left his wife and slaves in St. Louis. In August 1842 the army discharged Emerson, and he returned to St. Louis. He later moved to Iowa, a free territory, but Dred and Harriet Scott remained in St. Louis, hired out to various people. In December 1843 the forty-year-old Emerson died suddenly. His widow, Irene, inherited his estate. For the next three years the Scotts worked as hired slaves, with the rent going to Irene Emerson. During part of this time, an army captain rented Dred Scott and took him to the new state of Texas. Scott returned to St. Louis in early February 1846 and tried to purchase freedom for himself and his family. Irene Emerson refused to sell Scott to himself, and in April 1846 Scott filed suit for his freedom and that of his wife and his daughters, Eliza and Lizzie (the latter was born in St. Louis at about the time the suit began).

Why did Dred Scott suddenly sue for his freedom? He had not made such a claim while living in free jurisdictions and had not tried to escape when his master abandoned him at Fort Snelling or when he and Harriet were traveling alone down the Mississippi River to Louisiana. If Emerson had promised Scott his freedom — or at least the right to purchase his freedom—his sudden death may have led Scott to seek another route to liberty. This theory would explain Scott's behavior during his years at Forts Armstrong and Snelling and during his unsupervised trip to Louisiana.

It is also conceivable that only in 1846 did Scott discover he had a strong legal claim to freedom. He may have learned this from sympathetic whites, including the sons of his former master, Peter Blow. Sometime after his return to St. Louis, Scott had renewed contact with the Blows, who began to provide financial aid for his litigation.

DRED SCOTT SUES FOR FREEDOM

In 1846 Dred Scott's suit seemed to be an easy one to win. As early as 1806 slaves had successfully sued for their freedom in the St. Louis County Circuit Court. In 1818 a black woman named Winny sued in that court, and after some delays she gained her freedom in 1821. In 1824, in *Winny v. Whitesides*, the Missouri Supreme Court upheld that result, freeing Winny because she had been taken to Illinois. Over the next thirteen years, the Missouri Supreme Court heard another ten cases on the issue, always deciding that slaves gained their freedom by either working in a free jurisdiction or living there long enough to be considered a resident. During this period Missouri was one of the most liberal states in the nation on this question. By the time the Scotts sued for their freedom, about a hundred other slaves had gained their freedom in Missouri through suits, usually based on residence in a free state or territory. While Missouri may have had the most suits for freedom because of its geographical location, it was not the only slave state to release people from their bondage if they had lived in a free state. Courts in Kentucky, Louisiana, and Mississippi also upheld the freedom of slaves who had lived in a free state or territory.[32]

These decisions were based on the legal theory, first articulated in the English case of *Somerset v. Stewart* (1772), that the status of a "slave" was so contrary to the common law and natural law that only the enactment of specific legislation such as an act of Parliament could create it. In *Somerset* Lord Mansfield, chief justice of the Court of King's Bench, declared:

> So high an act of dominion [as the enslavement of a human being] must be recognized by the law of the country where it is used. . . . The state of slavery is of such a nature, that it is incapable of being introduced on any reasons, moral or political; . . . it's so odious, that nothing can be suffered to support it, but positive law.[33]

Under the *Somerset* precedent, when a master took a slave into a jurisdiction that lacked laws establishing slavery, the slave reverted to his natural status as a free person. Once he gained that status, he remained free. In *The Slave, Grace* (1827), the English High Court of Admiralty modified the *Somerset* rule.[34] Grace, a West Indian slave, had been taken to England but then returned to Antigua with her master. She sued for her freedom only after returning to Antigua. Lord Stowell, speaking for the English court, held that Grace was still a slave. He asserted that residence in England only suspended the status of a slave. He agreed that without positive law—that is, a specific statute—the master could not control a slave in England and could not force a slave to leave the realm. But if a slave did return to a slave jurisdiction, as Grace had, then the law of England would no longer be in force, and the person's status would once again be determined by the laws of the slave jurisdiction.

For the most part, southern states rejected the *Slave Grace* precedent.[35] Courts in Missouri, Kentucky, and Louisiana continued to free slaves who had lived or worked in free jurisdictions. Well after *Slave Grace*, the Missouri courts continued to liberate slaves who had lived in the North. Thus Scott's lawyers no doubt expected him to win his freedom.

Initially this did not happen. In June 1847 Scott lost in the St. Louis Circuit Court because of a technicality—he was suing Irene Emerson for his freedom, but he had no witness who could prove she actually owned him. Thus the jury found for Mrs. Emerson, and the Scotts were returned to her custody. As the historian Don Fehrenbacher noted, "The decision produced the absurd effect of allowing Mrs. Emerson to keep her slaves simply because no one had proved that they *were* her slaves."[36] In December 1847 the judge ordered a new trial, but Irene Emerson's attorneys challenged this order before the Missouri Supreme Court. In June 1848 the Missouri Supreme Court sided with Dred Scott. Two continuances, a major fire, and a cholera epidemic delayed the case for more than a year and a half. Finally, in January 1850 the case went to trial. The St. Louis Circuit Court judge charged the jury that residence in free jurisdictions would destroy Scott's status as a slave, and thus if the jurors determined he had in fact lived in a free state or territory, they should find him free. The jury sided with Scott and his family. This result was consistent with Missouri precedents dating from 1824. Emerson, hoping to keep her four slaves, appealed to the Missouri Supreme Court.

In late 1849 or early 1850 Irene Emerson left Missouri for Springfield, Massachusetts. In November 1850 she married Dr. Calvin C. Chaffee, a Springfield physician with antislavery leanings, who later became a Republican congressman. Although no longer in Missouri, Irene Emerson remained the defendant in Dred Scott's freedom suit. Her brother, John F. A. Sanford, continued to act on her behalf in defending the case. (Sanford, a prosperous New York merchant with strong personal and professional ties to St. Louis, actually spelled his name with only one *d*. However, the Supreme Court reporter mistakenly spelled it *Sandford*. Hence the Supreme Court case is called *Scott v. Sandford.*)

In 1852, in *Scott v. Emerson*, the Missouri Supreme Court reversed the lower court and declared that Scott was still a slave. The decision was frankly political. The makeup of the court had recently changed as Missouri went from an appointed court to an elected one. Two of the three judges were proslavery Democrats who were adamant about supporting slavery in the state. Thus the decision in *Scott v. Emerson* was made not on the basis of legal precedent but because of popular prejudice. Judge William Scott stated:

> Times are not now as they were when the former decisions on this subject were made. Since then, not only individuals but States have been possessed with a dark and fell spirit in relation to slavery, whose gratification is sought in the pursuit of measures, whose inevitable consequence must be the overthrow and destruction of our Government. Under such circumstances, it does not behoove the State of Missouri to show the least countenance to any measure which might gratify this spirit. She is willing to assume her full responsibility for the existence of slavery within her limits, nor does she seek to share or divide it with others.[37]

Thus Judge Scott overturned twenty-eight years of Missouri precedents.

IN THE FEDERAL COURT

The decision by the Missouri Supreme Court probably came as a relief to both Emerson and Sanford. After nearly six years, the case finally seemed to be over. However, the case was only entering a new phase.

Shortly before the Missouri Supreme Court decided *Scott v. Emerson*, one of Scott's lawyers died and another left the state. In 1854, however, Scott's new lawyer, Roswell M. Field, began a new case, this time in the federal courts. Scott now sued John Sanford, who, although a citizen of New York, exerted control over the Scotts. Sanford continued to defend the case because the Scott family constituted a valuable asset. Whether Sanford actually owned Scott is not clear. But in the end that does not matter.[38] Sanford had effective custody of the Scotts, kept them in servitude, and never denied he was their owner.

In addition to the value of the slaves themselves, there was another economic reason for pursuing the case. Since early in the litigation, Scott had been in the immediate custody of the sheriff of St. Louis County. The sheriff had been renting Scott and his family out, collecting the rent, and holding the money in escrow until the case was settled. By this time a tidy sum of money had accumulated. The winner of the case—either Scott or his owner—would get this money.

By 1854, when the case reached the U.S. Circuit Court in St. Louis, Charles Edmund LaBeaume, a brother-in-law of Peter Blow's sons, was renting the Scotts. The Blows had grown up with Scott (their father was his first owner) and were deeply involved in helping him gain his freedom. LaBeaume, in fact, was instrumental in helping Scott obtain the services of Roswell Field, a Vermont-born lawyer with strong antislavery convictions. Field brought the case into federal court for one simple reason—to win Scott's freedom.[39]

Dred Scott sued John Sanford in the U.S. Circuit Court for battery and wrongful imprisonment. Scott asked for nine thousand dollars in damages. This complaint was something of a legal fiction, designed to bring the issue of Scott's freedom into the court. Scott did not expect to win any substantial monetary damages from Sanford, but rather he hoped to win a token sum (as well as all of the accumulated wages being held by the court), which would prove that he was free. Scott's suit was against John Sanford because at this point either as the owner of Scott or as the legal representative of Irene (Emerson) Chaffee, Sanford was the one holding Scott in slavery. If Scott was legitimately free, Sanford was wrongfully imprisoning him.[40]

The Jurisdictional Issue and the Plea in Abatement

Before he could evaluate Scott's claim, federal district judge Robert W. Wells first had to determine whether he had the power to hear the case. In legal terms, this is known as *jurisdiction*, which is the authority or power that allows courts and judicial officers to hear and decide cases. A court, even the Supreme Court of the United States, can hear a case only if it has jurisdiction over the issues and parties involved.

The jurisdiction of the federal courts is limited to a number of rather well-defined areas, among them suits between citizens of different states. This jurisdiction, known as *diversity jurisdiction*, is based on a clause in article III, section 2, paragraph 1, of the U.S. Constitution, which allows citizens of one state to use the federal courts to sue citizens of another state. *Diversity* refers to the different state citizenship of the plaintiff and the defendant in the suit. Dred Scott sued in diversity, claiming that he was a citizen of Missouri and that the defendant, John Sanford, was a citizen of New York.[41] Sanford responded by denying that the court had jurisdiction over the parties. Sanford did not deny that he was a citizen of New York or that Scott resided in Missouri. But he did deny that Scott was a "citizen" of Missouri. Sanford's response, in the form of a plea in abatement, effectively asked the court to stop—or "abate"—the case immediately and throw Scott's suit out of court on the grounds that the court had no jurisdiction to hear the case.

In his plea in abatement Sanford argued that "Dred Scott, is not a citizen of the State of Missouri, as alleged in his declaration, because he is a negro of African descent; his ancestors were of pure African blood, and were brought into this country and sold as negro slaves."[42] In essence, Sanford argued that no black could be a citizen of Missouri, and thus, even if Dred Scott was legally free, the federal court did not have jurisdiction to hear the case. While such an argument seems harsh and racist by modern standards, it was based on the reality that in Missouri free blacks had very few rights and faced numerous legal burdens. They were not even allowed to live in the state without a special license. Thus Sanford was on strong ground in arguing that free blacks were not "citizens" of Missouri.[43]

Nevertheless, Judge Wells rejected Sanford's plea. Wells, a slaveowner originally from Virginia, was certainly neither an advocate of black equality nor an opponent of slavery. But he did believe that free blacks, even in the South, were entitled to minimal legal rights, including the right to sue in federal court. In reaching his conclusion in Scott's case, Wells did not declare that Scott, or any free black, was entitled to full legal, social, or political equality in Missouri or anywhere else in the country. He merely held that the term *citizen* in article III of the Constitution was equivalent to a free—nonslave—full-time resident or inhabitant of a state. If Dred Scott was in fact not a slave, then he met this minimal criterion and was a "citizen," at least for the purpose of suing in federal court.

The Case in the Federal District Court

By rejecting the plea in abatement, Judge Wells forced Sanford to defend himself in court. Sanford responded that he had not unlawfully harmed Scott. Sanford did not deny that he had "gently laid his hands upon" Scott and his family. Sanford admitted that he had "restrained them of their liberty," but he asserted "he had a right to do" this because Scott was his slave.[44] In essence, Sanford admitted that he had done all the things of which Scott complained. But Sanford argued that he was entitled to treat Scott in this manner because he legally owned Scott.

In May 1854 the case went to trial, and Judge Wells told the jury that Scott's status was to be determined by Missouri law. Since the Missouri Supreme Court had already decided that Scott was a slave, the federal jury upheld his status as a slave. If Scott had previously been declared free by a court in Illinois, then the result might have been different. Judge Wells might then have held that, under the full faith and credit clause of the Constitution, Missouri was obligated to recognize the judicial proceedings that had emancipated Scott. The clause, in article IV, section 1, of the Constitution, provides: "Full Faith and Credit shall be given in each State to the public Acts, Records, and judicial Proceedings of every other State." But no such proceeding had in fact ever taken place in Illinois or even in the Wisconsin Territory. Thus Scott and his family remained slaves.

BEFORE THE SUPREME COURT

The next stop in Dred Scott's legal odyssey was the U.S. Supreme Court. An appeal would be more expensive than the Blows, by now Scott's main financial patrons, could afford. However, Montgomery Blair, a Washington lawyer well connected to Missouri politics, agreed to take the case for free. Blair was not an opponent of slavery per se and did not care particularly how slavery affected blacks. But he was a member of the free-soil wing of the Democratic Party and thus was opposed to the spread of slavery into the territories. Sanford, meanwhile, retained Missouri's pro-slavery U.S. senator, Henry S. Geyer, and, more importantly, Reverdy Johnson of Maryland, who was one of the most distinguished constitutional lawyers in the nation, a former U.S. senator and U.S. attorney general, and a close friend of Chief Justice Taney. According to historian Don Fehrenbacher, Johnson was a "veteran of many famous court battles" who "added luster to any legal cause that he undertook" and who "made opposing attorneys apprehensive."[45]

Blair sought other attorneys to assist him, but no one stepped forward. Curiously, most people in the antislavery movement failed to see the potential danger—or opportunity—that this case presented.

Antislavery lawyers and politicians had always been available to take important cases involving slavery to the Supreme Court. For example, in *United States v. The Amistad* (1841), former president John Quincy Adams argued on behalf of a shipload of Africans who had recently—and illegally—been imported from Africa to Cuba, where they seized a ship that eventually landed off the coast of Connecticut. Eventually the Supreme Court ruled in favor of the Africans on the grounds that they had never been legally held as slaves under Spanish law.[46] Similarly, Senator William H. Seward of New York argued *Jones v. Van Zandt* before the Supreme Court in 1847, and Senator Salmon P. Chase argued the less-well-known case of *Moore v. Illinois* in 1852. Both involved whites accused of helping fugitive slaves escape.[47] But the antislavery community did not appreciate the importance of Scott's appeal. Doubtless, most lawyers expected the Supreme Court to reject Dred Scott's claim to freedom but to do it on narrow grounds and to set no new precedent.[48] No one foresaw Taney's sweeping assault on the Missouri Compromise and black rights.

Dred Scott appealed to the Supreme Court in December 1854, alleging that Judge Wells had made an error in charging the jury that Scott was not entitled to his freedom. The appeal reached Washington too late for the 1854 term, so the Supreme Court held the case over for the December 1855 term and finally heard arguments in February 1856.

The briefs and the oral arguments, the presentation of which lasted four days,[49] focused on whether blacks could be citizens of the United States, on the power of Congress to prohibit slavery in the territories, and on the constitutionality of the Missouri Compromise. In May the Court postponed a decision until the following year and scheduled reargument on two crucial questions: (1) whether the plea in abatement was legitimately before the Supreme Court and (2) whether a free Negro could be a citizen of a state or of the United States and as such bring a suit in diversity in federal court.

In December 1856 the Court heard new arguments on these two issues and on the constitutionality of the Missouri Compromise. The case was now attracting increased public attention. In this round the eminent constitutional lawyer George T. Curtis, the brother of Supreme Court Justice Benjamin R. Curtis, joined Blair in arguing for Scott's freedom. George Curtis was a political conservative who opposed the antislavery movement. His presence showed that even conservatives had become concerned that the Taney Court might overturn the Missouri Compromise and thus destroy what remained of sectional harmony in the nation. What had begun in 1846 as an attempt by Scott to gain freedom for himself and his family had become a case with potentially monumental legal and political significance.

Underscoring the political potential of the case was its timing. The Court declined to render a decision in the spring of 1856, just as the presidential campaign was heating up. Republicans would later argue that the Court intentionally delayed the case to avoid giving ammunition to the Republican party in the upcoming election. In his "House Divided" speech in 1858, Abraham Lincoln would suggest that the delay was part of a deliberate conspiracy to overturn the Missouri Compromise, force slavery into the territories, and elect James Buchanan president.

Some of the justices may have wanted to avoid making a decision that would affect presidential politics. However, this is quite different from the kind of conspiracy that Republicans later charged. Such a far-flung conspiracy seems unlikely, in part because Justice John McLean—who would eventually write a stinging dissent in the case—voted for the delay. McLean was vying for the 1856 Republican presidential nomination, and had he given his dissent in May of that year, it might very well have helped him get the nomination.[50] The justices were divided on a number of aspects of the case and believed that further argument would clarify the issues. In any event, if their goal was to keep the case out of presidential politics, it ultimately backfired, as the case became a central issue in the 1860 presidential campaign.

The Justices

The Court that heard Dred Scott's case was geographically balanced. Five justices (James Wayne of Georgia, John Catron of Tennessee, Peter V. Daniel of Virginia, John A. Campbell of Alabama, and Chief Justice Roger B. Taney of Maryland) were from slave states. All five of the southern judges came from slaveholding families, but by this time Justice Wayne no longer personally owned any slaves. As a young man, Taney had freed some of his slaves but not all of them. But as historian Timothy Huebner has argued, "Taney's beliefs about slavery changed substantially over the decades" as he "changed from a moderately anti-slavery lawyer into a zealous proslavery judge."[51] The remaining four justices—John McLean of Ohio, Robert C. Grier of Pennsylvania, Samuel Nelson of New York, and Benjamin R. Curtis of Massachusetts—were northerners who had always lived in free states.

This apparent balance was deceptive, both politically and geographically. Only two of the justices—Daniel and Curtis—had been nominated by northern presidents. The rest had been nominated by southern, slave-holding presidents. Moreover, the Court was politically out of balance: It was a Democratic stronghold at a time when that party was dominated by its southern, proslavery wing. Every justice except Curtis had been nominated by a Democrat, although by 1857 McLean had rejected his Democratic roots and was openly affiliated with the new Republican Party. The other two northerners on the Court, Nelson and Grier, were Democrats generally considered to be "doughfaces"—northern men with southern principles.[52] They could be counted on to support slavery along with the five southerners on the Court.

Chief Justice Taney came from a wealthy and well-connected Maryland family that made its fortune in landholding, slaves, and tobacco planting (Figure 2). Initially a Federalist, he served in the state legislature from 1799 to 1800, but he broke with the party when it failed to support the War of 1812. In 1816 he won a five-year term in the Maryland senate. During this period he began to manumit some of his own slaves, not out of any hostility to slavery but because he apparently had no need for them. His decision to free rather than sell his slaves suggests that as a young man he may have had some qualms about dealing in human beings. But by the time he became Andrew Jackson's attorney general in 1831, Taney was a firm supporter of the right to own slaves and a staunch opponent of black rights. By the 1850s Taney was a seething, angry, uncompromising supporter of the South and slavery and an implacable foe of racial equality, the Republican Party, and the antislavery movement.

In the early 1830s, as President Andrew Jackson's attorney general, Taney had argued that blacks in the United States had no political or legal rights, except those they "enjoy[ed]" at the "sufferance" and "mercy" of whites. Foreshadowing his later *Dred Scott* opinion, Taney denied that blacks had any political or constitutional rights. He wrote that blacks, "even when free," were a "degraded class" whose "privileges" were "accorded to them as a matter of kindness and benevolence rather than right." Despite the fact that free blacks in at least six states had the right to vote at the time of the adoption of the Constitution, as attorney general, Taney argued: "They [blacks] are not looked upon as citizens by the contracting parties who formed the Constitution. They were evidently not supposed to be included by the term *citizens*."[53] Thus by 1857 Chief Justice Taney was a longtime opponent of any rights for free blacks.

The other southerners on the Court universally supported slavery. Justice Wayne was a firm supporter of slavery and federal power.

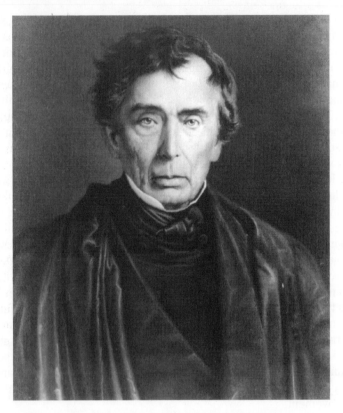

Figure 2. *Chief Justice Roger Brooke Taney (1777–1864)*
From a wealthy and prominent Maryland family, Taney married into the
equally important Key family. His brother-in-law, Francis Scott Key, wrote
"The Star-Spangled Banner." Taney was attorney general and secretary of
the treasury under President Andrew Jackson before becoming chief justice
in 1836. He served longer than any chief justice except John Marshall. Initially Taney made his mark in economic cases with decisions that favored
emerging industries. Despite freeing most of his own slaves as a young man,
Taney became almost fanatical in his defense of slavery and southern society.
His proslavery opinions in *Groves v. Slaughter* (1841), *Prigg v. Pennsylvania*
(1842), and *Strader v. Graham* (1851) offered no protection to free blacks
and favored the slave states. His *Dred Scott* opinion was consistent with his
earlier slavery jurisprudence.

Justices Campbell and Catron were more sympathetic to states' rights. Justice Daniel was almost a fanatic in his support of slavery and states' rights and in his opposition to black rights. In 1861 Campbell would leave the Court to join the Confederacy, while Catron and Wayne would remain loyal to the United States. Daniel died in 1860 but would doubtless have joined the Confederacy had he been alive.

The two northern Democrats on the Court, Justices Grier and Nelson, were certainly not secessionists. Indeed, they hoped for a moderate opinion upholding Scott's status as a slave but not dealing with either the Missouri Compromise or the status of free blacks in the nation. Scott's attorneys could expect little support from these two justices, who had consistently supported the South in Supreme Court cases dealing with slavery.[54]

In sum, this Court was unlikely to support Dred Scott's bid for freedom. Seven Democrats—five proslavery southerners and two northern doughfaces—dominated the Court. Justice Curtis, while not a Democrat, was a conservative tied by politics and family connections to the "Cotton Whigs" of Massachusetts, who usually supported southern interests. In 1836, as a young attorney, Curtis had defended the right of a master to bring a slave into Massachusetts.[55] Curtis's position on slavery was at best uncertain. In 1857, only one justice, John McLean, openly opposed slavery.

The Compromise Not Taken

While the Taney Court was unlikely to support Dred Scott's appeal, it need not have taken the extreme proslavery position that eventually emerged. The Court might have avoided any great political issues by simply reaffirming the ruling of *Strader v. Graham* (1851). In that case the Court had held that, with the exception of runaway slaves who had to be returned to their owners, every state had complete authority to decide for itself the status of all people within its borders. Thus the northern states could free visiting slaves, like Dred Scott, but the southern states had complete discretion to decide for themselves if a slave who had lived in the North had become free.[56]

The facts of *Strader* were somewhat different from those of *Dred Scott*, but nevertheless the legal precedent in *Strader* could easily have been applied to *Dred Scott*. Christopher Graham, a Kentuckian, was the owner of three slave musicians who boarded Jacob Strader's steamboat without Graham's permission and then escaped to Canada. Under Kentucky law a steamboat owner was liable for the value of any slaves who escaped under these circumstances. Strader argued that he did not owe Graham money for the three alleged slaves because they were actually free. Graham had previously allowed them to travel to Indiana and Ohio, where they worked as musicians. Strader asserted that under the laws of those states the slaves had become free and that, once free, they remained free. Strader also argued that the slaves had become free under the Northwest Ordinance. The Kentucky courts denied these claims, and in the appeal to the U.S. Supreme Court, Chief Justice Taney rejected both arguments, declaring that "every State has an undoubted right to determine the *status* or domestic condition, of the persons domiciled within its territory." Taney also argued that the Northwest Ordinance was no longer in force and thus could not free a slave. But even if it had been in force, Taney asserted that congressional legislation for a particular territory "could have no force beyond" the limits of that territory.

Strader was not perfectly analogous to *Dred Scott*. Graham's slaves had never sued for their freedom. They were already in Canada by the time Graham sued Strader. Moreover, the Kentucky court did not deny (as the Missouri court had) that slaves living in a free state became free. The Kentucky court merely asserted that a short visit to a free state would not end their bondage, and that in any event, the Court could not rule on the status of the slaves since they were not parties to the case and not even in the state. Nevertheless, the legal principle of *Strader*—that states were free to decide the status of slaves who had visited or lived in free states—would have allowed the Taney Court to settle *Dred Scott* without controversy. Most observers, in fact, expected the Court to reaffirm the principle of *Strader* that every state had the authority to determine the status of people in its jurisdiction. This may explain why the antislavery community ignored *Dred Scott* at first.

Initially the Court planned to use the *Strader* precedent to settle the case. In February 1857 Justice Samuel Nelson, a New York Democrat, began drafting an opinion that was to serve as the "Opinion of the Court." Nelson's draft, which eventually became his concurring opinion (Document 3), avoided all of the controversial aspects of the case. He asserted that Scott was not free because his status turned on Missouri law and that Missouri had already declared Scott to be a slave. Had the Court wished to avoid controversy, this was the path.

In the end the Court could not avoid controversy because the proslavery justices wanted a decision that would deal with the constitutionality of the Missouri Compromise and the rights of free blacks. In essence, by rejecting the Nelson approach, these justices sought confrontation rather than compromise.

For more than a decade, the nation had faced constant political turmoil and intense sectional tensions over the status of slavery in the territories and the Fugitive Slave Law of 1850. Even as Justice Nelson drafted his opinion, the southerners on the Court, especially Justice James Wayne of Georgia, pushed for a more comprehensive decision. They wanted Taney to write an opinion that would settle—in favor of the South—the issues of slavery in the territories and the rights of free blacks. If the Court held the Missouri Compromise unconstitutional, then all the territories would be open to slavery. If the Court declared that blacks could never be citizens of the United States, then alleged fugitive slaves and their white friends might be less able to resist the 1850 Fugitive Slave Law.

The southern majority on the Court wanted Taney to decide three questions in favor of the South:

1. Could free blacks sue in federal court as state citizens and as citizens of the United States?

2. Did Congress have the power to prohibit slavery in the territories? In other words, was the Missouri Compromise constitutional?

3. Was Missouri obligated to recognize Dred Scott's freedom based on his residence in either Illinois or the Wisconsin Territory?

The Jurisdictional Question

To reach these issues, the Supreme Court first had to deal with the jurisdictional issue, just as Judge Wells had had to do in the federal circuit court. This raised a confusing and technical question. Despite its complexity, the question went to the heart of the case and later became a major political issue after the Court handed down its decision.

If free blacks could be citizens of states, then Dred Scott had an apparent right to sue John Sanford in federal court so that he could test his freedom. However, if free blacks could not be citizens, then Dred Scott could not legally sue in a federal court, the case was not legitimately before the Supreme Court, and the Court would have to dismiss it.

Thus the following double quandary emerged. On the one hand, the southern majority wanted Taney to rule that blacks could never be citizens of the United States and could never sue in federal court as "citizens of a state." However, such a conclusion should have immediately ended the case, and then Chief Justice Taney could not rule on the constitutionality of the Missouri Compromise.

On the other hand, if Taney ruled on the constitutionality of the Missouri Compromise, he would presumably first have to acknowledge the Court's jurisdiction in the case, and that meant affirming (or at least not reversing) Judge Wells's ruling on the citizenship question—a ruling that allowed free blacks to sue in federal courts.

Some of the justices did not believe that the question of black citizenship was even before the Court. In the circuit court, John Sanford had filed the plea in abatement asking Judge Wells to immediately dismiss Dred Scott's suit on the grounds that a black could never be considered a citizen of Missouri. Judge Wells had ruled against the plea in abatement but then sided with Sanford on the question of Dred Scott's freedom. But no one appealed the ruling on the plea in abatement. When Scott appealed to the U.S. Supreme Court, he did not ask the Court to review Judge Wells's ruling that he had a right to sue, because Wells had ruled in his favor. But because Sanford won the case, he did not appeal any aspect of it. Because neither side appealed Judge Wells's ruling on the plea in abatement, some of the justices argued that the question of citizenship itself was not legitimately before the Court.

FREE BLACKS UNDER TANEY'S CONSTITUTION: "THEY HAD NO RIGHTS"

Taney thought that the question of citizenship was legitimately before the Court. He argued that the right of a black to sue in federal court was also before the Court, even though neither of the parties had raised the question. Taney believed this because every court has a right and an obligation to consider, on its own, whether it has jurisdiction to hear a case. On this point Taney was probably on firm legal ground, even though a number of his colleagues disagreed. He framed the issue to allow for a broad attack on the status of all free blacks in America:

> The question is simply this: Can a negro, whose ancestors were imported into this country, and sold as slaves, become a member of the political community formed and brought into existence by the Constitution of the United States, and as such become entitled to all the rights, and privileges, and immunities, guaranteed by that instrument to the citizen?

One of which rights is the privilege of suing in a court of the United States in the cases specified in the Constitution.[57]

Taney argued that free blacks—even those allowed to vote in the states where they lived—could never be citizens of the United States and have standing to sue in federal courts. Here Taney set up the novel concept of dual citizenship. He argued that being a citizen of a state did not necessarily make one a citizen of the United States.

Taney's argument, however, seems to be at odds with the text of the Constitution itself. Indeed, throughout the Constitution notions of national citizenship are tied to state citizenship. The right to vote for national legislators, for example, which is found in article I, section 2 of the Constitution, is based on state law and state citizenship. Article III, section 2 provides that the "Citizens of different States" can sue each other in federal courts. Article IV, section 1 requires the states to grant citizens of other states equal "Privileges and Immunities," which implies that citizenship in one state gives a person certain rights as a citizen throughout the country. Before *Dred Scott* most Americans therefore assumed that anyone who was considered a citizen of a state was also a citizen of the United States. Thus by 1857 the United States had "a long popular and judicial tradition of considering the two [state and national citizenship] as inseparable dimensions of the same status."[58]

But Taney had other ideas. He claimed:

> In discussing this question, we must not confound the rights of citizenship which a State may confer within its own limits, and the rights of citizenship as a member of the Union. It does not by any means follow, because he has all the rights and privileges of a citizen of a State, that he must be a citizen of the United States. He may have all of the rights and privileges of the citizen of a State, and yet not be entitled to the rights and privileges of a citizen in any other State.[59]

Taney based this argument entirely on race. He offered a slanted and one-sided history of the founding period that ignored the fact that free blacks had voted in six states at the time of the ratification of the Constitution. Ignoring this history, the chief justice asserted that, at the founding of the nation, blacks were either all slaves or, if free, without any political or legal rights. He declared that blacks

> are not included, and were not intended to be included, under the word "citizens" in the Constitution, and can therefore claim none of the rights and privileges which that instrument provides for and secures to citizens

Figure 3. *Justice Benjamin Robbins Curtis (1809–1874)*
Justice Curtis was a northern conservative with close ties to the cotton textile manufacturers in his home state of Massachusetts. Until the *Dred Scott* decision, he had shown no apparent hostility to slavery. Thus his opinion surprised abolitionists almost as much as it angered southerners. Chief Justice Taney was so hostile to him because of his dissent that Curtis resigned from the Court several months after the decision. Curtis's brother, also a northern conservative opponent of abolitionism, represented Dred Scott before the Supreme Court. Curtis's dissent and his brother's representation of Dred Scott underscore the radical nature of Taney's opinion. Northern conservatives, like Curtis, relied on the Missouri Compromise to maintain sectional harmony. Taney's opinion destroyed that harmony.

Library of Congress Prints and Photographs Division, Washington, D.C.

of the United States. On the contrary, they were at that time [1787] considered as a subordinate and inferior class of beings, who had been subjugated by the dominant race, and, whether emancipated or not, yet remained subject to their authority, and had no rights or privileges but such as those who held the power and the Government might choose to grant them.[60]

Blacks were "so far inferior," he continued, "that they had no rights which the white man was bound to respect."[61] Thus he concluded that blacks could never be citizens of the United States, even if they were born in the country and considered to be citizens of the states in which they lived.

This dual citizenship meant that Massachusetts, where blacks were full and equal citizens, could not force its notions of citizenship on the slave states. It also meant that southern states did not have to grant privileges and immunities, or any other rights, to the free black citizens of Massachusetts and other northern states.[62]

Having reached this conclusion, however, it seems that Taney could not then consider the constitutionality of the Missouri Compromise. If Dred Scott had no right to sue in federal court, then the Supreme Court should have dismissed the case for lack of jurisdiction. In his dissent Justice Benjamin R. Curtis argued precisely this point (Figure 3). However, the logic of the argument did not stop the determined chief justice, who went on to declare the Missouri Compromise unconstitutional.

Many Republicans would later argue that Taney's superfluous discussion of the Missouri Compromise was *dictum*—a statement that is unnecessary to the outcome of the case—and thus irrelevant and not legally binding. In 1858 Congressman Calvin C. Chaffee (who had married Irene Sanford Emerson) asserted, "The *dictum* of the Court is a very different affair from a *decision*."[63] From 1857 onward, Republicans argued that despite the *Dred Scott* decision, Congress retained the right to prohibit slavery in territories because all of Taney's discussion of the congressional power over slavery in the territories was *dictum*.

THE STATUS OF SLAVERY IN THE TERRITORIES UNDER *DRED SCOTT*

Whether it was *dictum* or not, Taney was determined to strike down the Missouri Compromise and to settle, finally and forever, and in favor of the South, the status of slavery in the territories. To do this Taney had to overcome two strong arguments in favor of congressional power over slavery in the territories. First was the clause in the Constitution that explicitly gave Congress the power to regulate the territories. Second was the political tradition, dating from the Northwest Ordinance in 1787, that Congress had such power. Taney approached this issue through an examination of two separate provisions of the Constitution: the territories clause and the Fifth Amendment.

The Territories Clause

Article IV, section 3, paragraph 2 of the Constitution provides that "Congress shall have Power to dispose of and make all needful Rules and Regulations respecting the Territory or other Property belonging to the United States." Congress had always assumed that this clause gave it the power to govern the territories. As we have seen, Congress had often exercised its power under this clause, prohibiting slavery in some territories and allowing it in others. In the Kansas-Nebraska Act (1854), Congress had even reversed course, allowing slavery in territories where it was previously prohibited. Except for the occasional voice of southern protest, no one seemed to doubt that Congress had the power to prohibit slavery in the territories. No one, that is, except Chief Justice Roger B. Taney.

To find the Missouri Compromise unconstitutional, Taney reread the territories clause in a way that few others had ever considered plausible. Taking his cue from a handful of extreme proslavery Democrats, including Senator Henry Geyer, who represented Sanford before the Supreme Court, Taney argued that the territories clause in article IV applied only to those territories the United States owned in 1787. Taney wrote that the clause was

> confined, and was intended to be confined, to the territory which at that time belonged to, or was claimed by, the United States, and was within their boundaries as settled by the treaty with Great Britain, and can have no influence upon a territory afterwards acquired from a foreign Government. It was a special provision for a known and particular territory, and to meet a present emergency, and nothing more.[64]

Taney offered no evidence, cited no judicial opinions, and quoted none of the founders to support this unpersuasive argument. Absurdly, Taney argued that the framers did not contemplate the acquisition of any new territories, and because they had none in mind, the clause could not be applied to them. He was wrong on two counts. The framers already had their eyes on acquiring New Orleans, which was then in Spanish hands. Moreover, the entire Constitution was written with expectations of a changing world. The logical extension of Taney's argument would be to prohibit congressional regulation of anything invented or discovered after 1787.[65]

Taney conceded that Congress had the power to provide a minimal government in the territories, at least at the earliest stages of settlement. He argued that this power did not come from the territories clause of the Constitution. Rather, he said, it came from the preceding paragraph in article IV, which says: "New States may be admitted by the Congress into this Union." This provision of the Constitution, Taney believed, allowed Congress to provide the initial government for a territory, but nothing beyond that. Taney claimed that allowing Congress to actually govern the territories would be equivalent to "establish[ing] or maintain[ing] colonies bordering on the United States or at a distance, to be ruled and governed at its own pleasure."[66] Taney's argument here was absurd. For example, in 1857 the United States had held some territory (which later became the eastern tip of Minnesota) for the entire period since the adoption of the Constitution, without making it a state. But Congress never treated the territory as a "colony."

The weakness of his argument did not stop Taney, who was determined, as few justices have been, to reach a specific result. Weak arguments or faulty logic would not stand in his way. His goal was to prohibit congressional regulation of slavery in the territories, and any argument, it seems, would do the trick.

Taney must have understood the inherent weakness of his arguments about the lack of congressional power to govern the territories. Even if, as Taney asserted, Congress had only minimal powers to prepare the territories for statehood, there was no reason why that minimal power could not include the right to prohibit slavery. Thus Taney turned to the Bill of Rights to plug the hole in his territories clause argument.

The Fifth Amendment

In his discussion of the Bill of Rights, Taney wanted to accomplish two goals. Most obviously he wanted to overrule the prohibition on slavery in the Missouri Compromise. Second, he wanted to make a preemptive strike against any western settlers using popular sovereignty to ban slavery in any of the territories. Taney achieved these goals with three interrelated arguments.

First he argued that Congress could not violate the Bill of Rights in the territories. This seems reasonable and persuasive. As an example, Taney asserted:

> [N]o one, we presume, will contend that Congress can make any law in a Territory respecting the establishment of religion, or the free exercise thereof, or abridging the freedom of speech or of the press, or the right of the people of the Territory peaceably to assemble, and to petition the Government for the redress of grievances.

Taney further argued that Congress could not prohibit the right to a jury trial or deny people their right against self-incrimination.[67]

Having established the obvious—that the Bill of Rights applied to the territories—Taney turned to the second part of his argument: that forbidding slavery in the territories violated the due process and just compensation clauses of the Fifth Amendment, which declares that under federal law no person can "be deprived of life, liberty, or property, without due process of law; nor shall private property be taken for public use without just compensation." Taney contended that "an act of Congress which deprives a citizen of the United States of his liberty or property, merely because he came himself or brought his property into a particular Territory of the United States, and who had committed no offence against the laws, could hardly be dignified with the name of due process of law."[68] In an analysis that scholars would later call *substantive due process*, Taney argued that no law could be constitutional if it arbitrarily denied a person his property, merely for taking that property into a federal territory.[69]

For many commentators, at the time and since, Taney's argument proved too much. No one believed that the Fifth Amendment prohibited Congress from banning dangerous, pernicious, or morally offensive forms of property from federal jurisdictions. In the nineteenth century, states banned things like liquor and lottery tickets from their jurisdictions. Congress surely had the same power in federal jurisdictions. For example, Congress, which had full lawmaking power for the District of Columbia, allowed local officials there to ban abolitionist publications, just as the southern states did. Since the Confederation period, Congress had always considered slavery to be a special sort of property that could be banned, in part because it was not normal property and could exist only if supported by positive law. The Northwest Ordinance and the Missouri Compromise both showed that slavery was a form of special property that required special laws and might be prohibited on grounds of public safety or public policy.

Taney, however, simply turned this argument inside out. He argued that slavery was indeed a special form of property, but one that deserved greater protection.

> [T]he right of property in a slave is distinctly and expressly affirmed in the Constitution. The right to traffic in it, like an ordinary article of merchandise and property, was guarantied to the citizens of the United States, in every State that might desire it, for twenty years. And the Government in express terms is pledged to protect it in all future time, if the slave escapes from his owner. This is done in plain words—too plain to be misunderstood. And no word can be found in the Constitution which gives Congress a greater power over slave property, or

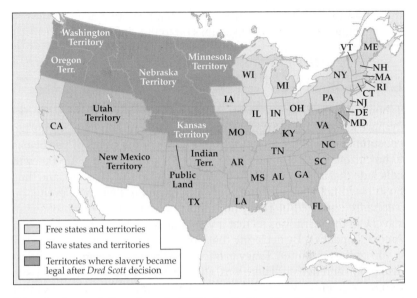

Map 4. *Free and Slave Areas in 1857 after the* Dred Scott *Decision*

which entitles property of that kind to less protection than property of any other description. The only power conferred is the power coupled with the duty of guarding and protecting the owner in his rights.[70]

With this analysis, Chief Justice Taney concluded that any prohibition on slavery in the territories violated the Fifth Amendment. Even the people of a territory could not ban slavery through the territorial legislature. Taney wrote, "And if Congress itself cannot do this—if it is beyond the powers conferred on the Federal Government—it will be admitted, we presume, that it could not authorize a Territorial Government to exercise them. It could confer no power on any local Government, established by its authority, to violate the provisions of the Constitution."[71] Like the Missouri Compromise, under Taney's interpretation of the Constitution, popular sovereignty was also unconstitutional during the territorial period. Thus under *Dred Scott* western settlers could only ban slavery after a territory became a state (Map 4). The practical application of this constitutional analysis was that southern settlers could establish slavery in any territory, while northern settlers could not establish freedom in any territory. Everyone in the nation understood it was far easier to prevent slavery from taking root in a territory before slavery than to dismantle slavery *after* statehood. Indeed, since

the ratification of the Constitution every territory that allowed slavery
had become a slave state upon admission to the Union.

LAW AS POLITICS

Taney's goals in *Dred Scott* were more political than legal. He could easily have upheld Dred Scott's slave status without commenting on the
constitutionality of the Missouri Compromise or the rights of free blacks
to be citizens of the United States. It would have been easy for Taney to
conclude that blacks, even if free, were not citizens of Missouri, and thus
Scott could not sue in federal court as a citizen of that state, even if he
were a free man.[72] But Taney hoped to resolve the festering problem of
slavery in the territories so that it would no longer be a central issue in
American politics. By declaring that Congress had no power to ban slavery from the territories, Taney in effect was trying to preempt all political
discussion and debate. There was, after all, no point in debating an issue
if Congress could not pass legislation on it. Taney seemed to expect that
when the Court ruled against congressional power over slavery in the
territories, political debate over the issue would end. Taney believed, or
at least hoped, that politicians would accept his resolution of the problem.

While this expectation seems naive, Taney had some good reasons for
believing he could accomplish this goal. Since the end of the Mexican-
American War in 1847, the nation had been bitterly divided—trauma-
tized—by the problem of slavery in the territories. During the war
almost all northern congressmen had backed the Wilmot Proviso,
which would have banned slavery in all land acquired from Mexico. The
House of Representatives, with its large northern majority, supported
the proviso, while the Senate, where the South had a temporary advantage, defeated it.[73] By 1850 the North had parity in the Senate, but in
the Compromise of 1850, Congress nevertheless allowed slavery in all
of the Mexican Cession except California, which entered the Union as
a free state. This huge territory encompassed most of the present-day
states of New Mexico, Arizona, Utah, Nevada, and Colorado, as well as
portions of other states. Finally, in 1854, in the Kansas-Nebraska Act, with
a free-state majority in both the House and the Senate, Congress repealed
the slavery prohibition of the Missouri Compromise as it applied to territories that included present-day Kansas, Nebraska, and all or part of the
Dakotas, Montana, Colorado, and Wyoming. By 1857 slavery was legal
in all but a handful of territories—those encompassing the present-day
states of Minnesota, Oregon, Washington, and Idaho. In *Dred Scott* Taney

may have seen himself as doing little more than finishing the job Congress had begun in 1850: opening all federal lands to slavery.

Taney may have also felt there was a political mandate for his decision. In the election of 1856 the new Republican Party pledged to stop the spread of slavery into the West. The new party made an excellent showing but lost the election. With hindsight we see that the 1856 election was a prelude to the Republican victory in 1860. But Taney interpreted the Democratic victory as a mandate for a continued deregulation of the territories and a national rejection of the free-soil principles of the Republicans.

A major goal of the Republican Party was to prevent the spread of slavery in the territories. From Taney's perspective the Republican Party was a dangerous, sectional organization that might push the nation toward civil war. Taney rejected the view of the Republicans—that slavery was an evil that must, in the words of Lincoln, be put "in course of ultimate extinction."[74] Taney believed it was the Republican Party that was the evil and hoped his decision would put *it* on the course of ultimate extinction.

If the nation accepted his ruling—that Congress could not prohibit slavery in the territories—then the raison d'être for the Republicans would disappear, the sectional party would die, and the nation could go back to politics as usual. Meanwhile, the settlement of the continent, which Taney, like so many other Americans, believed was part of the nation's "manifest destiny," could continue.

Many people in the country, including President-elect James Buchanan, wanted the Supreme Court to settle the issue of slavery in the territories once and for all. In his inaugural address, delivered just two days before Taney announced his opinion, Buchanan said that the issue of slavery in the territories was "a judicial question," which the Supreme Court would soon settle. Buchanan pledged to "cheerfully submit" to this decision, as he believed would "all good citizens."[75]

THE POLITICS OF LAW

Buchanan's prophecy was ill-fated. Instead, Taney's decision—and the legitimacy of that decision—became the focus of political debate in the nation. The ruling on the Missouri Compromise provided Republicans with political ammunition for the campaigns of 1858 and 1860.

Two justices, McLean and Curtis, offered extensive dissents to Taney's opinion. Curtis in particular undermined most of Taney's historical arguments, showing that blacks had voted in a number of states at the founding. He noted:

> At the time of the ratification of the Articles of Confederation, all free native-born inhabitants of the States of New Hampshire, Massachusetts, New York, New Jersey, and North Carolina, though descended from African slaves, were not only citizens of those States, but such of them as had the other necessary qualifications possessed the franchise of electors, on equal terms with other citizens.[76]

Thus, Curtis argued, they were constituent members of the nation and could not now be denied the right to claim citizenship.

Republicans around the nation embraced the dissents. Horace Greeley, the Republican editor of the New York *Tribune*, published a pamphlet edition of Taney's opinion and the Curtis dissent to help the Republican cause. Greeley's paper, the nation's leading Republican paper, responded to the decision with outrage, calling Taney's opinion "wicked," "atrocious," "abominable," and a "collation of false statements and shallow sophistries." The paper's editor thought Taney's decision had no more validity than the opinions that might be expressed in any "Washington barroom." The Chicago *Tribune* declared that Taney's statements on black citizenship were "inhuman dicta."[77]

The Republican Fear of a Conspiracy

For many Republicans, including Abraham Lincoln, the case symbolized the grave threat to the free states and to democracy itself posed by Chief Justice Taney and the Supreme Court. When nominated to run for the Senate in 1858, Lincoln spoke of a conspiracy to nationalize slavery that had been hatched by Taney, President Franklin Pierce, President James Buchanan, and Lincoln's opponent, Stephen A. Douglas. He saw the conspiracy as beginning with the Compromise of 1850, which Douglas had almost single-handedly guided through Congress; the Kansas-Nebraska Act (1854), which Douglas had sponsored; and then the *Dred Scott* decision. The final step in this process would be to open up the free states to slavery.

A conspiracy dating from the Compromise of 1850 seems a bit far-fetched, but the actions of both Taney and Buchanan gave the notion some credibility. On Inauguration Day, as Buchanan walked to the podium to take the oath of office and give his inaugural address, he stopped briefly to confer or chat with Chief Justice Taney. The crowd at the inauguration witnessed this conversation, and Americans later read about it in their newspapers. Republicans such as Senator William Seward of New York and Abraham Lincoln publicly speculated that Taney told Buchanan what the Court's decision would be. Seward claimed that the "whisperings" between Taney and Buchanan were part of a conspiracy to hang "the millstone of slavery" on the western territories.[78]

Only a few minutes after this "whispering," Buchanan, in his inaugural address, urged the nation to accept and support the forthcoming decision in *Dred Scott*. He argued that the status of slavery in the Territories was "a judicial question, which legitimately belongs to the Supreme Court of the United States, before whom it is now pending, and will, it is understood, be speedily and finally settled. To their decision, in common with all good citizens, I shall cheerfully submit."[79] Curiously, this is the only time when an American president endorsed the outcome of a Supreme Court decision *before* it was announced.

We will never know what Taney said to Buchanan, but we now know that Buchanan *already* knew what the Court was going to decide. In a major breach of Court etiquette, Justice John Catron of Tennessee and Justice Robert C. Grier, who, like Buchanan, was from Pennsylvania, had kept the president-elect fully informed about the progress of the case and the internal debates within the Court. So when Buchanan urged the nation to support the decision, he did already know what Taney would say.[80] Republican suspicions of impropriety turned out to be fully justified. There may not have been an ongoing conspiracy, but collusion abounded. The Court and the president-elect worked closely to get the decision Buchanan and Taney wanted and to urge the nation to accept it.

The Nationalization of Slavery

In 1858 Abraham Lincoln launched his bid for the U.S. Senate with an address to the Illinois Republican convention known as the "House Divided" speech, in which he warned that continued Democratic rule would soon lead to a nationalization of slavery. Lincoln told his fellow Republicans:

> We shall *lie down* pleasantly dreaming that the people of *Missouri* are on the verge of making their state *free*; and we shall *awake* to the *reality*, instead, that the *Supreme* Court has made *Illinois* a *slave* state.

Lincoln was convinced that the "logical conclusion" of *Dred Scott* was that "what Dred Scott's master might lawfully do with Dred Scott, in the free state of Illinois, every other master may lawfully do with any other *one*, or one *thousand* slaves, in Illinois, or in any other free state."[81] In an 1859 speech Lincoln warned of a future Supreme Court case—a "second *Dred Scott* decision"—that would make "slavery lawful in all the States."[82]

Such a case, *Lemmon v. The People*, was on its way through the New York courts. The Lemmons were Virginia slaveholders moving to Texas. The fastest route, although hardly the most direct, was to take a boat from Virginia to New York City and then change for a ship that was sailing directly for New Orleans. In 1852 they came to New York with their eight slaves. While they were there, a black dockworker named Louis Napoleon obtained a writ of habeas corpus, and a local judge ruled that under New York law the "eight colored Virginians," as the judge called them, became free the moment their owner brought them into the state. This decision was consistent with precedents dating from the *Somerset* case (1772). In 1857 a middle-level New York court upheld the *Lemmon* decision, but in the aftermath of *Dred Scott* the state of Virginia appealed the decision to New York's highest court, the Court of Appeals. In 1860 that court also upheld the original ruling in favor of freedom. Republicans predicted that an expected appeal to the U.S. Supreme Court would lead to the "second *Dred Scott* decision" that Lincoln feared.[83]

In 1859 Senator Salmon P. Chase of Ohio, who would become chief justice after Taney's death, predicted that if the Democrats won the presidency in 1860 there would be a new decision, allowing slavery in the North "just as after the election of Mr. Buchanan the Dred Scott case was decided in favor of the claim to carry slavery into the territories." Discussing *Lemmon*, Chase asked:

> What will the decision be? . . . It will be just as they claim, that they can take their slaves into New York over the railroads of New Jersey, through Pennsylvania and through Ohio, Indiana, Illinois . . . to any state of the North, and that they can hold them there during all the time that it is convenient for them to be passing through. In other words, it is a decision in favor, not of the African slave trade, but of the American slave trade, to be carried on in the free states.[84]

In Massachusetts the Springfield *Republican* asked, "If slavery is a national institution, recognized, protected, and carried into the territories, why does not the same authority recognize, protect, and carry it into all the several states?"[85]

Republicans focused—with fear—on the last paragraph of Justice Samuel Nelson's concurring opinion in *Dred Scott*. There Nelson declared, as if he had the *Lemmon* case in mind:

A question has been alluded to, on the argument, namely: the right of the master with his slave of transit into or through a free State, on Business or commercial pursuits, or in the exercise of a Federal right, or the discharge of a Federal duty, being a citizen of the United States, which is not before us. This question depends upon different considerations and principles from the one in hand, and turns upon the rights and privileges secured to a common citizen of the republic under the Constitution of the United States. When that question arises, we shall be prepared to decide it.[86]

Significantly Nelson was from New York and was certainly aware of the *Lemmon* case.

Had the Civil War not intervened, it is likely that the *Lemmon* case would have reached the Court and led to the "second *Dred Scott* decision" that Lincoln feared would nationalize slavery.

The Democratic Response

While northern Republicans viewed *Dred Scott* as a threat to their party and their region, Democrats, North and South, saw the decision as a valiant attempt to finally resolve the problem of slavery in the territories. They happily deferred to the Supreme Court to solve this seemingly impossible political issue. Stephen A. Douglas of Illinois, while running for reelection to the U.S. Senate in 1858, asserted, "The right and province of expounding the Constitution, and construing the law, is vested in the judiciary established by the Constitution." Unlike his opponent, Abraham Lincoln, Douglas declared that he had "no warfare to make on the Supreme Court." He was also happy to endorse the Court's holding that free blacks could never be citizens of the United States:

> I am opposed to negro equality. I repeat that this nation is a white people—a people composed of European descendants—a people that have established this government for themselves and their posterity, and I am in favor of preserving not only the purity of the blood, but the purity of the government from any mixture or amalgamation with inferior races.[87]

The New York *Journal of Commerce* declared that opponents of Taney's opinion, the Republicans, stood for "revolution and anarchy." Other northern Democratic papers took a similar position. Noting that the problem of slavery in the territories had been settled by the nation's highest court, the New York *Herald* boldly asserted: "Disobedience is rebellion, treason, and revolution."[88] Similarly, the Washington *Union* argued that "whoever now seeks to revive sectionalism arrays himself against the constitution, and consequently against the Union."[89]

Northern Democrats were relieved that, as the *Herald* put it, "the supreme law is expounded by the supreme authority," and thus the divisive issue of slavery in the territories would be gone forever. The unofficial organ of the Buchanan administration, the Washington *Union*, crowed, "The democratic party is now enjoying its greatest triumph—not merely that they have elected their candidates and secured four more years of party ascendancy in the executive branch of the government, but that their victory has been won on the most momentous issue that ever divided the public mind, and that their political triumph has been confirmed and endorsed by the highest judicial tribunal known to the Constitution." The paper declared that "the sectional question" was "settled, and that henceforth sectionalism will cease to be a dangerous element in our political contests."[90]

Southern Democrats were equally jubilant. South Carolina's Charleston *Daily Courier* cheered the Supreme Court's ruling "that the Missouri Compromise is unconstitutional . . . and that free negroes have no rights as citizens, under the Constitution of the United States." The paper's editors "confidently believe[d]" that the decision would "settle these vexed questions forever, quiet the country, and relieve it of abolition agitation, and tend greatly to perpetuate our Union—our Constitutional Union—the greatest political boon ever vouchsafed by God to man."[91]

The decision in the end did none of these things. Instead, it exacerbated sectional tensions, infuriated most northerners, helped set the stage for Lincoln's election to the presidency in 1860, and surely brought the nation closer to civil war.

EPILOGUE: PART I

In response to the *Dred Scott* decision, the black abolitionist Frederick Douglass displayed remarkable optimism. He told a New York audience: "You will readily ask me how I am affected by this devilish decision—this judicial incarnation of wolfishness! My answer is, and no thanks to the slaveholding wing of the Supreme Court, my hopes were never brighter than now." Douglass believed that the decision would raise "the National Conscience." Moreover, he saw in the decision the beginning of the great cataclysm that could destroy slavery:

> The Supreme Court of the United States is not the only power in
> this world. It is very great, but the Supreme Court of the Almighty
> is greater. Judge Taney can do many things, but he cannot perform

impossibilities. He cannot bale [*sic*] out the ocean, annihilate this firm old earth, or pluck the silvery star of liberty from our Northern sky. He may decide, and decide again; but he cannot reverse the decision of the Most High. He cannot change the essential nature of things—making evil good, and good, evil.[92]

The end of slavery came more quickly than Douglass could have imagined. On April 16, 1862, President Abraham Lincoln signed legislation ending slavery in the District of Columbia and on June 19 he signed legislation ending it in the territories. Congress and the president ignored Taney's views on the constitutional powers of the government to regulate slavery in the territories. Within six months, on January 1, 1863, Lincoln issued the Emancipation Proclamation. Secession, civil war, and Republican rule had effectively, if not actually, rewritten the Constitution. Slavery no longer had a special constitutional protection. Indeed, it now had almost no protection at all. U.S. soldiers had already ended slavery for hundreds of thousands of slaves. Before the war ended, nearly 200,000 of those blue-coated troops had black faces. Too old to serve, Frederick Douglass personally recruited more than a hundred blacks in upstate New York, including his two sons. In his newspaper Douglass "issued a stirring call, 'Men of Color, to Arms!'"[93] People who were written out of the Constitution in 1857 helped rewrite the constitutional arrangements only a few years later.

In early 1865 Congress passed, and sent on to the states, the Thirteenth Amendment, which ended slavery. A year later Congress passed the Fourteenth Amendment. Ratified in 1868, the amendment made all people born in the United States citizens of the state in which they lived as well as citizens of the nation. *Dred Scott* was now a dead letter.

Chief Justice Taney died on October 12, 1864, after the nation so emphatically rejected his judicial handiwork. Congress ended slavery in the District of Columbia and the territories, Lincoln used his power as commander-in-chief to issue the Emancipation Proclamation, and new legislation allowed the enlistment of black soldiers, including a small number of black officers. But by then he surely understood the depth of his failure in *Dred Scott*. His decision had helped put in motion forces that ended the controversy over slavery in the territories, but not in the way that he wanted.

In February 1865 the U.S. Senate debated a bill to appropriate money to honor the recently deceased Taney. The Senate bill would have provided money for a bust of the late chief justice to be placed with busts of all other deceased chief justices. This was almost a pro forma honor. No chief justice had ever been denied his place in the pantheon of American jurists, but no chief justice was like Roger B. Taney. At the time of his death in 1864, he was denounced and vilified. His opinion in *Dred Scott* was enough for antislavery senators, like Charles Sumner of Massachusetts, to oppose having Taney's bust given a place of honor in the Senate. Sumner argued, "If a man has done evil during his life he must not be complimented in marble," noting that England had never honored the hated Chief Justice Jeffries, "famous for his talents as for his crimes." Like Jeffries, the justice from Maryland had been "the tool of unjust power." Neither deserved honor. Taney had "administered his last justice wickedly, and degraded the judiciary of the country, and degraded the age." He was not to be remembered by a marble bust; rather, Taney was to be dealt with in the works of scholars. There, Sumner confidently predicted, "the name of Taney is to be hooted down the page of history."[94]

In the time since Sumner's speech, Chief Justice Taney's reputation has fluctuated. He was on the Court for nearly thirty years and wrote many important opinions. Much of his jurisprudence on economic issues is highly regarded by many scholars. But in the end, his reputation, and that of the antebellum Court, turns on *Dred Scott*.

Dred Scott did not live to see the demise of the case that bore his name or to witness the disgrace of Chief Justice Taney. Shortly after the Supreme Court decision, the son of Dred Scott's first owner, Peter Blow, purchased the Scotts and freed them. Thus the negative results of the case were in fact short-lived. Dred Scott remained a free man, and something of a celebrity, from May 26, 1857, until his death sixteen months later, on September 17, 1858.[95]

After the case ended, Scott and his family were remanded to the custody of John Sanford. On March 18, 1857, the St. Louis Circuit Court entered a final judgment in favor of Irene (Emerson) Chaffee, although it is not clear that she actually still claimed to own the Scotts. On May 5, 1857, John Sanford died in a mental hospital in New York City.

At this point it was not clear who owned the Scotts. Eight days after Sanford's death, Congressman Calvin Chaffee used a quitclaim deed to transfer ownership of the Scotts to Taylor Blow (the son of Peter Blow). A quitclaim deed does not actually prove title to the property being sold. The deed is simply a promise that the seller (in this case, Dr. and Mrs. Chaffee) abandoned any claim to the property.

Chaffee may have used a quitclaim deed because the Scotts had in fact become the property of John Sanford and were part of his estate, which had not yet been probated or distributed. Since Mrs. Chaffee was Sanford's sole heir, this was the easiest way to give up ownership of the Scotts. It also may be that, with Sanford's death, it would now be clear that the Scotts had always belonged to Mrs. Chaffee and thus her antislavery husband (who was a Republican Congressman) was, at least through marriage, a slaveowner. This was a strong incentive for Chaffee to sell the slaves to Taylor Blow, which he did, for the token sum of one dollar. The quitclaim deed was executed in Massachusetts on May 13 and then sent to St. Louis. The deed indicated that the Scotts were being transferred to Taylor Blow for the sole purpose of manumitting them. On May 26, 1857, Taylor Blow formally manumitted the Scotts.

The next day, lawyers for Chaffee obtained an order from the St. Louis County Court allowing them to receive all the accumulated wages of the Scotts since the case began in 1846. Thus, while Dr. Chaffee was happily no longer a slaveowner, he apparently had no moral or political qualms about profiting from the labor of the Scotts for the eleven years they worked while trying to obtain their liberty.

Dred and Harriet formally gained their freedom in May 1857, although it is not clear whether anyone exercised any control or dominion over them after the Supreme Court decision came down. Dred was regularly seen in the streets of St. Louis, where he had become something of a celebrity. After gaining his freedom, he remained in the city, famous but suffering from tuberculosis, from which he died on September 17, 1858. His widow, Harriet, lived for almost two more decades, dying in obscurity on June 17, 1876.[96]

EPILOGUE: PART II—REVERSING *DRED SCOTT*

By the time Chief Justice Taney died in 1864, his decision was under severe attack from Congress, the president, and the exigencies of the Civil War. In May and June 1862 Congress emancipated all the slaves in the District of Columbia, prohibited slavery in the federal territories, and emancipated all slaves living in them.[97] Congress simply ignored Taney's arguments in *Dred Scott* that slavery had special constitutional protection and that Congress had no power to ban slavery in the territories or to free any slaves in the territories. On January 1, 1863, President Lincoln issued the Emancipation Proclamation, freeing all slaves in the Confederacy. Chief Justice Taney privately fumed about these events and even began to draft an opinion declaring the Emancipation Proclamation unconstitutional. But no one challenged the proclamation or any of the other new laws dismantling slavery, and so the chief justice had no opportunity to formally respond to them.

In January 1865, shortly after Taney's death, Congress passed the Thirteenth Amendment, which ended slavery everywhere in the United

States. By December 1865 three quarters of the states had ratified this amendment, and slavery was now over. In the Civil Rights Act of 1866, passed over the veto of President Andrew Johnson, Congress declared that all former slaves, their descendants, and all other blacks born in the United States were citizens of the nation. At the same time, Congress passed the Fourteenth Amendment, which began with the words: "All persons born or naturalized in the United States, and subject to their jurisdiction, are citizens of the United States and of the state in which they reside." The language completely nullified Taney's ruling on black citizenship. The Amendment also prohibited the states from denying anyone "the privileges and immunities of citizens of the United States" or denying them "the equal protection of the laws." Two years later, in 1870, the United States ratified the Fifteenth Amendment, which prohibited discrimination in voting on the basis of "race, color, or previous condition of servitude." These amendments, along with a number of civil rights laws, meant that the damage of *Dred Scott* had been formally reversed. Blacks now had rights that were protected by the Constitution and the laws of the land.

NOTES

[1] Scott claimed freedom through his residence in Illinois and the Wisconsin Territory. Harriet's claim was based on her residence in the Wisconsin Territory. His older daughter, Eliza, was born in the Wisconsin Territory and was thus free from birth. His younger daughter, Lizzie, was born in Missouri but claimed her freedom on the ground that when she was born her mother was already a free woman.

[2] *Dred Scott v. Sandford*, 60 U.S. (19 How.) 393 (1857). Legal citations are relatively simple to read once the system is understood. After the case name (known as the *caption*), the first number is for the volume; next is a word, an abbreviation, or a name indicating the jurisdiction or the reporter (the person who edited the volume of reports in which the case appeared); the next number is the page on which the opinion begins; and the date in parentheses is the year the opinion was delivered. When the *Dred Scott* case was decided, court cases were cited by the name of the court reporter. Shortly after Reconstruction ended, the U.S. Supreme Court ceased to use the name of the reporter and began using the term *U.S.* for all Supreme Court reports. Old reports were subsequently renumbered. Thus *Dred Scott* was initially cited as 19 How. 393 (1857), indicating that it is on page 393 of the nineteenth volume of Howard's reports. The modern style is 60 U.S. 393 (1857), indicating that it is in volume 60 of *United States Reports*. Often both citations are used for older cases: Thus the full citation for *Dred Scott* is 60 U.S. (19 How.) 393 (1857). The names of the reporters are abbreviated, so Cranch becomes *Cr.*, Wheaton becomes *Wheat.*, Peters becomes *Pet.*, Howard becomes *How.*, and Wallace becomes *Wall.*

[3] Alexander M. Bickel, *The Supreme Court and the Idea of Progress* (New Haven, Conn.: Yale University Press, 1978), 41. Charles Evans Hughes, *The Supreme Court of the United States* (New York: Columbia University Press, 1928), 50. Hughes believed the two other cases to be *Hepburn v. Griswold*, 73 U.S. 603 (1870), and *Pollock v. Farmers Loan and Trust Company*, 157 U.S. 429 (1895). *Hepburn* denied the power of the United States to issue paper money. The Court reversed this decision two years later in *Knox v. Lee* and *Parker v. Davis*, 79 U.S. 457 (1872), which together are known as the *Legal Tender Cases*. *Pollock*

declared the federal income tax law to be unconstitutional. It was effectively reversed by the Sixteenth Amendment.

[4]Peter Wallsten, "Abortion Foes Call Bush's *Dred Scott* Reference Perfectly Clear," *Los Angeles Times*, October 13, 2004, http://articles.latimes.com/2004/oct/13/nation/na -dred13.

[5]*United States v. International Union United Automobile, Aircraft and Agricultural Implement Workers of America (UAW-CIO)*, 352 U.S. 567, 590–91 (1957).

[6]*Planned Parenthood of Southeastern Pennsylvania v. Casey*, 505 U.S. 833, 984 (1992). Justice Antonin Scalia quoted from Justice Curtis's dissent in *Dred Scott*.

[7]*Plessy v. Ferguson*, 163 U.S. 537, 559 (1896).

[8]*Williams v. North Carolina*, 325 U.S. 226, 274 (1945).

[9]Justice Frankfurter cited it in a majority opinion, but as a caution to courts to refrain "from avoidable constitutional pronouncements." *United States v. International Union United Automobile, Aircraft and Agricultural Implement Workers of America (UAW-CIO)*, 352 U.S. 567, 590–91.

[10]*McCleskey v. Kemp*, 481 U.S. 279, 343–44 (1987). In appealing his death penalty, McCleskey, an African American, presented overwhelming evidence that race was a major factor in death sentences and that blacks who killed whites, as McCleskey had, were 4.3 times more likely to be sentenced to death than defendants (white or black) who killed blacks. The Supreme Court rejected these statistics in upholding the death penalty. In his dissent, Justice Brennan cited *Dred Scott*.

[11]*Planned Parenthood of Southeastern Pennsylvania v. Casey*, 505 U.S. 833, 984 (1992). Opponents of reproductive choice often compare *Roe v. Wade*, 410 U.S. 113 (1973), to *Dred Scott*, claiming that both deny liberty to an oppressed group—fetuses and blacks. This is another example of using the *Dred Scott* case to discredit one's opponents.

[12]*Washington v. Glucksberg*, 521 U.S. 702, 758–59 (1997). Justice Souter is the only modern justice to cite *Dred Scott* favorably. Dissenting in *Seminole Tribe of Florida v. Florida*, 517 U.S. 44, 150–51 n. 43 (1996), he wrote: "Regardless of its other faults, Chief Justice Taney's opinion in *Dred Scott v. Sandford*, 19 How. 393 (1857), recognized as a structural matter that '[t]he new Government was not a mere change in a dynasty, or in a form of government, leaving the nation or sovereignty the same, and clothed with all the rights, and bound by all the obligations of the preceding one.'"

[13]Paul Finkelman, "The Constitution and the Intentions of the Framers: The Limits of Historical Analysis," *University of Pittsburgh Law Review* 50 (1989): 349, 390.

[14]*Marbury v. Madison*, 5 U.S. (1 Cr.) 137 (1803).

[15]The one minor exception to this is the positive use of *Dred Scott* by Justice Souter in *Seminole Tribe of Florida v. Florida*, discussed in note 12. *Dred Scott* could be used to argue that the Bill of Rights applies to U.S. military bases overseas, such as the one at Guantánamo Bay. See Paul Finkelman, "The Strange Career of *Dred Scott*: From Fort Armstrong to Guantánamo Bay," in *The Dred Scott Case: Historical and Contemporary Perspectives on Race and Law*, ed. David Thomas Konig, Paul Finkelman, and Christopher Alan Bracey (Athens: Ohio University Press, 2010), 227–51.

[16]*Dred Scott v. Sandford*, 60 U.S. (19 How.) 393, 404–5 (1857).

[17]See Mark A. Graber, *Dred Scott and the Problem of Constitutional Evil* (New York: Cambridge University Press, 2006).

[18]On the history of the slavery prohibition in the Northwest Ordinance, see Paul Finkelman, *Slavery and the Founders: Race and Liberty in the Age of Jefferson*, 3rd ed. (New York: Routledge, 2014), 46–101.

[19]An Act to Authorize the People of the Missouri Territory to Form a Constitution and State Government (March 6, 1820), *U.S. Statutes at Large* 3 (1846): 548.

[20]Paul Finkelman, "The Appeasement of 1850," in *Congress and the Crisis of the 1850's*, ed. Paul Finkelman and Don Kennon (Athens: Ohio University Press, 2012): 36–79. The compromise allowed slavery in the present-day states of New Mexico, Arizona, Utah, Nevada, Colorado, and Wyoming.

[21]Walter Ehrlich, *They Have No Rights: Dred Scott's Struggle for Freedom* (Westport, Conn.: Greenwood Press, 1979), is the best study of Scott's life; the most important and comprehensive book on the case remains Don E. Fehrenbacher, *The Dred Scott Case: Its Significance in American Law and Politics* (New York: Oxford University Press, 1978); Lea VanderVelde, *Mrs. Dred Scott: A Life on Slavery's Frontier* (New York: Oxford University Press, 2009), provides many useful details about the life of both Dred Scott and his wife, Harriet.

[22]Illinois was hostile to racial equality and allowed short-term visits by masters with slaves. But the state did not allow slavery or allow slaves to be kept there for long periods of time. Paul Finkelman, *An Imperfect Union: Slavery, Federalism, and Comity* (Chapel Hill: University of North Carolina Press, 1981), 96–98, 150–55; Finkelman, *Slavery and the Founders*, 34–79; and Stephen Middleton, ed., *The Black Laws in the Old Northwest: A Documentary History* (Westport, Conn.: Greenwood Press, 1993).

[23]An Act Establishing the Territorial Government of Wisconsin (April 20, 1836), *U.S. Statutes at Large* 5 (1856): 10. This law went into effect on July 23, 1836.

[24]Ibid., 15.

[25]In *Commonwealth v. Aves*, 18 Pick. (Mass.) 193 (1836), for example, the Massachusetts Supreme Judicial Court declared that a slave, Med, was free because her owner had brought her into Massachusetts. However, Med gained her freedom *only* because antislavery activists brought her case before the courts. For more analysis of *Aves*, see Finkelman, *An Imperfect Union*, 104–25.

[26]VanderVelde, *Mrs. Dred Scott.*

[27]See, for example, Protestant Episcopal Convention of South Carolina, *Duty of Clergymen in Relation to the Marriages of Slaves* (1859), reprinted in Paul Finkelman, *Defending Slavery: Proslavery Thought in the Old South* (Boston: Bedford Books, 2003), 114–20.

[28]Besides these legal issues, recognition of slave marriages would have undermined cultural assumptions about blacks, as well as the proslavery argument that slaves were childlike, immoral, and incapable of lasting affection and love. Most slaveowners agreed with the racist assumptions of Thomas Jefferson that "love seems with them [blacks] to be more an eager desire, than a tender mixture of sentiment and sensation. Their griefs are transient." See Thomas Jefferson, *Notes on the State of Virginia*, reprinted Merrill D. Peterson, ed., *The Portable Thomas Jefferson* (New York: Penguin, 1975), 187. Beliefs like this allowed masters to separate slave families whenever convenient without suffering any great pangs of conscience.

[29]Southern states also recognized this, in such cases as *Rankin v. Lydia*, 2 A.K. Marsh. (Ky.) 467 (1820), and *Winny v. Whitesides*, 1 Mo. 472 (1824). This issue is discussed at length in Finkelman, *An Imperfect Union.*

[30]In 1850 lawyers for Irene Emerson would make such arguments before the Missouri Supreme Court. Ehrlich, *They Have No Rights*, 56. However, the Missouri Supreme Court rejected similar arguments by a military officer in *Rachael v. Walker*, 4 Mo. 350 (1836).

[31]In *Lunsford v. Coquillon*, 2 Mart. N.S. 401 (1824), the Louisiana Supreme Court declared slaves free if they had lived in free territories, free states, or foreign countries, like France, where slavery was not legal. For a discussion of the cases in Louisiana, see Finkelman, *An Imperfect Union*, 206–16, and Judith Kelleher Schafer, *Slavery, the Civil Law, and the Supreme Court of Louisiana* (Baton Rouge: Louisiana State University Press, 1994), 250–88.

[32]*Winny v. Whitesides*, 1 Mo. 472 (1824). The material on Winny's suit and the statistics on freedom suits in St. Louis County are set out in David Thomas Konig, "The Long Road to *Dred Scott*: Personhood and Rule of Law in the Trial Court Records of St. Louis Slave Freedom Suits," *University of Missouri, Kansas City Law Review* 75 (2006): 53, 69, 71–72. The other Missouri cases are discussed in Finkelman, *An Imperfect Union*, 218–28. The last of these, *Rachael v. Walker*, led to freedom for a slave who had lived on military bases in the North and in federal territories where slavery was illegal. These facts are almost

identical to those in *Dred Scott.* See also *Rankin v. Lydia, Lunsford v. Coquillon,* and *Harry v. Decker and Hopkins,* Walker (Miss.) 36 (1818).

[33]*Somerset v. Stewart,* 1 Lofft (G.B.) 1 (1772). For a full discussion of *Somerset,* see William M. Wiecek, *"Somerset:* Lord Mansfield and the Legitimacy of Slavery in the Anglo-American World," *University of Chicago Law Review* 42 (1974): 86; William M. Wiecek, *The Sources of Antislavery Constitutionalism in America, 1760–1848* (Ithaca, N.Y.: Cornell University Press, 1978); and David Brion Davis, *The Problem of Slavery in the Age of Revolution, 1770–1823* (Ithaca, N.Y.: Cornell University Press, 1975). On the history of the application of *Somerset* in the United States, see Finkelman, *An Imperfect Union.*

[34]*The Slave, Grace,* 2 Hagg. Admir. (G.B.) 94 (1827).

[35]In the nineteenth century, American courts regularly cited English cases. English cases decided after the Revolution had value as intellectual "precedents" but were obviously not binding on American courts. A *precedent* is "an action or official decision that can be used as support for later actions or decisions." *Black's Law Dictionary,* 10th ed. (St. Paul: Thomson Reuters, 2014), 1366. Thus a case from another jurisdiction (or even another state or country) can be a precedent, even if it is not binding on a particular court. A *binding precedent* is one issued by a court that has the authority to compel another, lower court to follow its rule. Thus a decision by the U.S. Supreme Court is usually considered to be a binding precedent on all other courts in the United States. However, a decision of one state supreme court is not a binding precedent on another state supreme court.

[36]Fehrenbacher, *The Dred Scott Case,* 367.

[37]*Scott v. Emerson,* 15 Mo. 576, 586 (1852). Although in most supreme courts the jurists are called *justices,* in Missouri they were called *judges.*

[38]Walter Ehrlich, "Was the *Dred Scott* Case Valid?" *Journal of American History* 55 (1968): 256–65.

[39]See Kenneth C. Kaufman, *Dred Scott's Advocate: A Biography of Roswell M. Field* (Columbia: University of Missouri Press, 1996).

[40]Historians differ over whether Sanford actually owned the Scotts. Initially he simply took care of his sister's business interests, managing the case before and after Irene left St. Louis. Perhaps Irene Emerson sold or gave the Scotts to Sanford when she left the state. Or she may simply have let Sanford continue to manage her affairs. Sanford consistently maintained before the federal courts that he owned the Scotts, but it is possible they legally belonged to Irene all the time. Ultimately, as Don E. Fehrenbacher correctly concluded, "it makes little difference whether Sanford was acting as owner, agent, or executor when he accepted the role of defendant," in part because "the 'validity' of the case did not depend upon the source of his authority over the Scotts, but merely upon whether he had exercised such authority." Fehrenbacher, *The Dred Scott Case,* 274.

[41]Some scholars have questioned the legitimacy of Scott's suit, arguing that Sanford did not actually own Scott. These commentators have argued that Scott sued Sanford because the latter lived in New York and that this constituted the diversity of citizenship that allowed the case to come into the federal courts. However, this argument makes no sense. Had Scott not sued Sanford, he would have sued Dr. Emerson's widow, who was by this time a citizen of Massachusetts. Either way, Scott would have been able to claim diversity of state citizenship between the plaintiff (Scott) and the defendant (either Irene Emerson Chaffee or John Sanford).

[42]*Dred Scott v. Sandford,* 60 U.S. (19 How.) 393–94 (1857).

[43]For an elaboration of this position, see Paul Finkelman, "Was *Dred Scott* Correctly Decided? An 'Expert Report' for the Defendant," *Lewis & Clark Law Review* 12 (2008): 1219–52.

[44]Record of the circuit court case, quoted in Fehrenbacher, *The Dred Scott Case,* 279.

[45]Fehrenbacher, *The Dred Scott Case,* 282.

[46]*United States v. The Amistad,* 40 U.S. (15 Pet.) 518 (1841); Howard Jones, *Mutiny on the Amistad* (New York: Oxford University Press, 1987).

[47]*Jones v. Van Zandt*, 46 U.S. (5 How.) 215 (1847); *Moore v. Illinois*, 55 U.S. (14 How.) 13 (1852). Chase also argued, and won on a technicality, *Norris v. Crocker*, 54 U.S. (13 How.) 429 (1851), the only antislavery victory before the Supreme Court in the 1850s. For a discussion of this case and the surrounding events and litigation, see Paul Finkelman, "Fugitive Slaves, Midwestern Racial Tolerance, and the Value of 'Justice Delayed,'" *Iowa Law Review* 78 (1992): 89.

[48]Initially the Supreme Court headed in that direction, with a draft opinion by Justice Samuel Nelson that dodged the issues of black citizenship and the validity of the Missouri Compromise. But the Court eventually jettisoned that plan in favor of a strongly proslavery opinion by Chief Justice Taney.

[49]Today oral arguments before the Supreme Court rarely take up more than a few hours. In the nineteenth century it was not uncommon for arguments to take a day or two. The four days devoted to this case indicate how important the Court thought it was.

[50]Only in the last half of the twentieth century have Supreme Court justices been divorced from active involvement in partisan politics. Justice McLean was a viable candidate for the presidency in 1832, 1836, 1844, 1848, 1852, 1856, and 1860. Paul Finkelman, "John McLean: Moderate Abolitionist and Supreme Court Politician," *Vanderbilt Law Review* 62 (2009): 519–65. Chief Justice Salmon P. Chase considered seeking a presidential nomination from the bench. In 1916 Justice Charles Evans Hughes left the Court to run for president. In the 1940s Justice William O. Douglas was considered as a possible vice presidential candidate. In the 1960s Justice Arthur Goldberg left the bench to accept political office as U.S. ambassador to the United Nations.

[51]Timothy S. Huebner, "Roger B. Taney and the Slavery Issue: Looking beyond—and before—*Dred Scott*," *Journal of American History* 97 (June 2010): 39, 40.

[52]It was said their faces were made of dough and southerners could shape them into anything they wanted.

[53]Unpublished opinion of Attorney General Taney, quoted in Carl Brent Swisher, *Roger B. Taney* (New York: Macmillan, 1935), 154. In 1787 free blacks could vote in New Hampshire, Massachusetts, New York, New Jersey, Pennsylvania, and North Carolina. There is some evidence that some may have voted in Maryland as well. David Skillen Bogen, "The Maryland Context of *Dred Scott*: The Decline in the Legal Status of Maryland Free Blacks, 1776–1810," *American Journal of Legal History* 34 (1990): 381, 383.

[54]Only once did Grier fail to fully support the South. In 1851 the Fillmore administration had initiated treason prosecutions against white abolitionists and free blacks who had refused to aid in the capture of fugitive slaves at Christiana, Pennsylvania. Grier, who heard the case in the circuit court, held that refusal to support the law—even resistance to the law—did not constitute treason, although he would have upheld indictments under the 1850 Fugitive Slave Law. Paul Finkelman, "The Treason Trial of Castner Hanway," in *American Political Trials*, rev. ed., ed. Michal Belknap (Westport, Conn.: Greenwood Press, 1994), 77–96.

[55]The case is *Commonwealth v. Aves*, 18 Pick. 193 (1836), which Curtis lost. See Leonard W. Levy, *The Law of the Commonwealth and Chief Justice Shaw* (Cambridge, Mass.: Harvard University Press, 1957), 59–69; and Finkelman, *An Imperfect Union*, 103–28.

[56]*Strader v. Graham*, 51 U.S. (10 How.) 82 (1851). The status of fugitive slaves found in the North was governed by article IV, section 2, paragraph 3 of the U.S. Constitution and not by state law.

[57]*Dred Scott v. Sandford*, 60 U.S. (19 How.) 393, 403 (1857).

[58]The opposite was not true. It was possible to be a citizen of Washington, D.C., or a federal territory, and thus not be a citizen of a state, but still be a citizen of the United States. See *Hepburn v. Ellzey*, 6 U.S. (2 Cr.) 445 (1805), and *Prentiss v. Brennan*, 19 F. Cas. 1278 (1851). James H. Kettner, *The Development of American Citizenship, 1608–1870* (Chapel Hill: University of North Carolina Press, 1978), 248–86, quoted at 328.

[59]*Dred Scott v. Sandford*, 60 U.S. (19 How.) 393, 405 (1857).

[60]Ibid., 405–6.

[61]Ibid., 407.

[62]Article IV, section 2, paragraph 1 of the Constitution declares: "The Citizens of each State shall be entitled to all Privileges and Immunities of Citizens in the several States."

[63]*Congressional Globe*, 35th Cong., 1st sess., 852–55, quoted in Fehrenbacher, *The Dred Scott Case*, 473.

[64]*Dred Scott v. Sandford*, 60 U.S. (19 How.) 393, 432 (1857).

[65]Fehrenbacher, *The Dred Scott Case*, 367.

[66]*Dred Scott v. Sandford*, 60 U.S. (19 How.) 393, 446 (1857).

[67]Ibid., 449, 450. The Supreme Court would reject this analysis after the Spanish-American War, when it held in a series of cases, known as the *Insular Cases*, that the protections of the Bill of Rights did not apply to the territories that the United States had acquired from Spain, such as the Philippines, Puerto Rico, and Cuba.

[68]Ibid., 450.

[69]There are two kinds of "due process" in constitutional law: procedural and substantive. *Procedural due process* guarantees fair and unbiased procedures in a trial, hearing, or some other forum. *Substantive due process* deals with the denial of a right without a good reason, even if the process—the procedure—of denying the right is fair. A law violates substantive due process when it exceeds the reasonable and constitutional authority or power of the legislature that passed the law. An action violates substantive due process when

> the action, while adhering to the forms of law, unjustifiably abridges the Constitution's fundamental constraints upon the content of what government may do to people in the name of "law." As the Supreme Court put the matter most succinctly in *Hurtado v. California* (1884), "Law is something more than mere will exerted as an act of power. . . . [I]t exclud[es], as not due process of law . . . special, partial and arbitrary exertions of power under the forms of legislation. Arbitrary power, enforcing its edicts to the injury of the persons and property of its subjects is not law, whether manifested as the decree of a personal monarch or of an impersonal multitude."—Laurence H. Tribe, "Substantive Due Process of Law," in *Encyclopedia of the American Constitution*, ed. Leonard W. Levy (New York: Macmillan, 1986), 1796.

[70]*Dred Scott v. Sandford*, 60 U.S. (19 How.) 393, 451–52 (1857).

[71]Ibid., 451. Both of Taney's arguments on congressional power in the territories could have been powerfully turned against slavery. Taney's argument that Congress had no general power to legislate for the territories might have been used to assert that Congress had no power to pass any law *creating* or allowing slavery in the territories. Similarly, Taney's Fifth Amendment argument created a two-edged sword. The full text of the due process clause declares, "[N]or shall any person . . . be deprived of life, liberty, or property, without due process of law." Taney argued that it was a violation of "due process" to take property from people who merely entered a federal jurisdiction. By applying that logic to the slaves themselves, abolitionists might have argued that it was a denial of "liberty" to allow someone to be enslaved in a federal territory. Numerous abolitionists, including Theodore Dwight Weld, Salmon P. Chase, and William Goodell, made such arguments. Wiecek, *Sources of Antislavery Constitutionalism*, 190–98, 255, 265–67.

[72]Finkelman, "Was *Dred Scott* Correctly Decided?"

[73]Allocation of seats in the House of Representatives is based on population. The North, with its much larger population, had far more seats in the House than the South. In the Senate each state had two seats, and throughout this period the North and South usually had the same number of Senate seats, or one section had a short-term advantage of two or four seats. For example, in 1845 both Texas and Florida entered the Union, giving the South a four-seat advantage in the Senate until 1846 when Iowa became a state. The South then had a two-seat advantage until 1848, when Wisconsin entered the Union. The admission of California in 1850 gave the North a two-seat advantage in the Senate. But there was no reason to believe that new states like Utah or New Mexico might enter the Union

allowing slavery. There were slaves in both territories, and in 1860 the New Mexico Territory would adopt a slave code.

[74]Abraham Lincoln, "House Divided" speech at Springfield, Illinois, June 16, 1858. See Document 31.

[75]James Buchanan, Inaugural Address, March 4, 1857. See Document 29.

[76]*Dred Scott v. Sandford*, 60 U.S. (19 How.) 393, 572–73 (1857) (Curtis dissenting). Curtis should also have added Pennsylvania to the list of states where free blacks could vote.

[77]Both papers quoted in Fehrenbacher, *The Dred Scott Case*, 417.

[78]*Congressional Globe*, 35th Cong., 1st sess., 941, quoted in Fehrenbacher, *The Dred Scott Case*, 473.

[79]James Buchanan, Inaugural Address, March 4, 1857. See Document 29.

[80]Paul Finkelman, "James Buchanan, *Dred Scott*, and the Whisper of Conspiracy," in *James Buchanan and the Coming of the Civil War*, ed. John W. Quist and Michael. J. Birkner (Tallahassee: University of Florida Press, 2013), 20–45.

[81]Lincoln, "House Divided" speech. See Document 31.

[82]Abraham Lincoln, speech at Columbus, Ohio, in *Collected Works of Lincoln*, 3:404. See also 3:421, 423.

[83]The *Lemmon* case is discussed in Finkelman, *An Imperfect Union*, 285–338. On Louis Napoleon, see Eric Foner, *Gateway to Freedom: The Hidden History of the Underground Railroad* (New York: W. W. Norton, 2015).

[84]New York *Evening Post*, August 31, 1859.

[85]Springfield *Republican*, October 12, 1857.

[86]*Dred Scott v. Sandford*, 60 U.S. (19 How.) 393, 468 (1857).

[87]Stephen A. Douglas, speech at Chicago, July 9, 1858. See Document 32.

[88]Both papers quoted in Fehrenbacher, *The Dred Scott Case*, 420, 418. Significantly, and hypocritically, these papers ignored the fact that both Thomas Jefferson and Andrew Jackson — the presidential heroes of the Democratic Party — had denounced and ignored a number of Supreme Court opinions.

[89]Washington *Union*, March 11, 1857, p. 2.

[90]Ibid.

[91]Charleston *Daily Courier*, March 9, 1857.

[92]Frederick Douglass, speech at New York, May 11, 1857. See Document 30.

[93]Benjamin Quarles, *Frederick Douglass* (New York: Atheneum, 1970), 205.

[94]Charles Sumner, speech of February 23, 1865. See Document 37.

[95]Ehrlich, *They Have No Rights*, 182–83. For more discussion of Dred Scott after the case, see Adam Arenson, "Dred Scott versus the *Dred Scott* Case: The History and Memory of a Signal Moment in American Slavery, 1857–2007," in *The Dred Scott Case: Historical and Contemporary Perspectives on Race and Law*, ed. David Thomas Konig, Paul Finkelman, and Christopher Alan Bracey (Athens: Ohio University Press, 2010), 25–46.

[96]See also Arenson, "Dred Scott versus the *Dred Scott* Case," 25–46. On the death of Harriet, see VanderVelde, *Mrs. Dred Scott*, 322–26. I thank Dr. Robert Moore, the historian at the Old Court House in St. Louis, for providing many of the details of the purchase and emancipation of the Scott family.

[97]An Act for the Release of Certain Persons Held to Service or Labor in the District of Columbia (April 16, 1862), *U.S. Statutes at Large*, 12: 376; An Act to Secure Freedom to all Persons within the Territories of the United States (June 19, 1862), *U.S. Statutes at Large*, 12: 432.

PART TWO

The Documents

1

Opinions of the Justices

This chapter contains excerpts from the opinions of the justices in *Dred Scott*. This was the first time in the Court's history that all nine justices issued an opinion in a case. Some, like Chief Justice Taney's majority opinion and Justice Curtis's dissent, were incredibly long, especially by the standards of the mid-nineteenth century. On the other hand, Justice Grier's opinion (reprinted in full here) was only one paragraph long. All five southern justices agreed that the Scotts were not free, that the Constitution protected slavery, and that free blacks could not be citizens of the United States. But as their opinions show, they differed in their reasoning, the vehemence of their anti-black sentiments, and the power of Congress to regulate the territories. The two northern democrats on the Court—Nelson and Grier—supported the outcome, but with different reasoning. Nelson wrote a narrow opinion; he denied that the Court had jurisdiction to decide any issues regarding the regulation of slavery in the territories and in effect dissented from Taney's larger notions of black rights and congressional power. Justice Grier, in an opinion that was intellectually inconsistent, concurred with both Nelson and Taney, even though they disagreed with each other on major issues.

Justices John McLean of Ohio and Benjamin R. Curtis of Massachusetts dissented from all of Taney's conclusions. They did not disagree with each other, but they emphasized different issues.

1

CHIEF JUSTICE ROGER BROOKE TANEY

Opinion of the Court in Dred Scott, *Plaintiff in Error v. John F. A. Sandford*

March 6, 1857

Roger Brooke Taney (1777–1864) was born to a wealthy slaveowning family in Calvert County, Maryland. Taney served as chief justice longer than any individual except John Marshall.

At age eighteen Taney graduated from Dickinson College in Pennsylvania. He read law with Maryland Judge Jeremiah Chase and began practicing law in 1799. A Federalist state legislator in 1799 to 1800, he broke with the party when it failed to support the War of 1812. In 1816 he won a five-year term in the Maryland senate and in 1827 became Maryland's attorney general. The following year Taney chaired the Maryland central committee for Andrew Jackson's presidential campaign.

In 1831 Jackson appointed Taney attorney general of the United States, and in July and August of that year he also served as interim secretary of war. Taney was one of Jackson's key advisers, helping shape Jacksonian policies on slavery and the rights of blacks, federal-state relations, and the Bank of the United States. Taney drafted Jackson's famous veto of the recharter of the Bank of the United States, and then as secretary of the treasury he was responsible for removing the deposits of the U.S. government from the bank. President Jackson nominated him to the Supreme Court on December 28, 1835, and the Senate confirmed him on March 15, 1836.

During the nullification crisis of 1831 to 1832, when South Carolina asserted its right to nullify a federal law, Taney strongly supported President Jackson in insisting on the supremacy of the national government over the state governments. Here Taney was a proponent of federal power in the tradition of John Marshall. However, when confronted with questions of slavery and the rights of free blacks, Taney deferred to state authority and declined to assert federal power. He argued that neither under its commerce power nor its treaty power could the national government regulate slavery and race relations in the states.

Taney's early support of states' rights on issues of race and the rights of free blacks anticipated the views he later articulated in Dred Scott. *As attorney general, Taney had to comment on the constitutional power of southern states to prohibit free blacks (from other states or the British Empire) from entering their jurisdiction. In his official "Opinion of the Attorney General," Taney asserted:*

> *The African race in the United States even when free, are everywhere a degraded class, and exercise no political influence. The privileges they are allowed to enjoy, are accorded to them as a matter of kindness and benevolence rather than right. . . . They are not looked upon as citizens by the contracting parties who formed the Constitution. They were evidently not supposed to be included by the term* citizens.

In this opinion Taney also concluded that the Declaration of Independence was never meant to apply to blacks, who were, in the attorney general's mind, not entitled to the natural rights of "life, liberty, and the pursuit of happiness."

This official opinion of the attorney general demonstrates that the anti-black, proslavery views Taney expressed in Dred Scott *were not an aberration or a function of the changing politics of the 1850s. Rather, these views were part of his lifelong ideology.*

Mr. Chief Justice Taney delivered the opinion of the court. . . .

The Issues before the Court[1]

There are two leading questions presented by the record:

1. Had the Circuit Court of the United States jurisdiction to hear and determine the case between these parties? And

2. If it had jurisdiction, is the judgment it has given erroneous or not?

---

[1]The headings throughout this opinion have been inserted by the editor, as has all material in brackets.

The Plea in Abatement

The plaintiff [Dred Scott] . . . was, with his wife and children, held as slaves by the defendant [Sanford], in the State of Missouri; and he brought this action in the Circuit Court of the United States for [Missouri], to assert the title of himself and his family to freedom.

The declaration is . . . that he and the defendant are citizens of different States; that . . . he is a citizen of Missouri, and the defendant a citizen of New York.

[Sanford countered with a plea in abatement, asserting that Scott was] not a citizen of the State of Missouri [because he was] a negro of African descent, whose ancestors were of pure African blood, and who were brought into this country and sold as slaves.

[Taney explains that the federal judge ruled against Sanford on the plea in abatement, concluding that if Scott was free, then he was a citizen of Missouri for purposes of suing in federal court. However, after hearing the evidence in the suit, the judge ruled in favor of Sanford on the grounds that under Missouri law Scott was still a slave. Scott then appealed to the Supreme Court, where his lawyers argued that once the trial court had ruled on the plea in abatement, the Supreme Court could not reconsider the issue. Chief Justice Taney disagrees. He first turns to this question.]

If the question raised by [the plea in abatement] is legally before us, and the court should be of opinion that the facts stated in it disqualify the plaintiff from becoming a citizen, in the sense in which that word is used in the Constitution of the United States, then the judgment of the Circuit Court [on the plea in abatement] is erroneous, and must be reversed.

It is suggested, however, that this plea is not before us; and that as the judgment in the court below on this plea was in favor of the plaintiff, he does not seek to reverse it. . . .

We think . . . the plea in abatement is necessarily under consideration; and it becomes, therefore, our duty to decide [it]. . . .

The Constitutional Rights of Free Blacks

The question is simply this: Can a negro, whose ancestors were imported into this country, and sold as slaves, become a member of the political community formed and brought into existence by the Constitution of the United States, and as such become entitled to all the rights, and privileges, and immunities, guaranteed by that instrument to the citizen? One of which rights is the privilege of suing in a court of the United States in the cases specified in the Constitution. . . .

The words "people of the United States" and "citizens" are synonymous terms, and mean the same thing. They both describe the political body who . . . form the sovereignty, and who hold the power and conduct the Government through their representatives. . . . The question before us is, whether the class of persons described in the plea in abatement [people of African ancestry] compose a portion of this people, and are constituent members of this sovereignty? We think they are not, and that they are not included, and were not intended to be included, under the word "citizens" in the Constitution, and can therefore claim none of the rights and privileges which that instrument provides for and secures to citizens of the United States. On the contrary, they were at that time considered as a subordinate and inferior class of beings, who had been subjugated by the dominant race, and, whether emancipated or not, yet remained subject to their authority, and had no rights or privileges but such as those who held the power and the Government might choose to grant them.

It is not the province of the court to decide upon the justice or injustice, the policy or impolicy, of these laws. The decision of that question belonged . . . to those who formed the sovereignty and framed the Constitution. The duty of the court is, to interpret the instrument they have framed, with the best lights we can obtain on the subject, and to administer it as we find it, according to its true intent and meaning when it was adopted.

In discussing this question, we must not confound the rights of citizenship which a State may confer within its own limits, and the rights of citizenship as a member of the Union. It does not by any means follow, because he has all the rights and privileges of a citizen of a State, that he must be a citizen of the United States. He may have all of the rights and privileges of the citizen of a State, and yet not be entitled to the rights and privileges of a citizen in any other State. For, previous to the adoption of the Constitution of the United States, every State had the undoubted right to confer on whomsoever it pleased the character of citizen, and to endow him with all its rights. But this character of course was confined to the boundaries of the State, and gave him no rights or privileges in other States beyond those secured to him by the laws of nations and the comity of States. Nor have the several States surrendered the power of conferring these rights and privileges by adopting the Constitution of the United States. Each State may still confer them upon an alien, or any one it thinks proper, or upon any class or description of persons; yet he would not be a citizen in the sense in which that word is used in the Constitution of the United States, nor entitled to sue as such in one of its courts, nor to the privileges and immunities of a citizen in the other States. The rights which he would acquire would be restricted to the State which gave them. The Constitution has conferred on Congress the right to establish an uniform rule of naturalization, and this right is evidently exclusive, and has always been held by this court to be so. Consequently, no State, since the adoption of the Constitution, can by naturalizing an alien invest him with the rights and privileges secured to a citizen of a State under the Federal Government, although, so far as the State alone was concerned, he would undoubtedly be entitled to the rights of a citizen, and clothed with all the rights and immunities which the Constitution and laws of the State attached to that character.

It is very clear, therefore, that no State can, by any act or law of its own . . . introduce a new member into the political community created by the Constitution of the United States. It cannot make him a member of this community by making him a member of its own. . . .

The question then arises, whether the provisions of the Constitution, in relation to the personal rights and privileges to which the citizen of a State should be entitled, embraced the negro African race . . . made free in any State; and to put it in the power of a single State to make him a citizen of the United States, and endue him with the full rights of citizenship in every other State without their consent? Does the Constitution of the United States act upon him whenever he shall be made free under the laws of a State, and raised there to the rank of a citizen, and immediately clothe him with all the privileges of a citizen in every other State, and in its own courts?

Free Blacks Have No Rights under the Constitution

The court think the affirmative of these propositions cannot be maintained. And if it cannot, [Dred Scott] could not be a citizen of the State of Missouri, within the meaning of the Constitution of the United States, and, consequently, was not entitled to sue in its courts.

It is true, every person, and every class and description of persons, who were at the time of the adoption of the Constitution recognized as citizens in the several States, became also citizens of this new political body; but none other; it was formed by them, and for them and their posterity, but for no one else. And the personal rights and privileges guarantied to citizens of this new sovereignty were intended to embrace those only who were then members of the several State communities, or who should afterwards by birthright or otherwise become members, according to the provisions of the Constitution and the principles on which it was founded. . . .

The Citizenship Question

It becomes necessary, therefore, to determine who were citizens of the several States when the Constitution was adopted. . . .

. . . [T]he legislation and histories of the times, and the language used in the Declaration of Independence, show, that neither the class of persons who had been imported as slaves, nor their descendants, whether they had become free or not, were then acknowledged as a part of the people, nor intended to be included in the general words used in that memorable instrument.

It is difficult at this day to realize the state of public opinion in relation to that unfortunate race, which prevailed in the civilized and enlightened portions of the world at the time of the Declaration of Independence, and when the Constitution of the United States was framed and adopted. . . .

They had for more than a century before been regarded as beings of an inferior order, and altogether unfit to associate with the white race, either in social or political relations; and so far inferior, that they had no rights which the white man was bound to respect; and that the negro might justly and lawfully be reduced to slavery. . . . He was bought and sold, and treated as an ordinary article of merchandise and traffic, whenever a profit could be made by it. This opinion was at that time fixed and universal in the civilized portion of the white race. It was regarded as an axiom in morals as well as in politics, which no one thought of disputing, or supposed to be open to dispute; and men in every grade and position in society daily and habitually acted upon it in their private pursuits, as well as in matters of public concern, without doubting for a moment the correctness of this opinion.

And in no nation was this opinion more firmly fixed or more uniformly acted upon than by the English Government and English people. They not only seized them on the coast of Africa, and sold them or held them in slavery for their own use; but they took them as ordinary articles of merchandise to every country where they could make a profit on them, and were far more extensively engaged in this commerce than any other nation in the world.

The opinion thus entertained and acted upon in England was naturally impressed upon the colonies they founded on this side of the

Atlantic. And, accordingly, a negro of the African race was regarded by them as an article of property, and held, and bought and sold as such, in every one of the thirteen colonies which united in the Declaration of Independence, and afterwards formed the Constitution of the United States. The slaves were more or less numerous in the different colonies, as slave labor was found more or less profitable. But no one seems to have doubted the correctness of the prevailing opinion of the time.

The legislation of the different colonies furnishes positive and indisputable proof of this fact. . . .

The province of Maryland, in 1717, passed a law declaring "that if any free negro or mulatto intermarry with any white woman, or if any white man shall intermarry with any negro or mulatto woman, such negro or mulatto shall become a slave during life, excepting mulattoes born of white women, who, for such intermarriage, shall only become servants for seven years. . . ."

The other colonial law to which we refer was passed by Massachusetts in 1705. It is entitled "An act for the better preventing of a spurious and mixed issue," &c.; and it provides, that "if any negro or mulatto shall presume to smite or strike any person of the English or other Christian nation, such negro or mulatto shall be severely whipped. . . ."

. . . [T]hese laws . . . show, too plainly to be misunderstood, the degraded condition of this unhappy race. They were still in force when the Revolution began, and are a faithful index to the state of feeling towards the class of persons of whom they speak, and of the position they occupied throughout the thirteen colonies, in the eyes and thoughts of the men who framed the Declaration of Independence and established the State Constitutions and Governments. They show that a perpetual and impassable barrier was intended to be erected between the white race and the one which they had reduced to slavery, and governed as subjects with absolute and despotic power, and which they then looked upon as so far below them in the scale of created beings, that intermarriages between white persons and negroes or mulattoes were regarded as unnatural and immoral, and punished as crimes, not only in the parties, but in the person who joined them in marriage. And no distinction in this respect was made between the free negro or mulatto and the slave, but this stigma, of the deepest degradation, was fixed upon the whole race.

We refer to these historical facts for the purpose of showing the fixed opinions concerning that race, upon which the statesmen of that day spoke and acted . . . in order to determine whether the general terms used in the Constitution of the United States, as to the rights of man and the rights of the people, was intended to include them, or to give to them or their posterity the benefit of any of its provisions.

The Declaration of Independence and Equal Rights

The language of the Declaration of Independence is equally Conclusive: . . .

> We hold these truths to be self-evident: that all men are created equal; that they are endowed by their Creator with certain unalienable rights; that among them is life, liberty, and the pursuit of happiness; that to secure these rights, Governments are instituted, deriving their just powers from the consent of the governed.

The general words above quoted would seem to embrace the whole human family, and if they were used in a similar instrument at this day would be so understood. But it is too clear for dispute, that the enslaved African race were not intended to be included, and formed no part of the people who framed and adopted this declaration; for if the language, as understood in that day, would embrace them, the conduct of the distinguished men who framed the Declaration of Independence would have been utterly and flagrantly inconsistent with the principles they asserted; and instead of the sympathy of mankind, to which they so confidently appeared, they would have deserved and received universal rebuke and reprobation.

Yet the men who framed this declaration were great men—high in literary acquirements—high in their sense of honor, and incapable of asserting principles inconsistent with those on which they were acting. They perfectly understood the meaning of the language they used, and how it would be understood by others; and they knew that it would not in any part of the civilized world be supposed to embrace the negro race, which, by common consent, had been excluded from civilized Governments and the family of nations, and doomed to slavery. They spoke and acted according to the then established doctrines and principles, and in the ordinary language of the day, no one misunderstood them. The unhappy black race were separated from the white by indelible marks, and laws long before established, and were never thought of or spoken of except as property, and when the claims of the owner or the profit of the trader were supposed to need protection.

This state of public opinion had undergone no change when the Constitution was adopted, as is equally evident from its provisions and language. . . .

The Constitution and Racial Equality

[There] are two clauses in the Constitution which point directly and specifically to the negro race as a separate class of persons, and show clearly that they were not regarded as a portion of the people or citizens of the Government then formed.

One of these clauses reserves to each of the thirteen States the right to import slaves until the year 1808. . . . And by the other provision the States pledge themselves to each other to maintain the right of property of the master, by delivering up to him any slave who may have escaped from his service, and be found within their respective territories. . . . And these two provisions show, conclusively, that neither the description of persons therein referred to, nor their descendants, were embraced in any of the other provisions of the Constitution; for certainly these two clauses were not intended to confer on them or their posterity the blessings of liberty, or any of the personal rights so carefully provided for the citizen.

No one of that race had ever migrated to the United States voluntarily; all of them had been brought here as articles of merchandise. The number that had been emancipated at that time were but few in comparison with those held in slavery; and they were identified in the public mind with the race to which they belonged, and regarded as a part of the slave population rather than the free. It is obvious that they were not even in the minds of the framers of the Constitution when they were conferring special rights and privileges upon the citizens of a State in every other part of the Union.

State Laws of the Founding Era Used to Interpret the Constitution

Indeed, when we look to the condition of this race in the several States at the time, it is impossible to believe that these rights and privileges were intended to be extended to them.

It is very true, that in that portion of the Union where the labor of the negro race was found to be unsuited to the climate and unprofitable to the master, but few slaves were held at the time of the Declaration of Independence; and when the Constitution was adopted, it had entirely worn out in one of them, and measures had been taken for its gradual abolition in several others. But this change had not been produced by any change of opinion in relation to this race. . . .

And we may here again refer, in support of this proposition, to the plain and unequivocal language of the laws of the several States, some passed after the Declaration of Independence and before the Constitution was adopted, and some since the Government went into operation.

[The] . . . laws of the present slaveholding States . . . are full of provisions in relation to this class [and] . . . have continued to treat them as an inferior class, and to subject them to strict police regulations, drawing a broad line of distinction between the citizen and the slave races, and legislating in relation to them upon the same principle which prevailed at the time of the Declaration of Independence. As related to these States, it is too plain for argument, that they have never been regarded as a part of the people or citizens of the State, nor supposed to possess any political rights which the dominant race might not withhold or grant at their pleasure. . . .

And if we turn to the legislation of the States where slavery had worn out, or measures taken for its speedy abolition, we shall find the same opinions and principles equally fixed and equally acted upon.

Thus, [a] Massachusetts . . . Law of 1786 . . . forbids the marriage of any white person with any negro, Indian, or mulatto . . . and declares all such marriages absolutely null and void, and degrades thus the unhappy issue of the marriage by fixing upon it the stain of bastardy. . . .

And again, in 1833, Connecticut passed another law, which made it penal to set up or establish any school in that State for the instruction of persons of the African race not inhabitants of the State, or to instruct or teach in any such school or institution, or board or harbor for that purpose, any such person, without the previous consent in writing of the civil authority of the town in which such school or institution might be. . . .

By the laws of New Hampshire . . . no one was permitted to be enrolled in the militia of the State, but free white citizens; and the same provision is found in a subsequent collection of the laws, made in 1855. Nothing could more strongly mark the entire repudiation of the African race. . . . [W]hy are the African race, born in the State, not permitted to share in one of the highest duties of the citizen? The answer is obvious; he is not, by the institutions and laws of the State, numbered among its people. He forms no part of the sovereignty of the State, and is not therefore called on to uphold and defend it. . . .

It would be impossible to enumerate . . . the various laws, marking the condition of this race, which were passed from time to time after the Revolution, and before and since the adoption of the Constitution of the United States. In addition to those already referred to, it is sufficient to say, that Chancellor Kent,[2] whose accuracy and research no one will question, states in . . . his Commentaries . . . that in no part of the country except Maine, did the African race, in point of fact, participate equally with the whites in the exercise of civil and political rights.

The legislation of the States therefore shows, in a manner not to be mistaken, the inferior and subject condition of that race at the time the Constitution was adopted, and long afterwards, . . . and it is hardly consistent with the respect due to these States, to suppose that they regarded at that time, as fellow-citizens and members of the sovereignty, a class of beings whom they had thus stigmatized; . . . and upon whom they had impressed such deep and enduring marks of inferiority and degradation; or, that when they met in convention to form the Constitution, they looked upon them as a portion of their constituents, or designed to include them in the provisions so carefully inserted for the security and protection of the liberties and rights of their citizens. It cannot be supposed that they intended to secure to them rights, and privileges, and rank, in the new political body throughout the Union, which every one of them denied within the limits of its own dominion. More especially, it cannot be believed that the large slaveholding States regarded them as included in the word citizens, or would have consented to a Constitution which might compel them to receive them in that character from another State. For if they were so received, and entitled to the privileges and immunities of citizens, it would exempt them from the operation of the special laws and from the police regulations which they considered to be necessary for their own safety. It would give to persons of the negro race, who were recognized as citizens in any one State of the Union, the right to enter every other State whenever they pleased, singly or in companies, without pass or passport, and without obstruction, to sojourn there as long as they pleased, to go where they pleased at every hour of the day or night without molestation, unless they committed some violation of law for which a white man would be punished; and it would give them the full liberty of speech in public and in private upon all subjects upon which its own citizens might speak; to hold public meetings upon political affairs, and to keep and carry arms wherever

[2]James Kent (1763–1847) was a justice on the New York Supreme Court from 1798 to 1823, and he also served as chancellor of the state's court system from 1814 to 1823. He wrote the highly influential four-volume *Commentaries on American Law*. A forceful advocate of a strong judiciary, Kent was a Federalist in his politics and thus an advocate of a strong national government; he was a northerner and at least a nominal opponent of slavery. Here Taney shrewdly uses Kent to support his position that blacks have no rights under the Constitution.

they went. And all of this would be done in the face of the subject race of the same color, both free and slaves, and inevitably producing discontent and insubordination among them, and endangering the peace and safety of the State.

It is impossible, it would seem, to believe that the great men of the slaveholding States, who took so large a share in framing the Constitution of the United States, and exercised so much influence in procuring its adoption, could have been so forgetful or regardless of their own safety and the safety of those who trusted and confided in them. . . .

Federal Laws Used to Explain the Constitution

To all this mass of proof we have still to add, that Congress has repeatedly legislated upon the same construction of the Constitution that we have given. . . .

The first of these acts is the naturalization law . . . [of] March 26, 1790, [which] confines the right of becoming citizens *"to aliens being free white persons."* . . .

Another of the early laws of which we have spoken, is the first militia law, which was passed in 1792, at the first session of the second Congress. The language of this law is equally plain and significant. . . . It directs that every "free able-bodied white male citizen" shall be enrolled in the militia. The word *white* is evidently used to exclude the African race, and the word *citizen* to exclude unnaturalized foreigners; the latter forming no part of the sovereignty, owing it no allegiance, and therefore under no obligation to defend it. The African race, however, born in the country, did owe allegiance to the Government, whether they were slave or free; but it is repudiated, and rejected from the duties and obligations of citizenship in marked language.

The third act to which we have alluded is even still more decisive; it was passed as late as 1813, (2 Stat., 809) and it provides: "That from and after the termination of the war in which the United States are now engaged with Great Britain, it shall not be lawful to employ, on board of any public or private vessels of the United States, any person or persons except citizens of the United States, *or* persons of color, natives of the United States."

Here the line of distinction is drawn in express words. Persons of color, in the judgment of Congress, were not included in the word *citizens,* and they are described as another and different class of persons, and authorized to be employed, if born in the United States. . . .

The conduct of the Executive Department of the Government has been in perfect harmony upon this subject with this course of legislation. The question was brought officially before the late William Wirt, when he was the Attorney General of the United States, in 1821, and he decided that the words "citizens of the United States" were used in the acts of Congress in the same sense as in the Constitution; and that free persons of color were not citizens, within the meaning of the Constitution and laws; and this opinion has been confirmed by that of the late Attorney General, Caleb Cushing, in a recent case, and acted upon by the Secretary of State, who refused to grant passports to them as "citizens of the United States." . . .

"Original Intent" Analysis Used to Assert That the Constitution Protects Slavery

No one, we presume, supposes that any change in public opinion or feeling, in relation to this unfortunate race, in the civilized nations of Europe or in this country, should induce the court to give to the words of the Constitution a more liberal construction in their favor than they were intended to bear when the instrument was framed and adopted. Such an argument would be altogether inadmissible in any tribunal called on to interpret it. If any of its provisions are deemed unjust, there is a mode prescribed in the instrument itself by which it may be amended; but while it remains unaltered, it must be construed now as it was understood at the time of its adoption. It is not only the same in words, but the same in meaning, and delegates the same powers to the Government, and reserves and secures the same rights and privileges to the citizen; and as long as it continues to exist in its present form, it speaks not only in the same words, but with the same meaning and intent with which it spoke when it came from the hands of its framers, and was voted on and adopted by the people of the United States. Any other rule of construction would abrogate the judicial character of this court, and make it the mere reflex of the popular opinion or passion of the day. This court was not created by the Constitution for such purposes. Higher and graver trusts have been confided to it, and it must not falter in the path of duty. . . .

Taney's Ruling on Black Citizenship

And upon a full and careful consideration of the subject, the court is of opinion, that, . . . Dred Scott was not a citizen of Missouri within the meaning of the Constitution of the United States, and not entitled as such to sue in its courts; and, consequently, that the Circuit Court had no jurisdiction of the case, and that the judgment on the plea in abatement is erroneous. . . .

. . . [I]t appears affirmatively on the record that he is not a citizen, and consequently his suit against Sandford was not a suit between citizens of different States, and the court had no authority to pass any judgment between the parties. The suit ought, in this view of it, to have been dismissed by the Circuit Court, and its judgment in favor of Sandford is erroneous, and must be reversed.

It is true that the result either way, by dismissal or by a judgment for the defendant, makes very little, if any, difference in a pecuniary or personal point of view to either party. But the fact that the result would be very nearly the same to the parties in either form of judgment, would not justify this court in sanctioning an error in the judgment which is patent on the record, and which, if sanctioned, might be drawn into precedent, and lead to serious mischief and injustice in some future suit.

We proceed, therefore, to inquire whether the facts relied on by the plaintiff entitled him to his freedom.

[Here Taney recounts the facts of Dred Scott's residence in Illinois and Minnesota, his marriage to Harriet Robinson at Fort Snelling, and the birth of their two daughters.]

The Question of Residence in a Free Jurisdiction

In considering this part of the controversy, two questions arise: 1. Was he, together with his family, free in Missouri by reason of the stay in the territory of the United States . . . ? And 2. If they were not, is Scott himself free by reason of his removal to Rock Island, in the State of Illinois, as stated in the above admissions?

We proceed to examine the first question.

The act of Congress [the Missouri Compromise], upon which the plaintiff relies, declares that slavery and involuntary servitude, except as a punishment for crime, shall be forever prohibited in all that part of the territory ceded by France, under the name of Louisiana, which lies north of thirty-six degrees thirty minutes north latitude, and not included within the limits of Missouri. [But] . . . [was Congress] authorized to pass this law under any of the powers granted to it by the Constitution; for if the authority is not given by that instrument, it is the duty of this court to declare it void and inoperative, and incapable of conferring freedom upon any one who is held as a slave under the laws of any one of the States.

The counsel for the plaintiff [Dred Scott] has laid much stress upon that article in the Constitution which confers on Congress the power "to dispose of and make all needful rules and regulations respecting the territory or other property belonging to the United States" [article IV, section 3, paragraph 2]; but, in the judgment of the court, that provision has no bearing on the present controversy, and the power there given . . . was intended to be confined, to the territory which at that time belonged to, or was claimed by, the United States, and was within their boundaries as settled by the treaty with Great Britain, and can have no influence upon a territory afterwards acquired from a foreign Government. It was a special provision for a known and particular territory, and to meet a present emergency, and nothing more. . . .

It will be remembered that, from the commencement of the Revolutionary war, serious difficulties existed between the States, in relation to the disposition of large and unsettled territories which were included in the chartered limits of some of the States. . . .

The letters from the statesmen of that day will show how much this controversy occupied their thoughts, and the dangers that were apprehended from it. It was the disturbing element of the time, and fears were entertained that it might dissolve the Confederation by which the States were then united.

These fears and dangers were, however, at once removed, when the State of Virginia, in 1784, voluntarily ceded to the United States the immense tract of country lying northwest of the river Ohio, and which was within the acknowledged limits of the State. . . .

This was the state of things when the Constitution . . . was formed. The territory ceded by Virginia belonged to the several confederated States as common property, and they had united in establishing in it a system of government and jurisprudence, in order to prepare it for admission as States, according to the terms of the cession. . . . It was necessary that the lands should be sold to pay the war debt; that a Government and system of jurisprudence should be maintained in it, to protect the citizens of the United States who should migrate to the territory, in their rights of person and of property. . . . And, moreover, there were many articles of value besides this property in land, such as arms, military stores, munitions, and ships of war, which were the common property of the States, when acting in their independent characters as confederates, which neither the new Government nor any one else would have a right to take possession of, or control, without authority from them; and it was to place these things under the guardianship and protection of the new Government, and to clothe it with the necessary powers, that the clause was inserted in the Constitution which gives Congress the power "to dispose of and make all needful rules and regulations respecting the territory or other property belonging to the United States." It was intended for a specific purpose, to provide for the things we have mentioned. . . .

The . . . clause . . . does not speak of *any* territory, nor of *Territories*, but uses language which, according to its legitimate meaning, points to a particular thing. The power is given in relation only to *the* territory of the United States—that is, to a territory then in existence, and then known or claimed as the territory of the United States. [It] . . . gives the power which was necessarily associated with the disposition and sale of the lands—that is, the power of making needful rules and regulations respecting the territory. . . .

The words "needful rules and regulations" would seem, also, to have been cautiously used for some definite object. They are not the words usually employed by statesmen, when they mean to give the powers of sovereignty, or to establish a Government, or to authorize its establishment. Thus . . . in the Constitution, when granting the power to legislate over the territory that may be selected for the seat of Government independently of a State, it does not say Congress shall have power "to make all needful rules and regulations respecting the territory"; but it declares that "Congress shall have power to exercise exclusive legislation in all cases whatsoever over such District (not exceeding ten miles square) as may, by cession of particular States and the acceptance of Congress, become the seat of the Government of the United States.["] . . .

Whether, therefore, we take the particular clause in question, by itself, or in connection with the other provisions of the Constitution, we think it clear, that it applies only to the particular territory of which we have spoken, and cannot, by any just rule of interpretation, be extended to territory which the new Government might afterwards obtain from a foreign nation. Consequently, the power which Congress may have lawfully exercised in this Territory . . . can furnish no justification and no argument to support a similar exercise of power over territory afterwards acquired by the Federal Government. We put aside, therefore, any argument, drawn from precedents, showing the extent of the power which the General Government exercised over slavery in this Territory, as altogether inapplicable to the case before us. . . .

Interpretation of the Territories Clause of the Constitution

. . . The power to expand the territory of the United States by the admission of new States is plainly given; and in the construction of this power . . . it has been held to authorize the acquisition of territory, not fit for admission at the time, but to be admitted as soon as its population and situation would entitle it to admission. It is acquired to become a State, and not to be held as a colony and governed by Congress with absolute authority; and as the propriety of admitting a new State is committed to the sound discretion of Congress, the power to acquire territory for that purpose, to be held by the United States until it is in a suitable condition to become a state upon an equal footing with the other States, must rest upon the same discretion. . . .

Taking this rule to guide us, it may be safely assumed that citizens of the United States who migrate to a Territory belonging to the people of the United States, cannot be ruled as mere colonists, dependent upon the will of the General Government, and to be governed by any laws it may think proper to impose. The principle upon which our Governments rest, and upon which alone they continue to exist, is the union of States, sovereign and independent within their own limits in their internal and domestic concerns, and bound together as one people by a General Government, possessing certain enumerated and restricted powers, delegated to it by the people of the several States, and exercising supreme authority within the scope of the powers granted to it, throughout the dominion of the United States. A power, therefore, in the General Government to obtain and hold colonies and dependent territories, over which they might legislate without restriction, would be inconsistent with its own existence in its present form. . . .

Effect of the Bill of Rights on Slavery in the Territories

But until that time [of statehood] arrives, it is undoubtedly necessary that some Government should be established, in order to organize society, and to protect the inhabitants in their persons and property; and as the people of the United States could act in this matter only through the Government which represented them . . . it was not only within the scope of its powers, but it was its duty to pass such laws and establish such a Government as would enable . . . to gather there a population which would enable it to assume the position to which it was destined among the States of the Union. . . . But . . . what is the best form must always depend on the condition of the Territory at the time, and the choice of the mode must depend upon the exercise of a discretionary power by Congress, acting within the scope of its constitutional authority, and not infringing upon the rights of person or rights of property of the citizen who might go there to reside, or for any other lawful purpose . . . until it is fitted to be a State.

But the power of Congress over the person or property of a citizen . . . [is] regulated and plainly defined by the Constitution itself. And when the Territory becomes a part of the United States, the Federal Government enters . . . upon it with its powers over the citizen strictly defined, and limited by the Constitution. . . . It has no power of any kind beyond it; and it cannot, when it enters a Territory of the United States, put off its character, and assume discretionary or despotic powers which the Constitution has denied to it. . . . [A]nd the Federal Government can exercise no power over his person or property, beyond what that instrument confers, nor lawfully deny any right which it has reserved. . . .

For example, no one, we presume, will contend that Congress can make any law in a Territory respecting the establishment of religion, or the free exercise thereof, or abridging the freedom of speech or of the press, or the right of the people of the Territory peaceably to assemble, and to petition the Government for the redress of grievances.

Nor can Congress deny to the people the right to keep and bear arms, nor the right to trial by jury, nor compel any one to be a witness against himself in a criminal proceeding.

These powers, and others, in relation to rights of person, which it is not necessary here to enumerate, are, in express and positive terms, denied to the General Government; and the rights of private property have been guarded with equal care. Thus the rights of property are united with the rights of person, and placed on the same ground by the fifth amendment to the Constitution, which provides that no person shall be deprived of life, liberty, and property, without due process of law. And an act of Congress which deprives a citizen of the United States of his liberty or property, merely because he came himself or brought his property into a particular Territory of the United States, and who had committed no offence against the laws, could hardly be dignified with the name of due process of law.

So, too, it will hardly be contended that Congress could by law quarter a soldier in a house in a Territory without the consent of the owner, in time of peace; nor in time of war, but in a manner prescribed by law.

Nor could they by law forfeit the property of a citizen in a Territory who was convicted of treason, for a longer period than the life of the person convicted; nor take private property for public use without just compensation.

The powers over person and property of which we speak are not only not granted to Congress, but are in express terms denied, and they are forbidden to exercise them. And this prohibition . . . extend[s] to the whole territory over which the Constitution gives it power to legislate. . . . It is a total absence of power everywhere within the dominion of the United States, and places the citizens of a Territory, so far as these rights are concerned, on the same footing with citizens of the States, and guards them as firmly and plainly against any inroads which the General Government might attempt, under the plea of implied or incidental powers. And if Congress itself cannot do this—if it is beyond the powers conferred on the Federal Government—it will be admitted, we presume, that it could not authorize a Territorial Government to exercise them. It could confer no power on any local Government, established by its authority, to violate the provisions of the Constitution.

It seems, however, to be supposed, that there is a difference between property in a slave and other property, and that different rules may be applied to it in expounding the Constitution of the United States. And the laws and usages of nations, and the writings of eminent jurists upon the relation of master and slave and their mutual rights and duties, and the powers which Governments may exercise over it, have been dwelt upon in the argument.

But in considering the question before us, it must be borne in mind that there is no law of nations standing between the people of the United States and their Government, and interfering with their relation to each other. The powers of the Government, and the rights of the citizen under it, are positive and practical regulations plainly written down. . . . It has no power over the person or property of a citizen but what the citizens of the United States have granted. And no laws or usages of other nations, or reasoning of statesmen or jurists upon the relations of master and slave, can enlarge the powers of the Government, or take from the citizens the rights they have reserved. And if the Constitution recognises the right of property of the master in a slave, and makes no distinction between that description of property and other property owned by a citizen, no tribunal, acting under the authority of the United States, whether it be legislative, executive, or judicial, has a right to draw such a distinction, or deny to it the benefit of the provisions and guarantees which have been provided for the protection of private property against the encroachments of the Government.

Now, as we have already said . . . the right of property in a slave is distinctly and expressly affirmed in the Constitution. The right to traffic in it, like an ordinary article of merchandise and property, was guarantied to the citizens of the United States, in every State that might desire it, for twenty years. And the Government in express terms is pledged to protect it in all future time, if the slave escapes from his owner. This is done in plain words—too plain to be misunderstood. And no word can be found in the Constitution which gives Congress a greater power over slave property, or which entitles property of that kind to less protection than property of any other description. The only power conferred is the power coupled with the duty guarding and protecting the owner in his rights.

Upon these considerations, it is the opinion of the court that the act of Congress which prohibited a citizen from holding and owning property of this kind in the territory . . . is not warranted by the Constitution, and is therefore void; and that neither Dred Scott himself, nor any of his family, were made free by being carried into this territory; even if they had been carried there by the owner, with the intention of becoming a permanent resident. . . .

Did Scott's Residence in Illinois Affect His Status?

But there is another point in the case which depends on State power and State law. And it is contended, on the part of the plaintiff, that he is made free by being taken to Rock Island, in the State of Illinois, independently of his residence in the territory of the United States; and being so made free, he was not again reduced to a state of slavery by being brought back to Missouri.

Our notice of this part of the case will be very brief; for the principle on which it depends was decided in this court, upon much consideration, in the case of Strader et al. *v.* Graham [1851]. In that case, the slaves had been taken from Kentucky to Ohio, with the consent of the owner, and afterwards brought back to Kentucky. And this court held that their *status* or condition, as free or slave, depended upon the laws of Kentucky, when they were brought back into that State, and not of Ohio; and that this court had no jurisdiction to revise the judgment of a State court upon its own laws. This was the point directly before the court, and the decision that this court had no jurisdiction turned upon it, as will be seen by the report of the case.

So in this case. As Scott was a slave when taken into the State of Illinois by his owner, and was there held as such, and brought back in that character, his *status*, as free or slave, depended on the laws of Missouri, and not of Illinois. . . .

Conclusion: Scott Remains a Slave

Upon the whole, therefore, it is the judgment of this court, that it appears by the record before us that the plaintiff in error is not a citizen of Missouri, in the sense in which that word is used in the Constitution; and that the Circuit Court of the United States, for that reason, had no jurisdiction in the case, and could give no judgment in it. Its judgment for the defendant must, consequently, be reversed, and a mandate issued, directing the suit to be dismissed for want of jurisdiction.

2

JUSTICE JAMES M. WAYNE

Concurring Opinion

March 6, 1857

James Moore Wayne (c. 1790–1867) was born in Savannah, Georgia, the son of a rice planter. He received a degree from the College of New Jersey (now Princeton University) in 1808 and began law practice in Savannah in 1810. Wayne held various political positions and was in his fourth term in Congress when President Andrew Jackson nominated him to the Supreme Court. A slaveowner, Wayne generally took a moderately proslavery position. He concurred with Justice Joseph Story's majority opinion in Prigg v. Pennsylvania *(1842), the first fugitive slave case to come before the Supreme Court. While fully supporting the right of masters to regain their slaves, Wayne did not endorse Chief Justice Taney's more extreme concurring opinion in* Prigg. *Similarly, in 1858, the year after the* Dred Scott *decision, Wayne unsuccessfully urged a South Carolina jury to convict alleged slave traders of violating the federal ban on the African slave trade. At the beginning of the Civil War, Wayne chose loyalty to the nation of his birth and thus remained on the Court until his death in 1867.*

In Dred Scott *Wayne specifically concurred with Chief Justice Taney's opinion, asserting that Taney had the power and duty to decide every point in the case. Why did Wayne feel the need to write an opinion at all, if he completely agreed with Taney's opinion? Is Wayne's short opinion politically, rather than legally, motivated? Wayne also specifically endorsed Justice Nelson's position, while indicating that he believed Nelson should have joined him in finding the Missouri Compromise unconstitutional. After you have read Nelson's opinion, consider whether it is illogical, or inconsistent, to specifically endorse both the Taney opinion and the Nelson opinion. Does Wayne's opinion offer a way of mediating between the proslavery southern majority on the Court and their two northern allies?*

Mr. Justice Wayne.

[I concur] entirely in the opinion of the court, as it has been written and read by the Chief Justice—without any qualification of its reasoning or its conclusions. . . .

. . . [T]he court neither sought nor made the case. It was brought to us in the course of that administration of the laws which Congress has enacted, for the review of cases from the Circuit Courts by the Supreme Court.

In our action upon it, we have only discharged our duty as a distinct and efficient department of the Government, as the framers of the Constitution meant the judiciary to be, and as the States of the Union and the people of those States intended it should be, when they ratified the Constitution of the United States.

The case involves private rights of value, and constitutional principles of the highest importance, about which there had become such a difference of opinion, that the peace and harmony of the country required the settlement of them by judicial decision.

It would certainly be a subject of regret, that the conclusions of the court have not been assented to by all of its members, if I did not know from its history and my own experience how rarely it has happened that the judges have been unanimous upon constitutional questions of moment. . . .

Two of the judges, Mr. Justices McLean and Curtis, dissent from the opinion of the court. A third, Mr. Justice Nelson, gives a separate opinion, upon a single point in the case, with which I concur, assuming the Circuit Court had jurisdiction; but he abstains altogether from expressing any opinion on the eighth section of the act of 1820, known commonly as the Missouri Compromise law, and six of us declare that it was unconstitutional.

3

JUSTICE SAMUEL NELSON

Concurring Opinion
March 6, 1857

Born in upstate New York, Samuel Nelson (1792–1873) attended Middlebury College in Vermont, read law in Salem, New York, and was admitted to the bar in 1817. He served as a postmaster in Cortland, New York, from 1820 to 1823 and then served on various state courts from 1823 until 1845, when President James K. Polk nominated him to the U.S. Supreme Court. Nelson was a classic "doughface" Democrat—a northern man with southern principles. Initially Nelson was going to write the opinion of the Court in Dred Scott. *He planned to decide the case quickly and with little controversy. As his concurring opinion shows, he would have avoided most of the difficult issues surrounding slavery in the territories and the rights of free blacks by simply holding that Missouri had a right to decide for itself the status of blacks within its jurisdiction. The southern majority on the Court, however, wanted a more forcefully proslavery opinion, which Nelson would not write. Thus the four southern associate justices asked Taney to write a majority opinion that would strike down the Missouri Compromise.*

Would Nelson's opinion have been the wiser for the Court and the nation? Would Dred Scott *have become a major political issue if Nelson's had been the main opinion in the case? At the end of his opinion, Nelson wrote the following:*

> *A question has been alluded to, on the argument, namely: the right of the master with his slave of transit into or through a free State, on Business or commercial pursuits, or in the exercise of a Federal right, or the discharge of a Federal duty, being a citizen of the United States, which is not before us. This question depends upon different considerations and principles from the one in hand, and turns upon the rights and privileges secured to a common citizen of the republic under the Constitution of the United States. When that question arises, we shall be prepared to decide it.*

What are the implications of this statement? Does Nelson's statement support Lincoln's fears in his "House Divided" speech (Document 31) that the Court might nationalize slavery?

Mr. Justice Nelson.

[Nelson explains why he thinks the plea in abatement is not before the Court. He then turns to the issue of Dred Scott's residence in free jurisdictions.]

. . . Our opinion is, that the question is one which belongs to each State to decide for itself, either by its Legislature or courts of justice; and hence, in respect to the case before us . . . [it is] a question exclusively of Missouri law, and which, when determined by that State, it is the duty of the Federal courts to follow it. In other words, except in cases where the power is restrained by the Constitution of the United States, the law of the State is supreme over the subject of slavery within its jurisdiction.

As a practical illustration of the principle, we may refer to the legislation of the free States in abolishing slavery, and prohibiting its introduction into their territories. Confessedly, except as restrained by the Federal Constitution, they exercised, and rightfully, complete and absolute power over the subject. Upon what principle, then, can it be denied to the State of Missouri? The power flows from the sovereign character of the States of this Union; sovereign, not merely as respects the Federal Government . . . but sovereign as respects each other. Whether, therefore, the State of Missouri will recognise or give effect to the laws of Illinois within her territories on the subject of slavery, is a question for her to determine. . . .

Every State or nation possesses an exclusive sovereignty and jurisdiction within her own territory; and, her laws affect and bind all property and persons residing within it. It may regulate the manner and circumstances under which property is held, and the condition, capacity, and state, of all persons therein; and, also, the remedy and modes of administering justice. And it is equally true, that no State or nation can affect or bind property out of its territory, or persons not residing within it. No State, therefore, can enact laws to operate beyond its own dominions, and, if it attempts to do so, it may be lawfully refused obedience. Such laws can have no inherent authority extra-territorially. This is the necessary result of the independence of distinct and separate sovereignties. . . .

Judge Story[1] observes, in his Conflict of Laws, . . . "that a State may prohibit the operation of all foreign laws, and the rights growing out of them, within its territories." "And that when its code speaks positively on the subject, it must be obeyed by all persons who are within reach of its sovereignty; when its customary unwritten or common law speaks directly on the subject, it is equally to be obeyed."

Nations, from convenience and comity, and from mutual interest, and a sort of moral necessity to do justice, recognise and administer the laws of other countries. But, of the nature, extent, and utility, of them, respecting property, or the state and condition of persons within her territories, each nation judges for itself; and is never bound . . . to recognize them, if prejudicial to her own interests. The recognition is purely from comity, and not from any absolute or paramount obligation.

Judge Story again observes . . . "that the true foundation and extent of the obligation of the laws of one nation within another is the voluntary consent of latter, and is inadmissible when they are contrary to its known interests." . . .

These principles fully establish, that it belongs to . . . Missouri to determine by her laws the question of slavery within her jurisdiction, subject only to such limitations as may be found in the Federal Constitution; and, further, that the laws of other States of the Confederacy . . . can have no operation within her territory, or affect rights growing out of her own laws on the subject. This is the necessary result of the independent and sovereign character of the State. The principle is not peculiar to the State of Missouri, but is equally applicable to State belonging to the Confederacy. The laws of each have no extra-territorial operation within the jurisdiction of another, except such as may be voluntarily conceded by her laws or courts of justice. To the extent of such concession upon the rule of comity of nations, the foreign law may operate. . . .

[Dred Scott's attorneys] . . . insist that the removal and temporary residence with his master in Illinois, where slavery is inhibited, had the effect to set him free, and that the same effect is to be given to the law of Illinois, within the State of Missouri, after his return. Why was he set

---

[1]Joseph Story (1779–1845) was the most distinguished scholar to serve on the U.S. Supreme Court. During his years on the Court (1811–1845), he wrote numerous treatises on American law, including his *Commentaries on the Constitution*, 3 vols. (Boston: Hilliard and Gray, 1833) and the work cited by Nelson, *Commentaries on the Conflict of Laws* (Boston: Hilliard and Gray, 1834). His work was generally considered to be authoritative, and thus courts throughout the nation regularly cited him. On Story, see generally R. Kent Newmyer, *Supreme Court Justice Joseph Story: Statesman of the Old Republic* (Chapel Hill: University of North Carolina Press, 1985).

free in Illinois? Because the law of Missouri, under which he was held as a slave, had no operation by its own force extra-territorially; and the State of Illinois refused to recognize its effect within her limits, upon principles of comity, as a state of slavery was inconsistent with her laws, and contrary to her policy. But, how is the case different on the return of the plaintiff to the State of Missouri? Is she bound to recognize and enforce the law of Illinois? For, unless she is, the status and condition of the slave upon his return remains the same as originally existed. Has the law of Illinois any greater force within the jurisdiction of Missouri, than the laws of the latter within that of the former? Certainly not. They stand upon an equal footing. Neither has any force extra-territorially, except what may be voluntarily conceded to them. . . .

[In] Strader et al. v. Graham [1851] . . . [t]he question . . . was, whether certain slaves of Graham, a resident of Kentucky, who had been employed temporarily [in] . . . Ohio, with their master's consent, and had returned to Kentucky into his service, had thereby become entitled to their freedom. The Court of Appeals held that they had not. . . . This court held that it had no jurisdiction, for . . . the question was one that belonged exclusively to the State of Kentucky. The Chief Justice, in delivering the opinion of the court, observed that "every State has an undoubted right to determine the status or domestic and social condition of the persons domiciled within its territory, except in so far as the powers of the States in this respect are restrained, or duties and obligations imposed upon them, by the Constitution of the United States. There is nothing in the Constitution of the United States, he observes, that can in any degree control the law of Kentucky upon this subject. And the condition of the negroes, therefore, as to freedom or slavery, after their return, depended altogether upon the laws of that State, and could not be influenced by the laws of Ohio. It was exclusively in the power of Kentucky to determine, for herself, whether their employment in another State should or should not make them free on their return."

It has been supposed, in the argument on the part of the plaintiff, that the [Missouri Compromise] . . . possessed some superior virtue and effect, extra-territorially, and within the State of Missouri, beyond that of the laws of Illinois, or those of Ohio in the case of Strader et al. v. Graham. . . .

It must be admitted that Congress possesses no power to regulate or abolish slavery within the States; and that, if this act had attempted any such legislation, it would have been a nullity. And yet the argument here . . . leads to the result, that effect may be given to such legislation; for it is only by giving the act of Congress operation within the State of Missouri, that it can have any effect upon the question between the parties. Having no such effect directly, it will be difficult to maintain, upon any consistent reasoning, that it can be made to operate indirectly upon the subject. . . .

. . . [M]any of the most eminent statesmen and jurists of the country entertain the opinion that this provision of the act of Congress, even within the territory to which it relates, was not authorized by any power under the Constitution. The doctrine here contended for, not only upholds its validity in the territory, but claims for it effect beyond and within the limits of a sovereign State—an effect, as insisted, that displaces the laws of the State, and substitutes its own provisions in their place.

The consequences of any such construction are apparent. If Congress possesses the power, under the Constitution, to abolish slavery in a Territory, it must necessarily possess the like power to establish it. It cannot be a one-sided power, as may suit the convenience or particular views of the advocates. It is a power, if it exists at all, over the whole subject; and then, upon the process of reasoning which seek to extend its influence beyond the Territory, and within the limits of a State, if Congress should establish, instead of abolish, slavery, we do not see but that, if a slave should be removed from the Territory into a free State, his status would accompany him, and continue, notwithstanding its laws against slavery. The laws of the free State, according to the argument, would be displaced, and the act of Congress, in its effect, be substituted in their place. We do not see how this conclusion could be avoided, if the construction against which we are contending should prevail. We are satisfied, however, it is unsound, and that the true answer to it is, that even conceding, for the purposes of the argument, that this provision of the act of Congress is valid within the Territory for which it was enacted, it can have no operation or effect beyond its limits, or within the jurisdiction of a State. It can neither displace its laws, nor change the status or condition of its inhabitants.

Our conclusion, therefore, is, upon this branch of the case, that the question involved is one depending solely upon the law of Missouri, and that the Federal court sitting in the State, and trying the case before us, was bound to follow it.

The remaining question for consideration is, What is the law of the State of Missouri on this subject? . . . [As *Scott v. Emerson* (1852)] this case was originally brought in the Circuit Court of the State, which resulted in a judgment for the plaintiff [Scott]. The [Missouri Supreme Court] reversed the judgment . . . upon the principles of international law, that foreign laws have no extra-territorial force, except such as the State within which they are sought to be enforced may see fit to extend to them, upon the doctrine of comity of nations. . . .

Lord Stowell, in communicating his opinion in the case of the slave Grace[2] to Judge Story, states . . . : "Whether the emancipation of a slave brought to England insured a complete emancipation to him on his return to his own country, or whether it only operated as a suspension of slavery in England, and his original character devolved on him again upon his return." He observed, "the question had never been examined since an end was put to slavery fifty years ago," having reference to the decision of Lord Mansfield in the case of Somersett;[3] but the practice, he observed, "has regularly been, that on his return to his own country, the slave resumed his original character of slave." And so Lord Stowell held in the case.

Judge Story, in his letter in reply, observes: "I have read with great attention your judgment in the slave case, &c. Upon the fullest consideration which I have been able to give the subject, I entirely concur in your views. If I had been called upon to pronounce a judgment in a like case, I should have certainly arrived at the same result." Again he observes: "In my native State, (Massachusetts), the state of slavery not recognized as legal; and yet, if a slave should come hither, and afterwards return to his own home, we should certainly think that the local law attached upon him, and that his servile character would be reintegrated." . . .

[Nelson discusses similar cases from Maryland and Louisiana.]

Upon the whole, it must be admitted that the current of authority both in England and in this country, is in accordance with the law as declared by the courts of Missouri in the case before us, and we think the court below was not only right, but bound to follow it.

Some question has been made as to the character of the residence in this case in the free State. But we regard the facts as set forth in the agreed case as decisive. The removal of Dr. Emerson from Missouri to the military posts was in the discharge of his duties as surgeon in the army, and under the orders of his Government. He was liable at any moment to be recalled, as he was in 1838, and ordered to another

[2]*The Slave, Grace*, 2 Hagg. Admin. (G.B.) 94 (1827).
[3]*Somerset v. Stewart*, 1 Lofft (G.B.) 1 (1772).

post. . . . In such a case, the officer goes to his post for a temporary purpose, to remain there for an uncertain time, and not for the purpose of fixing his permanent abode. The question we think too plain to require argument. . . .

A question has been alluded to, on the argument, namely: the right of the master with his slave of transit into or through a free State, on Business or commercial pursuits, or in the exercise of a Federal right or the discharge of a Federal duty, being a citizen of the United States, which is not before us. This question depends upon different considerations and principles from the one in hand, and turns upon the right and privileges secured to a common citizen of the republic under the Constitution of the United States. When that question arises, we shall be prepared to decide it.

Our conclusion is, that the judgment of the court below should be affirmed.

4

JUSTICE ROBERT COOPER GRIER

Concurring Opinion
March 6, 1857

Born in Cumberland County, Pennsylvania, Robert C. Grier (1794– 1870) received a degree from Dickinson College in 1812 and read law until 1817, when he was admitted to the Pennsylvania bar. A loyal Jacksonian Democrat, he served as a state judge from 1833 until President James K. Polk nominated him to the U.S. Supreme Court in 1846. Grier generally supported states' rights. Until the Civil War he also always voted to support the interests of the South and slavery. After the election of President James Buchanan, but before his inauguration, Justice Grier wrote to his fellow Pennsylvanian and told him how the Court was going to decide Dred Scott. *Thus when Buchanan read his inaugural address and urged the nation to respect the forthcoming opinion, he already knew that the Court was about to declare the Missouri Compromise unconstitutional and allow slavery in all the federal territories. Grier's three-sentence opinion is the shortest of the nine delivered by the justices.*

Grier specifically concurs in Justice Nelson's opinion but also agrees with Justice Taney. Having read both opinions, do you think Grier was intellectually consistent? Why do you think Grier felt compelled to write this opinion, trying to side with both Nelson and Taney at the same time? Does his opinion add anything to the decision?

Mr. Justice Grier.

I concur in the opinion delivered by Mr. Justice Nelson on the questions discussed by him.

I also concur with the opinion of the court as delivered by the Chief Justice, that the act of Congress of 6th March, 1820, is unconstitutional and void; and that, assuming the facts as stated in the opinion, the plaintiff cannot sue as a citizen of Missouri in the courts of the United States. But, that the record shows a prima facie case of jurisdiction, requiring the court to decide all the questions properly arising in it; and as the decision of the pleas in bar shows that the plaintiff is a slave, and therefore not entitled to sue in a court of the United States. . . .

5

JUSTICE PETER VIVIAN DANIEL

Concurring Opinion

March 6, 1857

Born in Stafford County, Virginia, Peter Vivian Daniel (1784–1860) was the most proslavery member of the Court. He was also the Court's most adamant defender of states' rights. Daniel was educated by private tutors and briefly attended the College of New Jersey (later Princeton University). From 1805 to 1808 he studied law with Edmund Randolph, the former attorney general of the United States. Daniel then entered politics, becoming lieutenant governor of Virginia in 1818, at age thirty-four. In the 1830s he was Virginia's leading supporter of Presidents Andrew Jackson and Martin Van Buren. Jackson nominated him to the U.S. district court in 1836; in 1841, just nine days before he left the presidency, Van Buren elevated him to the Supreme Court. On the Court, Daniel was best known for his dissents—fifty between 1842 and 1859—in which he generally opposed banks, corporations, and a strong national government and generally supported states' rights and slavery. His Dred Scott *opinion is the most extreme of the nine opinions in its denial of federal power to regulate slavery. Unlike the other judges, Daniel argues that even the Northwest Ordinance of 1787, which prohibited slavery in the territories north and west of the Ohio River, was unconstitutional. What are the implications of Daniel's position on the Northwest Ordinance? If Taney was right about the unconstitutionality of the Missouri Compromise, why didn't Taney take such a position on the Northwest Ordinance?*

Mr. Justice Daniel.

. . . Now, the following are truths which a knowledge of the history of the world, and particularly of that of our own country, compels us to know—that the African negro race never have been acknowledged as belonging to the family of nations; that as amongst them there never has been known or recognized by the inhabitants of other countries anything partaking of the character of nationality, or civil or political polity; that this race has been by all the nations of Europe regarded as subjects of capture or purchase; as subjects of commerce or traffic; and that the introduction of that race into every section of this country was not as members of civil or political society, but as slaves, as *property* in the strictest sense of the term.

. . . And it now becomes the province of this court to determine whether the plaintiff . . . a *negro* of African descent, whose ancestors were of pure African blood, and were brought into this country and sold as negro slaves—such being his *status*, and such the circumstances surrounding his position—whether he can, by correct legal induction from that *status* and those circumstances, be clothed with the character and capacities of a citizen of the State of Missouri?

It may be assumed as a postulate, that to a slave, as such, there appertains and can appertain no relation, civil or political, with the State or the Government. He is himself strictly *property*, to be used in subserviency to the interests, the convenience, or the will, of his owner; . . . Hence it follows, necessarily, that a slave . . . possessing within himself no civil or political rights or capacities, cannot be a CITIZEN. . . .

But it has been insisted, in argument, that the emancipation of a slave, effected either by the direct act and assent of the master, or by causes operating in contravention of his will, produces a change in the *status* or capacities of the slave, such as will transform him from a mere subject of property, into a being possessing a social, civil, and political equality with a citizen. In other words, will make him a citizen of the State within which he was, previously to his emancipation, a slave.

It is difficult to conceive by what magic the [slave can become a citizen merely by private manumission]. Can it be pretended that an individual in any State, by his single act [of freeing a slave] . . . yet without the co-operation or warrant of the Government, perhaps in opposition to its policy or its guaranties, can create a citizen of that State? Much more emphatically may it be asked, how such a result could be accomplished by means wholly extraneous, and entirely foreign to the Government of the State? . . .

The institution of slavery, as it exists and has existed from the period of its introduction into the United States, though more humane and mitigated in character than was the same institution, either under the republic or the empire of Rome, bears, both in its tenure and in the simplicity incident to the mode of its exercise, a closer resemblance to Roman slavery than it does to the condition of *villanage*,[1] as it formerly existed in England. . . .

[In Rome] . . . citizenship was not conferred by the simple fact of emancipation. . . . The master might abdicate or abandon his interest or ownership in his property, but his act would be a mere abandonment. It seems to involve an absurdity to impute to it the investiture of rights which the sovereignty alone had power to impart. There is not perhaps a community in which slavery is recognized, in which the power of emancipation and the modes of its exercise are not regulated by law—that is by the sovereign authority; and none can fail to comprehend the necessity for such regulation, for the preservation of order, and even of political and social existence.

[Daniel argues that it would be despotism for one state to have the power to make slaves into citizens without the consent of all other states.]

By the argument for the plaintiff in error, a power equally despotic is vested in every member of the association, and the most obscure or unworthy individual it comprises may arbitrarily invade and derange its most deliberate and solemn ordinances. At assumptions anomalous as these, so fraught with mischief and ruin, the mind at once is revolted,

---

[1]Villenage (as it is spelled today) refers to the status of unfree peasants in medieval England. Villeins were legally tied to the land and owed service and other obligations to their feudal lords. However, they were not slaves. They had many legal rights, including the right to marry, make contracts, and own property, and they could not be bought or sold by their lords.

and goes directly to the conclusions, that to change or to abolish a fundamental principle of the society, must be the act of the society itself—of the *sovereignty*; and that none other can admit to a participation of that high attribute. It may further expose the character of the argument urged for the plaintiff, to point out some of the revolting consequences which it would authorize. If that argument possesses any integrity, it asserts the power in any citizen, or *quasi* citizen, or a resident foreigner of any one of the States, from a motive either of corruption or caprice, not only to infract the inherent and necessary authority of such State, but also materially to interfere with the organization of the Federal Government, and with the authority of the separate and independent States. He may emancipate his negro slave, by which process he first transforms that slave into a citizen of his own State; he may next, under color of article fourth, section second, of the Constitution of the United States, obtrude him, and on terms of civil and political equality, upon any and every State in this Union, in defiance of all regulations of necessity or policy, ordained by those States for their internal happiness or safety. Nay, more: [T]his manumitted slave may, by a proceeding springing from the will or act of his master alone, be mixed up with the institutions of the Federal Government, to which he is not a party, and in opposition to the laws of that Government which, in authorizing the extension by naturalization of the rights and immunities of citizens of the United States to those not originally parties to the Federal compact, have restricted that boon to *free white aliens alone*. If the rights and immunities connected with or practiced under the institutions of the United States can by any indirection be claimed or deduced from sources or modes other than the Constitution and laws of the United States, it follows that the power of naturalization vested in Congress is not exclusive—that it has *in effect* no existence, but is repealed or abrogated. . . .

The States, in the exercise of their political power, might, with reference to their peculiar Government and jurisdiction, guaranty the rights of person and property, and the enjoyment of civil and political privileges, to those whom they should be disposed to make the objects of their bounty; but they could not reclaim or exert the powers which they had vested exclusively in the Government of the United States. They could not add to or change in any respect the class of persons to whom alone the character of citizen of the United States appertained at the time of the adoption of the Federal Constitution. They could not create citizens of the United States by any direct or indirect proceeding. . . .

[Daniel argues that Congress had no power to limit slavery when it passed the Northwest Ordinance and the Missouri Compromise.]

The second or last-mentioned position assumed for the plaintiff under the pleas in bar, as it rests mainly if not solely upon . . . the *Missouri Compromise*, that assumption renews the question, formerly so zealously debated, as to the validity of the provision in the act of Congress, and upon the constitutional competency of Congress to establish it. . . .

There can exist no rational or natural connection or affinity between a pretension like this and the power vested by the Constitution in Congress with regard to the Territories. . . .

. . . Congress was made simply the agent or *trustee* for the United States, and could not, without a breach of trust and a fraud, appropriate the subject of the trust to any beneficiary . . . than the United States, or to the people of the United States, upon equal grounds legal or equitable. Congress could not appropriate that subject to any one class or portion of the people, to the exclusion of others, politically and constitutionally equals; but every citizen would, if any *one* could claim it, have the like rights of purchase, settlement, occupation, or any other right, in the national territory.

Nothing can be more conclusive to show the equality of this with every other right in all the citizens of the United States, and the iniquity and absurdity of the pretension to exclude or to disfranchise a portion of them because they are the owners of slaves, than the fact that the same instrument, which imparts to Congress its very existence and its every function, guaranties to the slaveholder the title to his property, and gives him the right to its reclamation throughout the entire extent of the nation; and, farther, that the only private property which the Constitution has *specifically recognised*, and has imposed it as a direct obligation both on the States and the Federal Government to protect and *enforce*, is the property of the master in his slave; no other right of property is placed by the Constitution upon the same high ground, nor shielded by a similar guaranty.

Can there be imputed to the sages and patriots by whom the Constitution was framed, or can there be detected in the text of that Constitution, or in any rational construction or implication deducible therefrom, a contradiction so palpable as would exist between a pledge to the slaveholder of an equality with his fellow-citizens, and of the formal and solemn assurance for the security and enjoyment of his property, and a warrant given . . . to another, to rob him of that property, or to subject him to proscription and disfranchisement for possessing or for endeavoring to retain it? The injustice and extravagance necessarily implied in a supposition like this, cannot be nationally imputed to the patriotic or the honest, or to those who were merely sane. . . .

. . . But apart from the superior control of the Constitution, and ante-
rior to the adoption of that instrument, it is obvious that the inhibition
in question never had and never could have any legitimate and binding
force. We may seek in vain for any power in the convention, either to
require or to accept a condition or restriction upon the cession like that
insisted on; a condition inconsistent with, and destructive of, the object
of the grant. [The prohibition of slavery in the Northwest Ordinance]
being contradictory to the terms and destructive of the purposes of
the cession, and after the cession was consummated, and the powers of
the ceding party terminated, and the rights of the grantees, *the people
of the United States*, vested, must necessarily, so far, have been *ab initio*
[from the beginning] void. . . .

6

JUSTICE JOHN ARCHIBALD CAMPBELL

Concurring Opinion
March 6, 1857

*John Archibald Campbell (1811–1889) was born in Washington, Georgia,
the son of a lawyer-planter. Campbell studied at both West Point and the
University of Georgia before beginning his legal career at the unusually
young age of eighteen. In 1830, at age nineteen, he moved to Alabama,
where he practiced law and held some local political offices. When
President Franklin Pierce chose him for the Supreme Court in 1853,
the New York* Tribune *commented that he was "a gentleman of shining
and profound talents, vast legal attainments and withal is irreproach-
able in character, but he is a fire-eater of the blazing school" in defending
southern nationalism.*[1] *A slaveholder for most of his life, Campbell's
lifelong sympathies were with slavery and the South. In 1861 he was the
only member of the Court to join the Confederate government, where he
became the assistant secretary of war.*

Campbell's twenty-five-page concurring opinion in Dred Scott *places
him clearly in the camp of the strongest advocates of slavery. Campbell uses*

---

[1]New York *Tribune*, quoted in Gordon Hylton Jr., " John Archibald Campbell," in *The
Supreme Court Justices: A Biographical Dictionary*, ed. Melvin I. Urofsky (New York:
Garland, 1994), 89.

various historical arguments, as well as the Ninth and Tenth Amendments to the Constitution, to justify his conclusion that the Missouri Compromise was unconstitutional and that slavery was a constitutionally protected form of property. In this opinion Campbell argues that slavery "is recognized by the law of nations" and could be found everywhere in the world and throughout human history. He also tries to demonstrate that involuntary servitude and bondage were found in England at the time of the Revolution.

Campbell seems to be arguing that slavery was part of American law at the time of the founding. Does such a historical argument strengthen his position that Congress cannot ban slavery in the territories? Throughout his opinion Campbell also favorably quotes such famous anti-Federalists as Patrick Henry, George Clinton, and Luther Martin. These men, who opposed the ratification of the Constitution in 1787–1788, were, like Campbell, unswerving supporters of states' rights and opponents of a strong central government. However, is it persuasive for Campbell to quote these opponents of the Constitution to support his view of how the Constitution should be interpreted?

Mr. Justice Campbell. . . .

The relation of domestic slavery is recognised in the law of nations, and the interference of the authorities of one State with the rights of a master belonging to another, without a valid cause, is a violation of that law. . . .

The public law of Europe formerly permitted a master to reclaim his bondsman, within a limited period, wherever he could find him, and one of the capitularies of Charlemagne . . . directs, "that wheresoever, within the bounds of Italy, either the runaway slave of the king, or of the church, or of any other man, shall be found by his master, he shall be restored. . . ." . . . [T]he clause in the Federal Constitution providing for the restoration of fugitive slaves is a recognition of this ancient right, and of the principle that a change of place does not effect a change of condition. . . .

. . . Historical research ascertains that at the date of the [Norman] Conquest [of England, 1066] the rural population of England were generally in a servile condition, and under various names, denoting slight variances in condition, they were sold with the land like cattle, and were a part of its living money. Traces of the existence of African slaves are to be found in the early chronicles. Parliament in the time of Richard II, and also of Henry VIII, refused to adopt a general law of emancipation. Acts of emancipation by the last-named monarch and by Elizabeth are preserved.

The African slave trade had been carried on, under the unbounded protection of the Crown, for near two centuries, when the case of Somersett[2] [1772] was heard, and no motion for its suppression had ever been submitted to Parliament; while it was forced upon and maintained in unwilling colonies by the Parliament and Crown of England at that moment. Fifteen thousand negro slaves were then living in that island, where they had been introduced under the counsel of the most illustrious jurists of the realm, and such slaves had been publicly sold for near a century in the markets of London. . . . No statute, from the Conquest till [1775] had been passed upon the subject of personal slavery. . . .

The clause [article IV, section 3 of the U.S. Constitution] which enables Congress to dispose of and make regulations respecting the public domain, was demanded by the exigencies of an exhausted treasury and a disordered finance, for relief by sales, and the preparation for sales, of the public lands; and the last clause, that nothing in the Constitution should prejudice the claims of the United States or a particular State, was to quiet the jealousy and irritation of those who claimed for the United States all the unappropriated lands. I look in vain, among the discussions of the time, for the assertion of a supreme sovereignty for Congress over the territory then belonging to the United States, or that they might thereafter acquire. I seek in vain for an annunciation that a consolidated power had been inaugurated, whose subject comprehended an empire, and which had no restriction but the discretion of Congress. This disturbing element of the Union entirely escaped the apprehensive previsions of Samuel Adams, George Clinton, Luther Martin, and Patrick Henry;[3] and, in respect to dangers from power vested in a central Government over distant settlements, colonies, or provinces, their instincts were always alive. Not a word escaped them, to warn their countrymen, that here was a power to threaten the landmarks of this federative Union, and with them the safeguards of popular and constitutional liberty; or that under this article there might be introduced, on our soil, a single Government over a vast extent of country—a Government foreign to the persons over whom it might be exercised, and capable of binding those not represented, by statutes, in all cases whatever. I find nothing to authorize these enormous pretensions, nothing in the expositions of the friends of the Constitution, nothing in the expres-

---

[2]*Somerset v. Stewart*, 1 Lofft (G.B.) 1 (1772).

[3]These four men were active in fighting against ratification of the Constitution in 1787–1788. Adams of Massachusetts eventually supported the Constitution, and Clinton of New York acquiesced when New York ratified it. Martin of Maryland and Henry of Virginia were two of the most vocal opponents of the Constitution in their states.

sions of alarm by its opponents—expressions which have since been developed as prophecies. . . .

The most dangerous of the efforts to employ a geographical political power, to perpetuate a geographical preponderance in the Union, is to be found in the deliberations upon the [Missouri Compromise]. The attempt consisted of a proposal to exclude Missouri from a place in the Union, unless her people would adopt a Constitution containing a prohibition upon the subject of slavery, according to a prescription of Congress. The sentiment is now general, if not universal, that Congress had no constitutional power to impose the restriction. This was frankly admitted at the bar, in the course of this argument. The principles which this court have pronounced condemn the pretension then made on behalf of the legislative department. . . .

[Campbell implies that the Missouri Compromise was like the oppressions of the British in the years before the American Revolution.]

Could it have been the purpose of Washington and his illustrious associates, by the use of ambiguous, equivocal, and expansive words, such as "rules," "regulation," "territory," to re-establish in the Constitution of their country [arbitrary government]? Are these words to be understood as the Norths, the Grenvilles, Hillsboroughs, Hutchinsons, and Dunmores[4]—in a word, as George III would have understood them—or are we to look for their interpretation to Patrick Henry or Samuel Adams, to Jefferson, and Jay, and Dickinson; to the sage Franklin, or to Hamilton, who from his early manhood was engaged in combating British constructions of such words? . . . In forming the Constitution . . . [t]he people were assured by their most trusted statesmen "that the jurisdiction of the Federal Government is limited to certain enumerated objects, which concern all members of the republic," and "that the local or municipal authorities form distinct portions of supremacy, no more subject within their respective spheres to the general authority, than the general authority is subject to them within its own sphere." Still, this did not content them. Under the lead of Hancock and Samuel Adams, of Patrick Henry and George Mason, they demanded an explicit

[4]Lords North, Grenville, and Hillsborough all headed the British government in the years leading up to the American Revolution. Americans held them responsible for the various laws, such as the Stamp Act, the tea tax, and the Intolerable Acts, that led to the Revolution. Thomas Hutchinson was the American-born lieutenant governor of Massachusetts who supported the closing of Boston Harbor after the Boston Tea Party. Hutchinson sided with the British during the Revolution and afterward went to England. Lord Dunmore was the royal governor of Virginia when the Revolution began. Southerners especially hated him because he offered to free any slave who would fight in the British army.

declaration that no more power was to be exercised than they had delegated. And the ninth and tenth amendments to the Constitution were designed to include the reserved rights of the States, and the people, within all the sanctions of that instrument, and to bind the authorities, State and Federal, by the judicial oath it prescribes, to their recognition and observance. Is it probable, therefore, that the supreme and irresponsible power, which is now claimed for Congress over boundless territories, the use of which cannot fail to react upon the political system of the States, to its subversion, was ever within the contemplation of the statesmen who conducted the counsels of the people in the formation of this Constitution? . . .

. . . My opinion is, that the claim for Congress of supreme power in the Territories, under the grant to "dispose of and make all needful rules and regulations respecting *territory*," is not supported by the historical evidence drawn from the Revolution, the Confederation, or the deliberations which preceded the ratification of the Federal Constitution. The ordinance of 1787 depended upon the action of the Congress of the Confederation, the assent of the State of Virginia, and the acquiescence of the people who recognized the validity of that plea of necessity which supported so many of the acts of the Governments of that time; and the Federal Government accepted the ordinance as a recognized and valid engagement of the Confederation. . . .

7

JUSTICE JOHN CATRON

Concurring Opinion
March 6, 1857

Born in Pennsylvania, John Catron (c. 1786–1865) grew up in poverty, served under Andrew Jackson in the War of 1812, and emerged as a lawyer in 1815. Between 1824 and 1834 Catron was a justice of the Tennessee Supreme Court. He was also an active supporter of President Jackson, who, on his last day in office, nominated Catron to the U.S. Supreme Court. Catron was generally a moderate on slavery, as his concurring opinion shows. Unlike Taney, he did not believe that Congress lacked all power to regulate the territories, although he denied that Congress could ban slavery in the territory acquired from France in the Louisiana Pur-

chase. Also indicative of his moderate position, Catron did not discuss whether free blacks could be citizens of the United States, perhaps because from the time it became a state, in 1796, until the late 1830s, free blacks were allowed to vote in Catron's home state of Tennessee.

Why does Catron refuse to deny Congress power to legislate for the territories? Does Taney's opinion on the unconstitutionality of all congressional regulation of the territories put Justice Catron in a morally ambiguous position?

Mr. Justice Catron. . . .

It is . . . insisted for the plaintiff, that his freedom . . . was obtained by . . . the Missouri compromise. . . .

The first question . . . is, whether Congress had power to make such compromise. For, if power was wanting, then no freedom could be acquired by the defendant under the act.

That Congress has no authority to pass laws and bind men's rights beyond the powers conferred by the Constitution, is not open to controversy. But it is insisted that, by the Constitution, Congress has power to legislate for and govern the Territories of the United States, and that by force of the power to govern, laws could be enacted, prohibiting slavery in any portion of the Louisiana Territory; and, of course, to abolish slavery *in all* parts of it, whilst it was, or is, governed as a Territory.

My opinion is, that Congress is vested with power to govern the Territories of the United States by force of the third section of the fourth article of the Constitution. . . .

It was hardly possible to separate the power "to make all needful rules and regulations" respecting the government of the territory and the disposition of the public lands. . . .

It is due to myself to say, that it is asking much of a judge, who had for nearly twenty years been exercising jurisdiction, from the western Missouri line to the Rocky Mountains, and, on this understanding of the Constitution, inflicting the extreme penalty of death for crimes committed where the direct legislation of Congress was the only rule, to agree that he had been all the while acting in mistake, and as an usurper.

More than sixty years have passed away since Congress has exercised power to govern the Territories, by its legislation directly, or by Territorial charters, subject to repeal at all times, and it is now too late to call that power into question. . . . The only question here is, as I think, how far the power of Congress is limited.

As to the Northwest Territory, Virginia had the right to abolish slavery there; and she did so agree in 1787, with the other States in the Congress of the Confederation, by assenting to and adopting the ordinance of 1787, for the government of the Northwest Territory. She did this also by an act of her Legislature, passed afterwards, which was a treaty in fact. . . .

My opinion is, that Congress had no power, in face of the compact between Virginia and the twelve other States, to *force* slavery into the Northwest Territory, because there, it was bound to that "engagement," and could not break it. . . .

And how does the [territorial] power of Congress stand west of the Mississippi river? The country there was acquired from France, by treaty, in 1803. It declares, . . . by article third, that "the inhabitants of the ceded territory shall be incorporated in the Union of the United States, and admitted as soon as possible, according to the principles of the Federal Constitution, to the enjoyment of all the rights, advantages, and immunities, of citizens of the United States; and, in the mean time, they shall be maintained and protected in the free enjoyment of their liberty, property, and the religion which they profess."

Louisiana was a province where slavery was not only lawful, but where property in slaves was the most valuable of all personal property. The province was ceded as a unit, with an equal right pertaining to all its inhabitants, in every part thereof, to own slaves. It was, to a great extent, a vacant country, having in it few civilized inhabitants. No one portion of the colony, of a proper size for a State of the Union[,] had a sufficient number of inhabitants to claim admission into the Union. To enable the United States to fulfill the treaty, additional population was indispensable, and obviously desired with anxiety by both sides, so that the whole country should, as soon as possible, become States of the Union. And for this contemplated future population, the treaty as expressly provided as it did for the inhabitants residing in the province when the treaty was made. . . .

At the date of the treaty, each inhabitant had the right to the *free* enjoyment of his property, alike with his liberty and his religion, in every part of Louisiana; the province then being one country, he might go everywhere in it, and carry his liberty, property, and religion, with him, and in which he was to be maintained and protected, until he became a citizen of a State of the Union of the United States. This cannot be denied to the original inhabitants and their descendants. And, if it be true that immigrants were equally protected, it must follow that they can also stand on the treaty. . . .

The Missouri compromise line of 1820 was very aggressive; it declared that slavery was abolished forever throughout a country reaching from the Mississippi river to the Pacific ocean. . . .

That the United States Government stipulated in favor of the inhabitants to the extent here contended for, has not been seriously denied . . . ; but the argument is, that Congress had authority to *repeal* the third article of the treaty of 1803, in so far as it secured the right to hold slave property, in a portion of the ceded territory. . . . In other words, that Congress could repeal the third article entirely, at its pleasure. This I deny. . . .

Congress cannot do indirectly what the Constitution prohibits directly. If the slaveholder is prohibited from going to the Territory with his slaves, who are parts of his family in name and in fact, it will follow that men owning lawful property in their own States, carrying with them the equality of their State to enjoy the common property, may be told, you cannot come here with your slaves, and he will be held out at the border. By this subterfuge, owners of slave property, to the amount of thousand[s] of millions, might be almost as effectually excluded from removing into the Territory of Louisiana north of thirty-six degrees thirty minutes, as if the law declared that owners of slaves, as a class, should be excluded, even if their slaves were left behind.

Just as well might Congress have said to those of the North, you shall not introduce into the territory south of said line your cattle or horses, as the country is already overstocked; nor can you introduce your tools of trade, or machines, as the policy of Congress is to encourage the culture of sugar and cotton south of the line, and so to provide that the Northern people shall manufacture for those of the South, and barter for the staple articles slaves labor produces. And thus the Northern farmer and mechanic would be held out, as the slaveholder was for thirty years, by the Missouri restriction.

If Congress could prohibit one species of property, lawful throughout Louisiana when it was acquired, and lawful in the State from whence it was brought, so Congress might exclude any or all property. . . .

My opinion is, that the third article of the treaty of 1803, ceding Louisiana to the United States, stands protected by the Constitution, and cannot be repealed by Congress.

And, secondly, that the act of 1820, known as the Missouri compromise, violates the most leading feature of the Constitution—a feature on which the Union depends, and which secures to the respective States and their citizens an entire EQUALITY of rights, privileges, and immunities.

On these grounds, I hold the compromise act to have been void; and, consequently, that the plaintiff, Scott, can claim no benefit under it. . . .

8

JUSTICE JOHN McLEAN

Dissenting Opinion

March 6, 1857

The son of Scotch-Irish immigrants, John McLean (1785–1861) was born in Morris County, New Jersey. Shortly after his birth the McLean family moved to the Ohio frontier. With little formal education, McLean studied law under Arthur St. Clair, the former governor of the Northwest Territory. He practiced law from 1807 to 1813, served in Congress from 1813 to 1816, and was a justice of the Ohio Supreme Court from 1816 to 1822. In 1823 President James Monroe appointed McLean to be postmaster general of the United States. He held this position until March 1829, when Andrew Jackson nominated him to the U.S. Supreme Court. A day later the Senate confirmed him. McLean remained on the Court until he died in April 1861. Although on the Court, McLean persistently pursued the presidency. He was considered for or actively pursued a presidential nomination with the Anti-Masonic Party (1832), the Whigs (1836, 1844, and 1848), the Free Soil Party (1848), the Free Democrats (1852), the Republicans (1856 and 1860), and the Constitutional Union Party (1860). By 1857 McLean was the only strong opponent of slavery on the Court. McLean's thirty-five-page dissent in Dred Scott *was the third longest of the opinions. He argues that the question of Dred Scott's right to sue is not even legitimately before the Court. McLean takes a traditional antislavery view of the law—that slavery can be established only through positive law and cannot exist without it—and emphatically argues that slavery is strictly a state institution, not national, and not protected by the Constitution per se. McLean stresses the fact that under Missouri law Dred Scott became free when his master took him to Illinois and Minnesota. Like Justice Curtis in his dissent, McLean argues that once Dred Scott became free he was free forever, and thus the Missouri Supreme Court cannot change that status simply by changing its jurisprudence. Justice McLean's opinion did not become as famous as Curtis's (Document 9). Why might this be so? Is McLean's opinion more "political" than Curtis's? Or is it possible that because McLean was an active Republican (who still hoped for a presidential nomination in 1860) people perceived his opinion as being more political?*

Mr. Justice McLean dissenting. . . .

In the first place, the plea to the jurisdiction is not before us. . . .

The decision on the [plea in abatement] was in favor of the plaintiff . . . [and] he does not complain of the decision on [it]. The defendant might have complained of this decision, as against him, and have prosecuted a writ of error, to reverse it. But as the case, under the instruction of the court to the jury, was decided in his favor, of course he had no ground of complaint.

But it is said, if the court, on looking at the record, shall clearly perceive that the Circuit Court had no jurisdiction, it is a ground for the dismissal of the case. This may be characterized as rather a sharp practice, and one which seldom, if ever, occurs. No case was cited in the argument as authority, and not a single case precisely in point is recollected in our reports. . . . Now, the plea which raises the question of jurisdiction, in my judgment, is radically defective. [Sanford's] plea is this: "That the plaintiff is a negro of African descent, his ancestors being of pure African blood, and were brought into this country, and sold as negro slaves."

. . . [B]ut this does not show that he is not a citizen of Missouri, within the meaning of the act of Congress authorizing him to sue in the Circuit Court. It has never been held necessary, to constitute a citizen within the act, that he should have the qualifications of an elector. Females and minors may sue in the Federal courts, and so may any individual who has a permanent domicil in the State under whose laws his rights are protected, and to which he owes allegiance.

Being born under our Constitution and laws, no naturalization is required, as one of foreign birth, to make him a citizen. The most general and appropriate definition of the term citizen is "a freeman." Being a freeman, and having his domicil in a State different from that of the defendant, he is a citizen within the act of Congress, and the courts of the Union are open to him. . . .

In the argument, it was said that a colored citizen would not be an agreeable member of society. This is more a matter of taste than of law. Several of the States have admitted persons of color to the right of suffrage, and in this view have recognized them as citizens; and this has been done in the slave as well as the free States.[1] On the question of citizenship, it must be admitted that we have not been very fastidious. Under the late treaty with Mexico, we have made citizens of all grades, combinations, and colors. The same was done in the admission of Louisiana and Florida. No one ever doubted, and no court ever held, that the people of these Territories did not become citizens under the treaty. They have exercised all the rights of citizens, without being naturalized under the acts of Congress. . . .

In the great and leading case of Prigg *v.* The State of Pennsylvania [1842], this court say that, by the general law of nations, no nation is bound to recognise the state of slavery, as found within its territorial dominions, where it is in opposition to its own policy and institutions, in favor of the subjects of other nations where slavery is organized. If it does it, it is as a matter of comity, and not as a matter of international right. The state of slavery is deemed to be a mere municipal regulation, founded upon and limited to the range of the territorial laws. This was fully recognized in Somersett's case, [Great Britain, 1772] which was decided before the American Revolution. . . .

In giving the opinion of the court [in *Somerset*], Lord Mansfield said: "The state of slavery is of such a nature that it is incapable of being introduced on any reasons, moral or political, but only by positive law, which preserves its force long after the reasons, occasion, and time itself, from whence it was created, is erased from the memory; it is of a nature that nothing can be suffered to support it but positive law." . . .

Slavery is emphatically a State institution. . . .

In the formation of the Federal Constitution, care was taken to confer no power on the Federal Government to interfere with this institution in the States. In the provision respecting the slave trade, in fixing the ratio of representation, and providing for the reclamation of fugitives from

---

[1]In mentioning the "slave" states in this sentence, McLean was undoubtedly referring to the fact that until the late 1830s free blacks had been allowed to vote in North Carolina and Tennessee.

labor, slaves were referred to as persons, and in no other respect are they considered in the Constitution.

We need not refer to the mercenary spirit which introduced the infamous traffic in slaves, to show the degradation of negro slavery in our country. This system was imposed upon our colonial settlements by the mother country, and it is due to truth to say that the commercial colonies and States were chiefly engaged in the traffic. But we know as a historical fact, that James Madison, that great and good man, a leading member in the Federal Convention, was solicitous to guard the language of that instrument so as not to convey the idea that there could be property in man.

I prefer the lights of Madison, Hamilton, and Jay,[2] as a means of construing the Constitution. . . .

Many of the States, on the adoption of the Constitution, or shortly afterward, took measures to abolish slavery within their respective jurisdictions; and it is a well-known fact that a belief was cherished by the leading men, South as well as North, that the institution of slavery would gradually decline, until it would become extinct. . . .

The power of Congress to establish Territorial Governments, and to prohibit the introduction of slavery therein, is the next point to be considered.

. . . [The Northwest Ordinance] was passed . . . while the Federal Convention was in session, about two months before the Constitution was adopted by the Convention. The members of the Convention must therefore have been well acquainted with the provisions of the Ordinance. It provided for a temporary Government, as initiatory to the formation of State Governments. Slavery was prohibited in the territory.

Can any one suppose that the eminent men of the Federal Convention could have overlooked or neglected a matter so vitally important to the country, in the organization of temporary Governments for the vast territory northwest of the river Ohio? In the 3d section of the 4th article of the Constitution, they did make provision for the admission of new States, the sale of the public lands, and the temporary Government of the territory. Without a temporary Government, new States could not have been formed, nor could the public lands have been sold.

---

[2]James Madison, Alexander Hamilton, and John Jay were the three authors of the *Federalist Papers,* a series of essays written to support the ratification of the Constitution and to explain its meaning. This is McLean's response to Justice Campbell, who relied on opponents of the Constitution, like Patrick Henry and George Mason, to support his views.

If the third section were before us now for consideration for the first time, under the facts stated, I could not hesitate to say there was adequate legislative power given in it. The power to make all needful rules and regulations is a power to legislate. . . . But it is argued that the word territory is used as synonymous with the word land; and that the rules and regulations of Congress are limited to the disposition of lands and other property belonging to the United States. That this is not the true construction of the section appears from the fact that in the first line of the section "the power to dispose of the public lands" is given expressly, and, in addition, to make all needful rules and regulations. The power to dispose of is complete in itself, and requires nothing more. It authorizes Congress to use the proper means within its discretion, and any further provision for this purpose would be a useless verbiage. . . .

In the discussion of the power of Congress to govern a Territory, in the case of the Atlantic Insurance Company *v.* Canter [1828], Chief Justice Marshall, speaking for the court, said, in regard to the people of Florida, "they do not, however, participate in political power; they do not share in the Government till Florida shall become a State; in the mean time, Florida continues to be a Territory of the United States, governed by virtue of that clause in the Constitution which empowers Congress to make all needful rules and regulations respecting the territory or other property belonging to the United States."

And . . . in the close of the opinion, the court say, "in legislating for them [the Territories,][3] Congress exercises the combined powers of the General and State Governments." . . .

If Congress should deem slaves or free colored persons injurious to the population of a free Territory, as conducing to lessen the value of the public lands, or on any other ground connected with the public interest, they have the power to prohibit them from becoming settlers in it. This can be sustained on the ground of a sound national policy, which is so clearly shown in our history by practical results, that it would seem no considerate individuals can question it. And, as regards any unfairness of such a policy to our Southern brethren, as urged in the argument, it is only necessary to say that, with one-fourth of the Federal population of the Union, they have in the slave States a larger extent of fertile territory than is included in the free States; and it is submitted, if masters of slaves be restricted from bringing them into free territory, that the restriction on the free citizens of non-slaveholding States, by bringing slaves into free territory, is four times greater than that complained of

[3]McLean's addition.

by the South. But, not only so; some three or four hundred thousand holders of slaves, by bringing them into free territory, impose a restriction on twenty millions of the free States. The repugnancy to slavery would probably prevent fifty or a hundred freemen from settling in a slave Territory, where one slaveholder would be prevented from settling in a free Territory.

This remark is made in answer to the argument urged, that a prohibition of slavery in the free Territories is inconsistent with the continuance of the Union. Where a Territorial Government is established in a slave Territory, it has uniformly remained in that condition until the people form a State Constitution; the same course where the Territory is free, both parties acting in good faith, would be attended with satisfactory results.

The sovereignty of the Federal Government extends to the entire limits of our territory. Should any foreign power invade our jurisdiction, it would be repelled. There is a law of Congress to punish our citizens for crimes committed in districts of [the] country where there is no organized Government. Criminals are brought to certain Territories or States, designated in the law, for punishment. Death has been inflicted in Arkansas and in Missouri, on individuals, for murders committed beyond the limit of any organized Territory or State; and no one doubts that such a jurisdiction was rightfully exercised. If there be a right to acquire territory, there necessarily must be an implied power to govern it. When the military force of the Union shall conquer a country, may not Congress provide for the government of such country? This would be an implied power essential to the acquisition of new territory. This power has been exercised, without doubt of its constitutionality, over territory acquired by conquest and purchase. . . .

[I now] consider whether the status of slavery attached to the plaintiff and wife, on their return to Missouri. . . .

The States of Missouri and Illinois are bounded by a common line. The one prohibits slavery, the other admits it. This has been done by the exercise of that sovereign power which appertains to each. We are bound to respect the institutions of each, as emanating from the voluntary action of the people. Have the people of either any right to disturb the relations of the other? Each State rests upon the basis of its own sovereignty, protected by the Constitution. Our Union has been the foundation of our prosperity and national glory. Shall we not cherish and maintain it? This can only be done by respecting the legal rights of each State.

If a citizen of a free State shall entice or enable a slave to escape from the service of his master, the law holds him responsible, not only for the loss of the slave, but he is liable to be indicted and fined for the misdemeanor. And I am bound here to say, that I have never found a jury in the four States which constitute my circuit, which have not sustained this law, where the evidence required them to sustain it. And it is proper that I should also say, that more cases have arisen in my circuit, by reason of its extent and locality, than in all other parts of the Union. This has been done to vindicate the sovereign rights of the Southern States, and protect the legal interests of our brethren of the South.

Let these facts be contrasted with the case now before the court. Illinois has declared in the most solemn and impressive form that there shall be neither slavery nor involuntary servitude in that State, and that any slave brought into it, with a view of becoming a resident, shall be emancipated. And effect has been given to this provision of the Constitution by the decision of the Supreme Court of that State. With a full knowledge of these facts, a slave is brought from Missouri to Rock Island, in the State of Illinois, and is retained there as a slave for two years, and then taken to Fort Snelling, where slavery is prohibited by the Missouri compromise act, and there he is detained two years longer in a state of slavery. Harriet, his wife, was also kept at the same place four years as a slave, having been purchased in Missouri. They were then removed to the State of Missouri, and sold as slaves, and in the action before us they are not only claimed as slaves, but a majority of my brethren have held that on their being returned to Missouri the status of slavery attached to them.

I am not able to reconcile this result with the respect due to the State of Illinois. Having the same rights of sovereignty as the State of Missouri in adopting a Constitution, I can perceive no reason why the institutions of Illinois should not receive the same consideration as those of Missouri. Allowing to my brethren the same right of judgment that I exercise myself, I must be permitted to say that it seems to me the principle laid down will enable the people of a slave State to introduce slavery into a free State, for a longer or shorter time, as may suit their convenience; and by returning the slave to the State whence he was brought, by force or otherwise, the status of slavery attaches, and protects the rights of the master, and defies the sovereignty of the free State. There is no evidence before us that Dred Scott and his family returned to Missouri voluntarily. The contrary is inferable . . . : "In the year 1838, Dr. Emerson removed the plaintiff and said Harriet, and their daughter Eliza, from Fort Snelling to the State of Missouri, where they have ever since resided." This is the agreed case; and can it be inferred from this that Scott and family returned to Missouri voluntarily? He was removed; which shows that he was passive, as a slave, having exercised no volition on the subject. He did not resist the master by absconding or force. . . . It would be a mockery of law and an outrage on his rights to coerce his return, and then claim that it was voluntary, and on that ground that his former status of slavery attached.

If the decision be placed on this ground, it is a fact for a jury to decide, whether the return was voluntary, or else the fact should be distinctly admitted. A presumption against the plaintiff in this respect, I say with confidence, is not authorized from the facts admitted. . . .

In every decision of a slave case prior to that of Dred Scott *v.* Emerson, the Supreme Court of Missouri considered it as turning upon the Constitution of Illinois, the ordinance of 1787, or the Missouri compromise act of 1820. The court treated these acts as in force, and held itself bound to execute them, by declaring the slave to be free who had acquired a domicil under them with the consent of his master.

The late decision reversed this whole line of adjudication, and held that neither the Constitution and laws of the States, nor acts of Congress in relation to Territories, could be judicially noticed by the Supreme Court of Missouri. This is believed to be in conflict with the decisions of all the courts in the Southern States, with some exceptions of recent cases.

[McLean discusses cases from Louisiana, Mississippi, Virginia, the District of Columbia, and Kentucky, in which slaves gained their liberty because of residence or transit in a free state.]

In the case of Rankin *v.* Lydia [1820] Judge Mills, speaking for the Court of Appeals of Kentucky, says:

"If, by the positive provision in our code, we can and must hold our slaves in the one case, and statutory provisions equally positive decide against that right in the other, and liberate the slave, he must, by an authority equally imperious, be declared free. Every argument which supports the right of the master on one side, based upon the force of written law, must be equally conclusive in favor of the slave, when he can point out in the statute the clause which secures his freedom."

And he further said:

"Free people of color in all the States are, it is believed, quasi citizens, or, at least, denizens. Although none of the States may allow them the privilege of office and suffrage, yet all other civil and conventional rights are secured to them; at least, such rights were evidently secured to them by the ordinance in question for the government of Indiana. If these rights are vested in that or any other portion of the United States, can it be compatible with the spirit of our confederated Government to deny their existence in any other part? Is there less comity existing between State and State, or State and Territory, than exists between the despotic Governments of Europe?"

These are the words of a learned and great judge, born and educated in a slave State. . . .

But there is another ground which I deem conclusive, and which re-state.

The Supreme Court of Missouri refused to notice the act of Congress or the Constitution of Illinois, under which Dred Scott, his wife and children, claimed that they are entitled to freedom.

This being rejected by the Missouri court, there was no case before it, or least it was a case with only one side. And this is the case which in the opinion of this court, we are bound to follow. The Missouri court disregards the express provisions of an act of Congress and the Constitution of a sovereign State, both of which laws for twenty-eight years it had not only regarded, but carried into effect.

If a State court may do this, on a question involving the liberty of human being, what protection do the laws afford? So far from this being a Missouri question, it is a question, as it would seem, within the twenty-fifth section of the judiciary act, where a right to freedom being set up under the act of Congress, and the decision being against such right, it may be brought for revision before this court, from the Supreme Court of Missouri.

I think the judgment of the court below should be reversed.

9

JUSTICE BENJAMIN ROBBINS CURTIS

Dissenting Opinion
March 6, 1857

Born in Watertown, Massachusetts, Benjamin Robbins Curtis (1809–1874) graduated from Harvard College in 1829 and Harvard Law School in 1832. Supreme Court Justice Joseph Story, who taught at Harvard Law School, considered Curtis to be one of his best students. Curtis was politically conservative and never sympathetic to the opponents of slavery. As a young man he had, in Commonwealth v. Aves *(1836), represented a slaveowner who had brought a slave to Massachusetts. In* Aves *Curtis argued that Massachusetts should not free a slave accompanying a visiting master. Unlike most Bostonians, Curtis supported the Fugitive Slave Law of 1850. He was not personally proslavery, but like many northern doughfaces, he despised abolitionists and was a staunch nationalist willing to placate the South. Indeed, his endorsement of the Fugitive Slave Law led President Millard Fillmore to nominate him to the U.S. Supreme Court in 1851. In 1854 Curtis supported the indictment of Massachusetts abolitionists who had tried to rescue the fugitive slave Anthony Burns. Not surprisingly, many of his fellow Bostonians called him the "slave-catcher judge." Thus Curtis's vigorous dissent in* Dred Scott *was somewhat surprising.*

His seventy-page dissent—sixteen pages longer than Taney's majority opinion—is remembered primarily because he so overwhelmingly refutes Chief Justice Taney's assertions that free blacks had no political rights when the United States adopted the Constitution. Curtis shows that blacks were in fact citizens of a number of states in 1787. Curtis also argues that in Anglo-American law, birth has always been tied to citizenship and that allowing slavery into the territories requires allowing all of the laws of a slave society into the territories. He writes:

> *[T]he rights, powers, and obligations, which grow out of that status [of a slave], must be defined, protected, and enforced, by such laws. The liability of the master for the torts and crimes of his slave, and of third persons for assaulting or injuring or harboring or kidnapping him, the forms and modes of emancipation and sale, their subjection to the debts of the master, succession by death of the master, suits for freedom, the capacity of the slave to be party to a suit, or to be a witness, with such police regulations as have existed in all civilized States where slavery has been tolerated, are among the subjects upon which municipal legislation becomes necessary when slavery is introduced.*

Curtis's dissent, widely read in the North, was used by some northern legislatures as the basis for resolutions opposing Taney's opinion. Curtis's opinion became a political document during the elections of 1858 and 1860, with Republicans reprinting it in whole or part. But Curtis was no radical and no fan of the Republicans. His dissent does not endorse racial equality; it argues that the states are free to deny citizenship to blacks. During the Civil War, Curtis reverted to his conservative doughface views. He supported the war but opposed almost all of Lincoln's domestic policies, opposed the Emancipation Proclamation, and in 1868 defended Andrew Johnson during his impeachment trial.

How does Curtis's opinion compare with Taney's? Who has the better argument on the citizenship of blacks and the meaning of the Constitution? Why would a northern conservative, who often supported the interests of the South, write this opinion?

Mr. Justice Curtis dissenting. . . .

[The] . . . question is, whether any person of African descent, whose ancestors were sold as slaves in the United States, can be a citizen of the United States. If any such person can be a citizen, this plaintiff has the right to the judgment of the court . . . ; for no cause is shown . . . why he is not so, except his descent and slavery of his ancestors.

The first section of the second article of the Constitution uses the language, "a citizen of the United States at the time of the adoption of the Constitution." One mode of approaching this question is, to inquire who were citizens of the United States at the time of the adoption if the Constitution. . . .

To determine whether any free persons, descended from Africans held in slavery, were citizens of the United States . . . at the time of the adoption of the Constitution of the United States, it is only necessary to know whether any such persons were citizens of either of the States under the Confederation, at the time of the adoption of the Constitution.

Of this there can be no doubt. At the time of the ratification of the Articles of Confederation, all free native-born inhabitants of the States of New Hampshire, Massachusetts, New York, New Jersey, and North Carolina, though descended from African slaves, were not only citizens of those States, but such of them as had the other necessary qualifications possessed the franchise of electors, on equal terms with other citizens.[1] . . .

[In Massachusetts] . . . persons of color, descended from African slaves, were by [the 1780 state] Constitution made citizens of the State; and such of them as have had the necessary qualifications, have held and exercised the elective franchise, as citizens, from that time to the present. . . .

The [1784] Constitution of New Hampshire conferred the elective franchise upon "every inhabitant of the State having the necessary qualifications," of which color or descent was not one.

---

[1] Oddly, Curtis failed to note that in the 1780s, when the Constitution was written and ratified, free black men could also vote in Pennsylvania.

The Constitution of New York gave the right to vote to "every male inhabitant . . ." making no discrimination between free colored persons and others. . . .

That of New Jersey, to "all inhabitants of this colony, of full age who are worth £50 proclamation money, clear estate."

New York, by its Constitution of 1820 [actually, it was 1821], required colored persons have some qualifications as prerequisites for voting, which white persons need not possess. And New Jersey, by its present Constitution restricts the right to vote to white male citizens. But these changes can have no other effect upon the present inquiry,[2] except to show, that before they were made, no such restrictions existed; and colored in common with white persons, were not only citizens of those States, but entitled to the elective franchise on the same qualifications as white persons, as they now are in New Hampshire and Massachusetts. . . . And . . . no argument can obscure, that in some of the original thirteen States, free colored persons, before and at the time of the formation of the Constitution, were citizens of those States.

The fourth of the fundamental articles of the Confederation was as follows: "The free inhabitants of each of these States, paupers vagabonds, and fugitives from justice, excepted, shall be entitled to all the privileges and immunities of free citizens in the several States."

The fact that free persons of color were citizens of some of the several States, and the consequence, that this fourth article of the Confederation would have the effect to confer on such persons the privileges and immunities of general citizenship, were not only known to those who framed and adopted those articles, but the evidence is decisive, that the fourth article was intended to have that effect, and that more restricted language, which would have excluded such persons, was deliberately and purposely rejected.

On the 25th of June, 1778 . . . the delegates from South Carolina moved to amend this fourth article, by inserting after the word "free and before the word "inhabitants," the word "white," so that the privileges and immunities of general citizenship would be secured only to white persons. Two States voted for the amendment, eight States against it, and the vote of one State was divided. The language of article stood unchanged, and both by its terms of inclusion, "free inhabitants," and the strong implication from its terms of exclusion "paupers, vagabonds, and fugitives from justice," who alone were excepted, it is clear, that

---

[2]Curtis might also have noted that blacks could no longer vote in North Carolina, Pennsylvania, or Tennessee (which became a state in 1796), but they could vote in Vermont, Maine, and Rhode Island by the time *Dred Scott* was decided.

under the Confederation, and at the time of the adoption of the Constitution, free colored persons of African descent might be, and, by reason of their citizenship in certain States, were entitled to the privileges and immunities of general citizenship of the United States.

Did the Constitution of the United States deprive them or their descendants of citizenship?

That Constitution was ordained and established by the people of the United States, through the action, in each State, of those persons who were qualified by its laws to act thereon, in behalf of themselves and all other citizens of that State. In some of the States, as we have seen, colored persons were among those qualified by law to act on this subject. These colored persons were not only included in the body of "the people of the United States," by whom the Constitution was ordained and established, but in at least five of the States they had the power to act, and doubtless did act, by their suffrages, upon the question of its adoption. It would be strange, if we were to find in that instrument anything which deprived of their citizenship any part of the people of the United States who were among those by whom it was established.

I can find nothing in the Constitution which, *proprio vigore* [by its own force], deprives of their citizenship any class of persons who were citizens of the United States at the time of its adoption, or who should be native-born citizens of any State after its adoption; nor any power enabling Congress to disfranchise persons born on the soil of any State, and entitled to citizenship of such State by its Constitution and laws. And my opinion is, that, under the Constitution of the United States, every free person born on the soil of a State, who is a citizen of that State by force of its Constitution or laws, is also a citizen of the United States. . . .

Undoubtedly . . . it is a principle of public law, recognized by the Constitution itself, that birth on the soil of a country both creates the duties and confers the rights of citizenship. . . .

But, further: though . . . I do not think the enjoyment of the elective franchise essential to citizenship, there can be no doubt it is one of the chiefest attributes of citizenship under the American Constitution; and the just and constitutional possession of this right is decisive evidence of citizenship. The provisions made by a Constitution on this subject must therefore be looked to as bearing directly on the question what persons are citizens under that Constitution; and as being decisive, to this extent, that all such persons as are allowed by the Constitution to exercise the elective franchise, and thus, to participate in the Government of the United States, must be deemed citizens of the United States. . . .

It has been often asserted that the Constitution was made exclusively by and for the white race. It has already been shown that in five [actually it was six states since Curtis failed to note black voting in Pennsylvania] of the thirteen original States, colored persons then possessed the elective franchise, and were among those by whom the Constitution was ordained and established. If so, it is not true, in point of fact, that the Constitution was made exclusively by the white race. And that it was made exclusively for the white race is, in my opinion, not only an assumption not warranted by anything in the Constitution, but contradicted by its opening declaration, that it was ordained and established by the people of the United States, for themselves and their posterity. And as free colored persons were then citizens of at least five States, and so in every sense part of the people of the United States, they were among those for whom and whose posterity the Constitution was ordained and established. . . .

It has been further objected, that if free colored persons, born within a particular State, and made citizens of that State by its Constitution and laws, are thereby made citizens of the United States, then . . . such persons would be entitled to all the privileges and immunities of citizens in the several States; and if so, then colored persons could vote, and be eligible to not only Federal offices, but offices even in those States whose Constitutions and laws disqualify colored persons from voting or being elected to office.

But this position rests upon an assumption which I deem untenable. Its basis is, that no one can be deemed a citizen of the United States who is not entitled to enjoy all the privileges and franchises which are conferred on any citizen. . . . That this is not true, under the Constitution of the United States, seems to me clear.

A naturalized citizen cannot be President of the United States, nor a Senator till after the lapse of nine years, nor a Representative till after the lapse of seven years, from his naturalization. Yet, as soon as naturalized, he is certainly a citizen of the United States. Nor is any inhabitant of the District of Columbia, or . . . of the Territories, eligible to the office of Senator or Representative in Congress, though they may be citizens of the United States. So, in all the States, numerous persons, though citizens, cannot vote, or cannot hold office, either on account of their age, or sex, or the want of the necessary legal qualifications. The truth is, that citizenship, under the Constitution of the United States, is not dependent on the possession of any particular political or even of all civil rights; and any attempt so to define it must lead to error. To what citizens the elective franchise shall be confided, is a question to be

determined by each State, in accordance with its own views of the neces-
sities or expediencies of its condition. What civil rights shall be enjoyed
by its citizens, and whether all shall enjoy the same, or how they may be
gained or lost, are to be determined in the same way.

One may confine the right of suffrage to white male citizens; another
may extend it to colored persons and females; one may allow all persons
above a prescribed age to convey property and transact business; another
may exclude married women. But whether native-born women, or persons under age, or under guardianship because insane or spendthrifts, be
excluded from voting or holding office, or allowed to do so, I apprehend
no one will deny that they are citizens of the United States. . . .

It has sometimes been urged that colored persons are shown not to
be citizens of the United States by the fact that the naturalization laws
apply only to white persons. But whether a person born in the United
States be or be not a citizen, cannot depend on laws which refer only to
aliens, and do not affect the *status* of persons born in the United States.
The utmost effect which can be attributed to them is, to show that Congress has not deemed it expedient generally to apply the rule to colored
aliens. That they might do so, if thought fit, is clear. The Constitution
has not excluded them. . . .

I do not deem it necessary to review at length the legislation of Congress having more or less bearing on the citizenship of colored persons. . . . Undoubtedly they have been debarred from the exercise of
particular rights or privileges extended to white persons, but, I believe,
always in terms which, by implication, admit they may be citizens. Thus
the [1792] act . . . for the organization of the militia, directs the enrol-
ment of "every free, able-bodied, white male citizen." An assumption that
none but white persons are citizens, would be as inconsistent with the just
import of this language, as that all citizens are able-bodied, or males. . . .

The conclusions at which I have arrived on this part of the case are:

First. That the free native-born citizens of each State are citizens of
the United States.

Second. That as free colored persons born within some of the States
are citizens of those States, such persons are also citizens of the United
States.

Third. That every such citizen, residing in any State, has the right
to sue and is liable to be sued in the Federal courts, as a citizen of that
State in which he resides.

Fourth. That as the plea to the jurisdiction in this case shows no facts,
except that the plaintiff was of African descent, and his ancestors were

sold as slaves, and as these facts are not inconsistent with his citizenship of the United States, and his residence in the State of Missouri, the plea to the jurisdiction was bad, and judgment of the Circuit Court overruling it was correct.

I dissent, therefore, from that part of the opinion of the majority of the court, in which it is held that a person of African descent cannot be a citizen of the United States; and I regret I must go further, and dissent both from what I deem their assumption of authority to examine the constitutionality of the act of Congress commonly called the Missouri compromise act. . . .

Having first decided that they were bound to consider the sufficiency of the plea to the jurisdiction of the Circuit Court, and having decided that this plea showed that the Circuit Court had not jurisidiction, and consequently that this is a case to which the judicial power of the United States does not extend, they have gone on to examine the merits of the case . . . and so have reached the question of the power of Congress to pass the act of 1820. . . . [I]n my opinion, such an exertion of judicial power transcends the limits of the authority of the court. . . .

I do not consider it to be within the scope of the judicial power of the majority of the court to pass upon any question respecting the plaintiff's citizenship in Missouri, save that raised by the plea to the jurisdiction; and I do not hold any opinion of this court, or any court, binding, when expressed on a question not legitimately before it. . . . The judgment of this court is, that the case is to be dismissed for want of jurisdiction, because the plaintiff was not a citizen of Missouri. . . . Into that judgment, according to the settled course of this court, nothing appearing after a plea to the merits can enter. A great question of constitutional law, deeply affecting the peace and welfare of the country, is not, in my opinion, a fit subject to be thus reached.

But as, in my opinion, the Circuit Court had jurisdiction, I am obliged to consider the question whether its judgment on the merits of the case should stand or be reversed. . . .

The general question may be stated to be, whether the plaintiff's *status*, as a slave, was so changed by his residence within that territory, that he was not a slave in the State of Missouri, at the time this action was brought. . . .

[If] the acts of Congress on this subject are valid, the law of the Territory of Wisconsin, within whose limits the residence of the plaintiff and his wife, and their marriage and the birth of one or both of their children, took place, . . . is a law operating directly on the *status* of the slave. [The Missouri Compromise] enacted that, within this Territory, "slavery and involuntary servitude, otherwise than in the punishment of crimes whereof the parties shall have been duly convicted, shall be, and is hereby, forever prohibited. . . ."

[Curtis explains why under international law and American domestic law the state of Missouri was obligated to enforce any change Dred Scott's status caused by his residence in the Wisconsin Territory.]

It becomes necessary, therefore, to inquire whether the operation of the laws of the Territory of Wisconsin upon the *status* of the plaintiff was or was not such an operation as these principles of international law require other States to recognise and allow effect to. . . .

The material facts agreed, bearing on this part of the case, are, that Dr. Emerson, the plaintiff's master, resided about two years at the military post of Fort Snelling. . . .

On what ground can it be denied that all valid laws of the United States, constitutionally enacted by Congress for the government of the Territory, rightfully extended over an officer of the United States and his servant who went into the Territory to remain there for an indefinite length of time, to take part in its civil or military affairs? They were not foreigners, coming from abroad. Dr. Emerson was a citizen of the country which had exclusive jurisdiction over the Territory; and not only a citizen, but he went there in a public capacity, in the service of the same sovereignty which made the laws. . . . Whether the laws now in question were constitutionally enacted, I repeat once more, is a separate question. But, assuming that they were, . . . I consider that no other State or country could question the rightful power of the United States so to legislate, or, consistently with the settled rules of international law, could refuse to recognise the effects of such legislation upon the *status* of their officers and servants, as valid everywhere.

This alone would, in my apprehension, be sufficient to decide this question.

But there are other facts stated on the record which should not be passed over. It is agreed that, in the year 1836, the plaintiff, while residing in the Territory, was married, with the consent of Dr. Emerson, to Harriet. . . . And the inquiry is, whether, after the marriage of the plaintiff in the Territory, with the consent of Dr. Emerson, any other State or Country can, consistently with the settled rules of international law, refuse to recognise and treat him as a free man, when suing for the liberty of himself, his wife, and the children of that marriage. . . .

If the laws of Congress governing the Territory of Wisconsin were constitutional and valid laws, there can be no doubt these parties were capable of contracting a lawful marriage, attended with all the usual civil rights and obligations of that condition. In that Territory they were absolutely free persons, having full capacity to enter into the civil contract of marriage.

It is a principle of international law, settled beyond controversy in England and America, that a marriage, valid by the law of the place where it was contracted, and not in fraud of the law of any other place, is valid everywhere. . . .

What, then, shall we say of the consent of the master, that the slave may contract a lawful marriage, attended with all the civil rights and duties which belong to that relation; that he may enter into a relation which none but a free man can assume — a relation which involves not only the rights and duties of the slave, but those of the other party to the contract, and of their descendants to the remotest generation? In my judgment, there can be no more effectual abandonment of the legal rights of a master over his slave, than by the consent of the master that the slave should enter into a contract of marriage, in a free State, attended by all the civil rights and obligations which belong to that condition.

And any claim by Dr. Emerson . . . the effect of which is to deny the validity of this marriage, and the lawful paternity of the children born from it, wherever asserted, is, in my judgment, a claim inconsistent with good faith and sound reason, as well as with the rules of international law. And I go further: in my opinion, a law of . . . Missouri, which should thus annul a marriage, lawfully contracted by these parties while resident in Wisconsin, not in fraud of any law of Missouri . . . would be a law impairing the obligation of a contract, and within the prohibition of the Constitution of the United States. . . .

To avoid misapprehension on this important and difficult subject, I will state, distinctly, the conclusions at which I have arrived. They are:

First. The rules of international law respecting the emancipation of slaves, by the rightful operation of the laws of another State or country upon the *status* of the slave, while resident in such foreign State or country, are part of the common law of Missouri, and have not been abrogated by any statute law of that State.

Second. The laws of the United States, constitutionally enacted, which operated directly on and changed the *status* of a slave coming into the Territory of Wisconsin with his master, who went thither to reside for an indefinite length of time, in the performance of his duties as an officer of the United States, had a rightful operation on the *status* of the slave, and it is in conformity with the rules of international law that this change of *status* should be recognised everywhere.

Third. The laws of the United States, in operation in the Territory of Wisconsin at the time of the plaintiffs residence there, did act directly on the *status* of the plaintiff, and change his *status* to that of a free man.

Fourth. The plaintiff and his wife were capable of contracting, and with the consent of Dr. Emerson, did contract a marriage in that Territory, valid under its laws; and the validity of this marriage cannot be questioned in Missouri, save by showing that it was fraud of the laws of that State, or of some right derived from them; which cannot be shown in this case, because the master consented to it.

Fifth. That the consent of the master that his slave, residing in a country which does not tolerate slavery, may enter into a lawful contract of marriage, attended with the civil rights and duties which belong to that condition, is an effectual act of emancipation. And the law does not enable Dr. Emerson, or any one claiming under him assert a title to the married persons as slaves, and thus destroy the obligation of the contract of marriage, and bastardize their issue, and reduce them to slavery. . . .

I have thus far assumed, merely for the purpose of the argument, that the laws of the United States, respecting slavery in this Territory, were constitutionally enacted by Congress. It remains to inquire whether they are constitutional and binding laws. . . .

. . . [W]hen the Federal Constitution was framed, and presented to the people of the several States for their consideration, the unsettled [Northwest] territory was viewed as justly applicable to the common benefit, so far as it then had or might attain thereafter a pecuniary value; and so far as it might become the seat of new States, to be admitted into the Union upon an equal footing with the original States. . . . The ordinance of 1787 had made provision for the temporary government of so much of the territory actually ceded as lay northwest of the river Ohio. . . .

The Congress of the [Articles of] Confederation [in passing the Northwest Ordinance] had assumed the power not only to dispose of the lands ceded, but to institute Governments and make laws for their inhabitants. . . . The Convention for framing the Constitution was then in session at Philadelphia. The proof is direct and decisive, that it was known to the Convention. . . .

The importance of conferring on the new Government regular powers commensurate with the objects to be attained, and thus avoiding the alternative of a failure to execute the trust assumed by the acceptance of the cessions made and expected, or its execution by usurpation, could scarcely fail to be perceived. That it was in fact perceived, is clearly shown by the Federalist[1] (No. 38,) where this very argument is made use of in commendation of the Constitution. . . .

Any other conclusion would involve the assumption that a subject of the gravest national concern, respecting which the small States felt so much jealousy that it had been almost an insurmountable obstacle to the formation of the Confederation, and as to which all the States had deep pecuniary and political interests, and which had been so recently and constantly agitated, was nevertheless overlooked; or that such a subject was not overlooked, but designedly left unprovided for, though it was manifestly a subject of common concern, which belonged to the care of the General Government, and adequate provision for which could not fail to be deemed necessary and proper. . . .

[Curtis discusses the debates in the constitutional convention over the territories and the admission of new states. This led to two clauses in the final Constitution:]

"New States may be admitted by the Congress into this Union; but no new State shall be formed or erected within the jurisdiction of any other State, nor any State be formed by the junction of two or more States, or parts of States, without the consent of the Legislatures of the States concerned, as well as of Congress.

"The Congress shall have power to dispose of and make all needful rules and regulations respecting the territory or other property belonging to the United States; and nothing in this Constitution shall be so construed as to prejudice any claims of the United States or any particular State" [article IV, section 3]. . . .

It is said this provision has no application to any territory save that then belonging to the United States. . . . [But] when the Constitution was framed, a confident expectation was entertained, which was speedily realized, that North Carolina and Georgia would cede their claims to that great territory which lay west of those States. No doubt has

---

[1] The *Federalist Papers* were a series of essays written by James Madison, Alexander Hamilton, and John Jay in 1787–1788 to gain support for the Constitution. Curtis, like McLean, is trying to tie his position to that of the framers of the Constitution and the founders of the nation.

been suggested that the first clause of this same article, which enabled Congress to admit new States, refers to and includes new States to be formed out of this territory, expected to be thereafter ceded by North Carolina and Georgia, as well as new States to be formed out of territory northwest of the Ohio, which then had been ceded by Virginia. It must have been seen, therefore, that the same necessity would exist for an authority to dispose of and make all needful regulations respecting this territory, when ceded, as existed for a like authority respecting territory which had been ceded.

No reason has been suggested why any reluctance should have been felt, by the framers of the Constitution, to apply this provision to all the territory which might belong to the United States, or why any distinction should have been made, founded on the accidental circumstance of the dates of the cessions; a circumstance in no way material as respects the necessity for rules and regulations, or the propriety of conferring on the Congress power to make them. And if we look at the course of the debates in the Convention on this article, we shall find that the then unceded lands, so far from having been left out of view in adopting this article, constituted, in the minds of members, a subject of even paramount importance.

Again, in what an extraordinary position would the limitation of this clause to territory then belonging to the United States, place the territory which lay within the chartered limits of North Carolina and Georgia. The title to that territory was then claimed by those States, and by the United States . . . ; so that it was impossible then, and has ever since remained impossible, to know whether this territory did or did not then belong to the United States; and, consequently, to know whether it was within or without the authority conferred by this clause, to dispose of and make rules and regulations respecting the territory of the United States. This attributes to the eminent men who acted on this subject a want of ability and forecast, or a want of attention to the known facts upon which they were acting, in which I cannot concur.

There is not, in my judgment, anything in the language, the history, or the subject-matter of this article, which restricts its operation to territory owned by the United States when the Constitution was adopted. . . .

I construe [the territories] clause, therefore, as if it had read, Congress shall have power to make all needful rules and regulations respecting those tracts of country, out of the limits of the several States, which the United States have acquired, or may hereafter acquire, by cessions, as well of the jurisdiction as of the soil, so far as the soil may be the property of the party making the cession, at the time of making it. . . .

If, then, this clause does contain a power to legislate respecting the territory, what are the limits of that power?

To this I answer, that, in common with all the other legislative powers of Congress, it finds limits in the express prohibitions on Congress not to do certain things; that, in the exercise of the legislative power, Congress cannot pass an ex post facto law or bill of attainder; and so in respect to each of the other prohibitions contained in the Constitution.

Besides this, the rules and regulations must be needful. But undoubtedly the question whether a particular rule or regulation be needful, must be finally determined by Congress itself. Whether a law be needful, is a legislative or political, not a judicial, question. Whatever Congress deems needful is so, under the grant of power. . . .

But it is insisted, that whatever other powers Congress may have respecting the territory of the United States, the subject of negro slavery forms an exception.

The Constitution declares that Congress shall have power to make "*all* needful rules and regulations" respecting the territory belonging to the United States.

The assertion is, though the Constitution says all, it does not mean all—though it says all, without qualification, it means all except such as allow or prohibit slavery. It cannot be doubted that it is incumbent on those who would thus introduce an exception not found in the language of the instrument, to exhibit some solid and satisfactory reason, drawn from the subject-matter or the purposes and objects of the clause, the context, or from other provisions of the Constitution, showing that the words employed in this clause are not to be understood according to their clear, plain, and natural signification. . . .

There is nothing in the context which qualifies the grant of power. The regulations must be "respecting the territory." An enactment that slavery may or may not exist there, is a regulation respecting the territory. Regulations must be needful; but it is necessarily left to the legislative discretion to determine whether a law be needful. No other clause of the Constitution has been referred to at the bar . . . which imposes any restrictions or makes any exception concerning the power of Congress to allow or prohibit slavery in the territory belonging to the United States.

A practical construction, nearly contemporaneous with the adoption of the Constitution, and continued by repeated instances through a long series of years, may always influence, and in doubtful cases should determine, the judicial mind, on a question of the interpretation of the Constitution. . . .

It has already been stated, that after the Government of the United States was organized under the Constitution, the temporary Government of the Territory northwest of the river Ohio could no longer exist, save under the powers conferred on Congress by the Constitution. . . . And accordingly, an act was passed on the 7th day of August, 1789 [reenacting the substance of the Northwest Ordinance, including the prohibition of slavery]. . . .

Here is an explicit declaration of the will of the first Congress, of which fourteen members, including Mr. Madison,[2] had been members of the Convention which framed the Constitution, that the ordinance, one article of which prohibited slavery, "should continue to have full effect." Gen. Washington, who signed this bill, as President, was the President of that Convention. . . .

I consider the passage of this law to have been an assertion by the first Congress of the power of the United States to prohibit slavery within this part of the territory of the United States; for it clearly shows that slavery was thereafter to be prohibited there, and it could be prohibited only by an exertion of the power of the United States, under the Constitution; no other power being capable of operating within that territory after the Constitution took effect. . . .

[Curtis discusses eight separate federal laws regulating slavery in the territories that became the free states of Indiana, Illinois, Michigan, Wisconsin, Iowa, and Oregon and the slave states of Tennessee, Louisiana, Mississippi, Alabama, Florida, and Arkansas.]

Here are eight distinct instances, beginning with the first Congress and coming down to the year 1848, in which Congress has excluded slavery from the territory of the United States; and six distinct instances in which Congress organized Governments of Territories by which slavery was recognised and continued, beginning also with the first Congress, and coming down to the year 1822. These acts were severally signed by seven Presidents of the United States, beginning with General Washington, and coming regularly down as far as Mr. John Quincy Adams, thus including all who were in public life when the Constitution was adopted.

---

[2]As he does elsewhere in his opinion, Curtis ties his interpretation to the most famous of the constitutional framers, the "father of the Constitution," James Madison.

If the practical construction of the Constitution contemporaneously with its going into effect, by men intimately acquainted with its history from their personal participation in framing and adopting it, and continued by them through a long series of acts of the gravest importance, be entitled to weight in the judicial mind on a question of construction, it would seem to be difficult to resist the force of the acts above adverted to.

It appears, however, from what has taken place at the bar, that notwithstanding the language of the Constitution, and the long line of legislative and executive precedents under it, three different and opposite views are taken of the power of Congress respecting slavery in the Territories.

One is, that though Congress can make a regulation prohibiting slavery in a Territory, they cannot make a regulation allowing it; another is, that it can neither be established nor prohibited by Congress, but that the people of a Territory, when organized by Congress, can establish or prohibit slavery; while the third is, that the Constitution itself secures to every citizen who holds slaves, under the laws of any State, the indefeasible right to carry them into any Territory, and there hold them as property.

No particular clause of the Constitution has been referred to at the bar in support of either of these views. The first seems to be rested upon general considerations concerning the social and moral evils of slavery, its relations to republican Governments, its inconsistency with the Declaration of Independence and with natural right.

The second is drawn from considerations equally general, concerning the right of self-government, and the nature of the political institutions which have been established by the people of the United States.

While the third is said to rest upon the equal right of all citizens to go with their property upon the public domain, and the inequality of a regulation which would admit the property of some and exclude the property of other citizens; and, inasmuch as slaves are chiefly held by citizens of those particular States where slavery is established, it is insisted that a regulation excluding slavery from a Territory operates, practically, to make an unjust discrimination between citizens of different States, in respect to their use and enjoyment of the territory of the United States.

With the weight of either of these considerations, when presented to Congress to influence its action, this court has no concern. One or the other may be justly entitled to guide or control the legislative judgment upon what is a needful regulation. The question here is, whether they are sufficient to authorize this court to insert into this clause of the Constitution an exception of the exclusion or allowance of slavery, not found therein, nor in any other part of that instrument. To engraft on any instrument a substantive exception not found in it, must be admitted to be a matter attended with great difficulty. And the difficulty increases with the importance of the instrument, and the magnitude and complexity of the interests involved in its construction. To allow this to be done with the Constitution, upon reasons purely political, renders its judicial interpretation impossible—because judicial tribunals, as such, cannot decide upon political considerations. Political reasons have not the requisite certainty to afford rules of judicial interpretation. They are different in different men. They are different in the same men at different times. And when a strict interpretation of the Constitution, according to the fixed rules which govern the interpretation of laws, is abandoned, and the theoretical opinions of individuals are allowed to control its meaning, we have no longer a Constitution; we are under the government of individual men, who for the time being have power to declare what the Constitution is, according to their own views of what it ought to mean. When such a method of interpretation of the Constitution obtains, in place of a republican Government, with limited and defined powers, we have a Government which is merely an exponent of the will of Congress; or what, in my opinion, would not be preferable, an exponent of the individual political opinions of the members of this court.

If it can be shown, by anything in the Constitution itself, that when it confers on Congress the power to make *all* needful rules and regulations respecting the territory belonging to the United States, the exclusion or the allowance of slavery was excepted; or if anything in the history of this provision tends to show that such an exception was intended by those who framed and adopted the Constitution to be introduced into it, I hold it to be my duty carefully to consider, and to allow just weight to such considerations in interpreting the positive text of the Constitution. But where the Constitution has said *all* needful rules and regulations, I must find something more than theoretical reasoning to induce me to say it did not mean all. . . .

[But the opinion of the Court suggests that the slavery prohibition in the Missouri Compromise violates] that clause in the fifth article of the amendments of the Constitution which declares that no person shall be deprived of his life, liberty, or property, without due process of law. . . .

Slavery, being contrary to natural right, is created only by municipal law. This is not only plain in itself, and agreed by all writers on the subject, but is inferable from the Constitution, and has been explicitly declared by this court. The Constitution refers to slaves as "persons held to service in one State, under the laws thereof." Nothing can more clearly describe a *status* created by municipal law. In Prigg v. Pennsylvania, [1842] this court said: "The state of slavery is deemed to be a mere municipal regulation, founded on and limited to the range of territorial laws." In Rankin *v.* Lydia [1820], the Supreme Court of Appeals of Kentucky said: "Slavery is sanctioned by the laws of this State, and the right to hold them under our municipal regulations is unquestionable. But we view this as a right existing by positive law of a municipal character, without foundation in the law of nature or the unwritten common law." I am not acquainted with any case or writer questioning the correctness of this doctrine. . . .

Nor, in my judgment, will the position, that a prohibition to bring slaves into a Territory deprives any one of his property without due process of law, bear examination.

It must be remembered that this restriction on the legislative power is not peculiar to the Constitution of the United States; it was borrowed from *Magna Charta*;[3] was brought to America by our ancestors, as part of their inherited liberties, and has existed in all the States, usually in the very words of the great charter. It existed in every political community in America in 1787, when the ordinance prohibiting slavery north and west of the Ohio was passed.

And if a prohibition of slavery in a Territory in 1820 violated this principle of *Magna Charta*; the ordinance of 1787 also violated it; and what power had, I do not say the Congress of the Confederation alone, but the Legislature of Virginia, or the Legislature of any or all the States of the Confederacy, to consent to such a violation? . . . I think I may at least say, if the Congress did then violate *Magna Charta* by the ordinance, no one discovered that violation. Besides, if the prohibition upon all persons . . . to bring slaves into a Territory, and a declaration that if brought they shall be free, deprives citizens of their property without due process of law, what shall we say of the legislation of many of the slaveholding States which have enacted the same prohibition? As early as October, 1778, a law was passed in Virginia, that thereafter no slave should be imported into that Commonwealth by sea or by land, and that every slave who should be imported should become free. A citizen of

---

[3]In 1215 the leading barons and lords of England forced King John to sign the Magna Carta (Latin for "great charter"; sometimes spelled "Magna Charta," as above). In the Magna Carta the king promised to respect the rights and liberties of "all free men of our kingdom." The document declares that "no freed man shall be taken, imprisoned, disseised, outlawed, banished, or in any way destroyed . . . except by the lawful judgment of his peers and by the LAW OF THE LAND." Four other clauses of the Magna Carta were designed to prevent the king from taking private property without permission of the owner or without payment. While initially seen as protecting the barons and lords of England from abuses by the king, over the centuries the Magna Carta came to stand for the fundamental rights of all Englishmen and, by extension, all Americans.

Virginia purchased in Maryland a slave who belonged to another citizen of Virginia, and removed with the slave to Virginia. The slave sued for her freedom, and recovered it; as may be seen in Wilson *v.* Isabel, (Va., 1805) . . . I am not aware that such laws, though they exist in many States, were ever supposed to be in conflict with the principle of *Magna Charta.* . . . It was certainly understood by the Convention which framed the Constitution, and has been so understood ever since, that, under the power to regulate commerce, Congress could prohibit the importation of slaves; and the exercise of the power was restrained till 1808. A citizen of the United States owns slaves in Cuba, and brings them to the United States, where they are set free by the legislation of Congress. Does this legislation deprive him of his property without due process of law? If so, what becomes of the laws prohibiting the slave trade? If not, how can a similar regulation respecting a Territory violate the fifth amendment of the Constitution? . . .

In my opinion, the judgment of the Circuit Court should be reversed, and the cause remanded for a new trial.

2

Newspaper Responses to the *Dred Scott* Decision

In the nineteenth century, newspapers were rarely politically neutral. They were usually affiliated with a political party, or even a wing of a political party. For example, the Washington *Union* was the unofficial voice of the Buchanan administration and the proslavery wing of the Democratic Party. Similarly, the New York *Tribune*, edited by the famous publisher-politician Horace Greeley, spoke for the antislavery wing of the new Republican Party. Newspapers also actively participated in political debates, and editors debated one another in print. The editorials and articles from the newspapers reprinted in this chapter offer a wide variety of responses to *Dred Scott*.

Varieties of Southern Proslavery Opinion

In the 1850s virtually all southern leaders supported slavery and "southern rights." They did not all agree, however, on the best way to protect the South and its "peculiar institution," as both northerners and southerners referred to slavery.

Some southerners favored states' rights, arguing that the South, with its distinct culture and identity, had to be free of federal interference. The end result of this argument would be secession and the creation of an independent southern nation. An editorial in the Charleston Mercury *(Document 11) illustrates this position. Other southern papers, like the Richmond* Enquirer, *advocated states' rights with strong support for the national union and belief that the national government should protect slavery. The more moderate New Orleans* Picayune, *which was affiliated with the Whig Party, understood that the southern way of life required the economic and military support of the North. In 1857 southern moderates saw no great need to create an independent southern nation. After the election of Lincoln all three of these papers supported secession.*

The sweeping opinion in Dred Scott *pleased southern whites of all political stripes, although the responses varied. The three articles reprinted here reflect the fears and hopes of southerners. Pleased about the result of the case, some southerners nevertheless saw clouds on the horizon.*

The Richmond Enquirer *gleefully praises the decision, seeing it as a nationalist opinion that ends debate over slavery. Significantly, the Richmond paper takes the position that the South has won the constitutional struggle, thus implying that supporters of black rights and opponents of slavery are subversive to the American constitutional order.*

The Charleston Mercury, *which represents the most extreme southern nationalism, expresses surprise that the Supreme Court would so openly support the interests of the South and slavery. Even in the wake of this sweeping victory, the Charleston paper fears the political implications of a national discussion of slavery. The paper correctly predicts that the Republicans will use* Dred Scott *to consolidate their position in the North.*

The more moderate New Orleans Picayune *rejoices in Taney's opinion. Like the Charleston* Mercury, *the* Picayune *believes that the Republicans of the North will try to exploit the opinion. But the* Picayune *reminds its readers that the Court and the Constitution support the South. The* Picayune *also underscores the racism of proslavery thought by declaring that it would not "lament" denying free blacks any political rights, even in the North.*

The debate among these papers is over the best way to protect slavery. The Mercury *favors an approach that combines extreme states' rights ideas with eventual secession. The* Mercury *would have each state free to totally control its own institutions, but only in a nation made up of slave states. For the* Mercury *the United States, as then constituted, presents a constant threat to the South and slavery. The* Mercury *believes that southern rights and southern institutions can never be protected in the national Union and understands that if one Supreme Court decision can nationalize slavery and protect it, another decision might do the opposite. The* Enquirer *had long been a proponent of states' rights as a way of protecting slavery. However, in the* Dred Scott *decision, the Richmond paper sees the value of a more nationalist position. If the Constitution thoroughly protects slavery, then states' rights is not as necessary a political theory. The* Picayune *sees* Dred Scott *as a vindication of its views that the South can safely remain within the Union. The New Orleans*

*paper seems to believe that the debate over slavery in the territories is
now over and the South has won.*

Both the Mercury *and the* Picayune *refer to members of the Republican Party as "black Republicans." This phrase suggests the racial fears
of southerners, who somehow believed that the Republicans would bring
about black equality throughout the nation. Although many Republican
leaders, such as Senators Salmon P. Chase of Ohio and Charles Sumner
of Massachusetts, fervently believed in racial equality, the stated goal of
the Republicans was neither racial equality nor even an end to slavery;
rather, it was the more modest goal that slavery be prohibited from the
western territories and that there be no new slave states admitted to the
Union. Ironically, of course, after eleven slave states attempted to leave
the nation in 1861, sparking the Civil War, the Republican Party became
an advocate of racial equality, and after the war southern blacks almost
unanimously supported the Republicans.*

10

ENQUIRER (RICHMOND)

The Dred Scott *Case*

March 10, 1857

In anticipation of the definitive decision of the Supreme Court of the
United States in the Dred Scott case, some two months or more ago,
its adjudication was announced through a respectable proportion of the
press, emanating, we do not now recollect precisely, whence or how;
but, as the sequel shows, not from mere conjecture, or without reliable
data, for it was then stated that seven of the nine judges constituting the
court, agreed in the opinion that the Missouri Compromise was unconstitutional, and consequently, that the rights originating in it and under
it, were even factitious and ineffective. And it will be seen by the authentic annunciation of the grave and deliberate decision of that august body,
in another column, that what was rumor then is reality now.—Thus
has a politico-legal question, involving others of deep import, been
decided emphatically in favor of the advocates and supporters of the

Constitution and the Union, the equality of the States and the rights of the South, in contradistinction to and in repudiation of the diabolical doctrines inculcated by factionists and fanatics; and that too by a tribunal of jurists, as learned, impartial and unprejudiced as perhaps the world has ever seen. A prize, for which the athletes of the nation have often wrestled in the halls of Congress, has been awarded at last, by the proper umpire, to those who have justly won it. The *nation* has achieved a triumph, *sectionalism* has been rebuked, and abolitionism has been staggered and stunned. Another supporting pillar has been added to our institutions; the assailants of the South and enemies of the Union have been driven from their *point d'appui*;[1] a patriotic principle has been pronounced; a great national, conservative, union saving sentiment has been proclaimed. An adjudication of the constitutionality of the Missouri Compromise, in the *Dred Scott* case, inseparably embraced collateral questions of such character, as also to involve incidental issues, not unfrequently arising in the councils of the country, and which have ever proved, points of irreconcilable antagonism between the friends and enemies of the institutions of the South; all of which, it will be seen, have been unequivocally established in accordance with the sense of the Southern people. And thus it is, that reason and right, justice and truth, always triumph over passion and prejudice, ignorance and envy, when submitted to the deliberations of honest and able men: that the dross and the genuine metal are separated when the ore is accurately assayed.

[1] Foundation or base.

11

MERCURY (CHARLESTON)

The Dred Scott *Case —*
Supreme Court on the Rights of the South

April 2, 1857

The Supreme Court has never been thought the special guardian of State Rights and the interests of the South. With few honorable exceptions, as Judge Daniel, of [Virginia], and Judge Campbell, of Alabama, the most scrupulous sticklers for strict construction have quietly lapsed into extreme Federalism,[1] after their elevation to the Supreme Bench. And so it happened that in the general tenor of its decisions, as in special memorable cases, this august tribunal has shown itself inimical to the interests of the South and State Rights. Its judgment in the *Dred Scott* case comes, then, with the exaggerated effect of surprise; and everybody in the South is disposed to unite in the chorus of congratulation. And certainly it is not easy to overrate the importance of the principles propounded in that decision, in their relation to the constitutional rights of the South. They give to our claim to equality of privilege in the Confederacy,[2] the sanction of the deliberate judgment of the highest tribunal in the land. They show that in its most extreme demand the south contends only for its rights under the Constitution; and that we *ultras*,[3] as they stigmatise us, take no step in which we are not supported by the letter and spirit of the law. In the final conflict between Slavery and Abolitionism, which this very decision will precipitate rather than retard, the principles of the judgment in the Dred Scott case may be of some avail to the South in giving an appearance of justice and moderation to its position. Of these advantages the South is secure; but let us not

---

[1] The *Mercury*, an extreme states' rights paper, was hostile to the idea of a strong central government, which it associated with the Federalist Party of the 1790s and the constitutional doctrine of John Marshall. In fact, none of the majority in the *Dred Scott* decision was remotely "Federalist" in his beliefs. The *Mercury* used the term to warn against the nationalist implication of Taney's decision.

[2] Southern nationalists often used the term *Confederacy* in referring to the United States, implying a loose union rather than the stronger "federal" union that the Constitution created.

[3] Extremists among southern nationalists, especially those who advocated secession or disunion.

abandon ourselves to the delirium of a premature triumph. The victory is not yet gained; and it is a question whether the decision may not add as much to the material strength of the North as it deducts from its moral power. Another such success as was achieved in the Kansas Nebraska act, and the South would have been undone—so hardly was the victory won, and so much of resentment and ferocious energy did it infuse into the ranks of the adversary. It seems as if the same consequence will follow from our recent triumph in the Supreme Court. The Abolitionists are not at all abashed or dismayed; on the contrary, they accept this repulse as another blow in the work of imparting compactness and strength to their organization, and, from the fire that consumes *Dred Scott*, they appear to anticipate a conflagration which will again set the popular sentiment of the North in a blaze of indignation. They know well enough that the Supreme Court is infallible only in a technical sense; and that even its decision may be reversed by the vote of a popular majority. They remember that this same august tribunal, after elaborate argument, pronounced a National Bank to be constitutional, and that the people reversed the decision in the triumphant re-election of Andrew Jackson; and with this instructive example in their eye, they betray a resolution to contend for a like victory in the end. The Black Republican party will go into the canvass[4] of 1860, strengthened rather than discredited and weakened by the adverse judgment of the Supreme Court; and we might as well prepare for the struggle. At least, let not the South cherish the delusion that its cause is triumphant and its rights secure.

[4]*Canvass* is a nineteenth-century term for an election. Thus the reference here is to the Republican Party's upcoming presidential campaign. Note that the *Mercury* refers to the party as the "Black Republicans."

12

DAILY PICAYUNE (NEW ORLEANS)

Citizenship

March 21, 1857

The decision of the Supreme Court of the United States in the *Dred Scott* case is the theme of bitter comment in the anti-slavery journals of the North. There is enough in it, in fact, to overthrow their favorite theories and upset their political plans. It clears away the mists through which many honest men have had distorted views of the rights of the Southern people, and have mistakenly lent themselves to the cause of oppression and aggression, when they supposed themselves to be merely on their defense against attack. It gives the sanction of established law, and the guarantees of the constitution, for all that the South has insisted upon in the recent struggles, and forces her adversaries to surrender their political organization against her rights, or assume openly the position of agitators against the constitution. It is a heavy blow to Black Republicanism and its allies, the force of which they are attempting to break, in some slight degree, by raising a clamor against the judgment of the court for what it does not contain, and alarming the Northern mind for consequences which do not belong to it at all. It is pretended that it will work the necessity of extensive changes in the constitutions of the non-slaveholding states, and compel them to amend important provisions, and abolish old standing laws and take away long conceded rights, against their own declared views of internal policy. This complaint is made with most vehemence against that part of the decision that Africans and their descendants cannot become citizens of the United States. It is stated with alarm that all the States where colored persons have any political rights must proceed immediately to make the changes in their systems which are necessary to make them conform to this rule.

For our own part we should not at all lament to see such a result brought about; but there is no such compulsory effect in the decision of the court in this case. On the contrary, the capacity of every State to confer political rights within its own limits, on any class of persons, at discretion, is broadly affirmed by the court, and the distinction as broadly taken that these, while they may create citizenship for the State, do not give rights as citizens of the United States. . . .

But the Supreme Court decision does not affect any right of a State over its own internal regulations; it rather seems to concede more than has been claimed by some persons who think themselves rigid constructionists of Federal powers, and the clamor about the overthrow of State laws and State constitutions is entirely unnecessary.

The Buchanan Administration's Paper Endorses the Decision

The Washington Union *was the unofficial voice of the administration of President James Buchanan and the proslavery mainstream of the Democratic Party. The following editorial illustrates the position of the administration on* Dred Scott. *Buchanan was both proslavery and proSouth, even though he was a lifelong political leader in his home state of Pennsylvania. Many southerners endorsed the views of the* Union. *The* Richmond Enquirer *and the Charleston* Mercury *often reprinted its editorials, although the* Mercury *considered the* Union *overly optimistic in its assessments of the effectiveness of the decision in ending antislavery agitation in the North and undermining the Republican Party.*

13

UNION (WASHINGTON, D.C.)

The Dred Scott *Case*

March 12, 1857

On the 6th instant the Chief Justice of the United States delivered an elaborate opinion of the Supreme Court declaring the Missouri Compromise unconstitutional. . . .

We cherish a most ardent and confident expectation that this decision will meet a proper reception from the great mass of our intelligent countrymen; that it will be regarded with soberness and not with passion; and that it will thereby exert a mighty influence in diffusing sound opinions and restoring harmony and fraternal concord throughout the country. It comes at an auspicious period. Had it been pronounced—which could hardly have been possible—during the excitement of a presidential canvass,[1] its useful effect, for the present at least, would have been lost. Though no less just and constitutional than it is, it would have been temporarily overwhelmed in the surges of party clamor. Now, however, the excitement and strife of the late canvass are happily abated. The sober second thought has returned to the people; and they are well prepared to receive the judgment of the highest tribunal in the land, even if it, in many instances, differs from their own favorite political opinions.

The court which has settled the vexed constitutional question as to the power of Congress over Territories is entirely independent of the legislative branch of the government. It is elevated above the schemes of party politics, and shielded alike from the effects of sudden passion and of popular prejudice. Little motive, therefore, can the venerable jurists who compose that tribunal have for a deviation from the true principles of law.

It would be fortunate, indeed, if the opinion of that court on this important subject could receive the candid and respectful acquiescence which it merits. Such an exhibition of the moral conservatism of the people would well correspond with that sublime example of the fitness of the people for self-government lately witnessed in the laying down and taking up of high executive trusts in the midst of orderly enthusiasm. But we expect this decision will for a while be questioned, and even ridiculed by the anti-slavery press. The judges who concurred in it will be abused. "We have a race of agitators all over the country," said Daniel Webster[2] in his speech at Buffalo in 1851, "their livelihood consists in agitating; their freehold, their copyhold, their capital, their all in all, depend on the excitement of the public mind." To this class, which still exists, this decision will be a fresh topic of sectional agitation. . . .

We refer to the judgment of the court in this case in no spirit of triumph. We would not subject it to the mere uses of party. Many men supported the Nebraska-Kansas act who believed Congress had the right to exclude slavery from the Territories, but who deemed it inexpedient to have the right exercised. They wished to keep the subject out of

---

[1]Election.

[2]Daniel Webster (1782–1852) was a leading Whig Party politician, longtime U.S. senator from Massachusetts, and secretary of state in the administrations of Presidents John Tyler and Millard Fillmore. Webster startled his Massachusetts constituents by supporting the Fugitive Slave Law as part of the Compromise of 1850. This made him something of a hero among northern conservatives and "doughfaces." The Democratic *Union* happily quotes the Massachusetts Whig to attack those who might oppose *Dred Scott*.

Congress. They thought as Mr. Webster did when he favored the organization of New Mexico without the application of the Wilmot proviso. These men may be unprepared for this decision. We know that in the non-slaveholding States there are many who sincerely deprecated the repeal of the Missouri Compromise. There are many who have been brought up in the faith of the Wilmot proviso. They, perhaps, have not examined both sides of the question, and will feel a regret at this decision as deep as the pleasure of our southern friends is ardent. We would appeal to such men in a spirit of candor and patriotism; and, without censuring them for sentiments which they have long honestly cherished, only invite them to review their opinions, and to conform their action to the adjudication of the highest judicial tribunal in the land.

Never perhaps, in the history of the country, has there existed so much bitterness between the North and the South as within the past year. And it is remarkable that this bitterness has resulted not from measures so much as from transient excesses. The troubles in Kansas and some other accidental acts contributed to this state of things. But the chief cause of alienation was the unbridled license of a portion of the press and the intemperate language employed by many of our public speakers. It has been common for some of the ablest journals of the North to misrepresent and vilify the institutions and the people of the South. And these attacks have been reciprocated by some of the radical papers of the South. Orators have resorted to the same practice. Under such circumstances, what else but bitterness and alienation could follow? What else but distrust be excited? No State or community is perfect. The North and the South have different institutions. Each State is alone responsible for its institutions, and it is morally and constitutionally wrong for the people of one State to assail the institutions of another State. Nor is it at all remarkable to expect that people who have been differently educated by social habits, by tradition, by parental precept, will think entirely alike. There must be toleration, and there must be forbearance.

It is gratifying to see that a better feeling is beginning to exist between both sections of the country; and we invoke the temperate and intelligent public opinion of the country, so potent for wise purposes, to withhold every vestige of support from that class whose livelihood is to create sectional animosity. In this way their shafts will fall impotent in the dust, and the wounds they have before made will become healed.

Northern Support for the *Dred Scott* Decision

Many northerners, especially Democrats and some businessmen, supported the Dred Scott *decision. Northern support stemmed from three interrelated sources: party politics, racism, and business concerns.*

Democrats hoped the decision would finally end the debate over slavery in the territories and thus allow Democrats to get on with their agenda of western settlement and manifest destiny, while at the same time maintaining their political power. Since 1828 the Democratic Party had dominated U.S. politics. But at least since the mid-1830s slavery had threatened to disrupt the party and its political hegemony. Democrats, such as Stephen A. Douglas of Illinois, saw the Dred Scott *decision as finally ending the debate. (See Chapter 3 for excerpts from Douglas's speeches and his debates with Lincoln in 1858.)*

Some northerners also supported the decision out of racism. Most northern whites, along with virtually all southern whites, did not believe in racial equality. Abolitionists, antislavery activists, and some Republicans advocated an end to racial discrimination, but they were clearly in the minority. Northern Democrats used race to attack their political opponents. Thus many northern whites, especially northern Democrats, saw the decision as a way to exclude blacks from American public life.

Finally, northern business interests saw the debate over slavery as a threat to national commerce and the economy. Some business leaders hoped Dred Scott *not only would end the debate but would minimize the divisiveness of the issue.*

The New York Journal of Commerce, *whose editorials are reprinted here, spoke for business interests in vigorously supporting the decision. The editorial from the Pittsburgh* Post *reflects the views of mainstream northern Democrats, arguing that the* Dred Scott *decision was "the law." Here the* Post *accuses Republicans of trying to politicize the Supreme Court.*

14

JOURNAL OF COMMERCE (NEW YORK)

The Decision of the Supreme Court
March 11, 1857

The Decision of the Supreme Court.—It was not to be expected that the Abolition press would readily concur in the wisdom, justice and constitutionality of the decision recently delivered in the Supreme Court of the United States in the case of *Scott vs. Sandford*, but it was hardly to be supposed that journals claiming to be respectable should so forget what is due to public decency and decorum as to assert that unique and deliberate judgment of the highest court of the land is entitled to no more "moral weight than would be the judgment of a majority of those congregated in any Washington bar-room,"[1] or to impugn the honesty and purity of the great Constitutional lawyers who occupy the exalted position of supreme and final judges of all matters relating to the interpretation of the Constitution and the laws. We believe, however, that those indecent and contemptible calumnies will meet with no approving response beyond the limited circle of disappointed factionists whose vocation it is to foment strife and discord to subserve individual and selfish ends; that by the great masses of the people who prefer truth to error, light to darkness, upon important political questions, the decision will be respected and honored, and that it will be accepted as a permanent record stamped with the absolute authenticity of the Constitution itself.

It is now decided on authority which admits of no appeal or question, and which few will presume to dispute, that negroes whether bond or free cannot be citizens of the United States according to the Constitution; that it is not in the power of any one particular State by conferring citizenship within its limits on a negro, to endow him with full citizenship in the other States of the Union without their consent; that . . . the Act of 1820, known as the Missouri Compromise, is void, and unwarranted by the Constitution. . . .

The vast and comprehensive social and political importance of this lucid and convincing judgment of the first constitutional authorities in

---

[1] See the New York *Tribune* editorial (Document 17).

the Republic, cannot be too highly estimated. It dissipates the mist in which we have been enveloped for years; it exposes in all their deformity the slavery heresies by which we have been disturbed for more than half a century; it lays down, in language stripped of all sophistry or sectional bias, the relations which should exist between the States and Territories of the Union; it gives to the North, to the South, to the East, and to the West the true chart and compass by which to steer, and it proclaims to the people that they alone have the right, at all times and under all circumstances, to provide their own local government, to regulate their own affairs, and to decide for themselves whether they will or will not adopt domestic servitude as one of their institutions.

15

JOURNAL OF COMMERCE (NEW YORK)

The Dred Scott *Case*

March 12, 1857

Our Republican friends have fairly raised the standard of insurrection, and are giving us the higher law in all its moods and tenses with a vengeance. They declare in every way and shape—in every form of language, and with every possible manifestation of temper, except that of reason and sense—that the decision in the *Dred Scott* Case is not law, that the Judges who decided it don't know what law means, that their decision is absurd and nonsensical, oppressive and tyrannical, that nobody is bound by it, that nobody ought to obey it, and finally, that it shall not be submitted to.

After the flurry is over, we shall respectfully request the organs, whether of party or of the press, which have taken the Goddess of Liberty into their especial keeping, to be pleased to let us know the platform or program, upon which they propose to carry out this government after the year 1860, or whenever the Millennium shall arrive, which is to induct them into power and place.

If the present Supreme Court is to be overthrown and its decrees trampled under foot—if the fundamental clauses of the Constitution are to be scoffed at and obliterated, we take it for granted that some other arbiter of controversies, some other ultimate tribunal, some other form of government in short, is to be adopted; and we are curious to know what it is to be.

For, the present question raises no issue like that presented by the Fugitive Slave Law, as to the competency of Congress to pass the law—no question of State Right or Federal Authority—on which men may plausibly differ. On the contrary, nobody pretends to deny that by the very words of the fundamental charter, the Supreme Court is vested with the power that it has exercised—that in deciding this *Dred Scott* Case—be the results right or wrong, the Court has done no more than it is authorized to do, and that every obligation of Constitution and of compact, of honor and of law, bind us to obey the decisions of that high tribunal.

But if all these considerations are to be derided—if the present is, in a word, a case for revolution, then do pray let us know what we are to have next. Are we to go for our law to the Tribune, or to the Post—to town meeting, or to a Vigilance Committee?

We have here, in practical shape, the tangible results of the very sensible doctrine of the Higher Law, by infiltrating which into the minds of our people, it is hoped to prepare them for some violent outbreak against our system of government.

What is the decision in the *Dred Scott* case? Let us see what the precise points are, which are considered so very novel, awful, and subversive of liberty.

First. The Court has decided that this government was made to secure the freedom of the white race, and that people of African descent are not citizens of the United States. This very point was decided administratively by Mr. Secretary [of State William L.] Marcy not three months since, when he refused passports to certain free persons of color. The refusal hardly attracted attention. It is arrant trash and nonsense, an anachronism, and a historical absurdity to assert that the Declaration of Independence, when it speaks of the "freedom and equality of mankind," intended to comprehend the black race. The Declaration of Independence was made by the representatives of communities every one of which were then slaveholding communities. If the truth could be got at, it would no doubt appear that with perhaps a few exceptions, every man who signed the Declaration of Independence, was at the time a slaveholder. Very sensible and logical, is it not, to assert that these slaveholders intended to declare that their slaves were all free, and equal to themselves?

Second. The Court has decided that property in slaves is recognized by the Constitution, and that Congress has no power to prevent the citizen of South Carolina from going into the common territory of the United States with property recognized as such by his State, any more than it has to prohibit the citizen of Massachusetts from going into the Territories with property recognized as such by *his* State.

Third. The Court has decided that if a slave is taken into a free State and then taken back into a slave State by his or her master, that by this act of removal, the owner does not lose his right of property.

16

POST (PITTSBURGH)

Seeking an Issue

March 17, 1857

The Republican presses just now are very busy in hunting up an issue on which to contend with the Democrats in the next election. Some of them seem to think that the late decision of the Supreme Court of the United States in the Dred Scott case will do to quarrel about. But others consider it too heavy a subject for a State election issue. The decision affects this State very little, and the people cannot be roused to activity by a matter that is of no practical importance to them. The decision was what was all along expected, and excites no great interest any where except with political agitators who are seeking an issue with the Democrats. Nothing can be made out of it as a political issue. It is law, and cannot be reversed by any other tribunal. The Judges cannot be removed. To contend about such a matter leads to no practical results whatever, and can excite no general interest.

Opposition to the *Dred Scott* Decision:
A Spectrum of Northern Opinion

Negative responses to Dred Scott *in the North were far more varied than the positive responses in the South. Illustrative of the diversity of northern opinion are editorials in five papers: the New York* Tribune, *the New York* Daily Times, *the New York* Evening Post, *the New York* Independent, *and the Salem (Mass.)* Register. *All five papers attacked the decision but from rather different perspectives.*

Historians often quote the New York Tribune *editorial of March 7, 1857, which argues that the* Dred Scott *decision deserves no more "moral weight" than "would be the judgment of a majority of those congregated in any Washington bar-room." Note also that the* Tribune *accuses Taney and the Court of being part of a political conspiracy.*

Taney's decision left moderate opponents of slavery perplexed. The New York Daily Times, *for example, was horrified that the Supreme Court had "nationalized" slavery and thought that in the end the decision would strengthen northern resolve against the expansion of slavery. The* Daily Times *thought Taney's opinion was revolutionary but saw few political options for northerners opposed to the decision.*

The New York Evening Post, *a mainstream moderate opponent of slavery, considered the action of the Supreme Court to be treasonous. Its editorial comes very close to endorsing the view of abolitionist William Lloyd Garrison that, in the aftermath of* Dred Scott, *politics was useless. Not surprisingly, Garrison's paper, the* Liberator, *reprinted this* Post *editorial.*

The Independent, *a Protestant religious paper, was unconcerned with the political implications of the decision. Its editors simply denounced the "wickedness" of the decision while exposing the weakness of Taney's arguments. Pointing out that Taney was a Roman Catholic, the* Independent *played on anti-Catholic sentiments common among many northern Protestants. This religious bigotry was tied to party politics; most Catholics, especially Irish Catholics, were Democrats and thus for political reasons were likely to support Taney's opinion.*

The editorial from the Salem Register *also reflects the disillusion and frustration of northerners. The Salem paper sees the decision as revolutionary.*

17

TRIBUNE (NEW YORK)

Editorial

March 7, 1857

The long Trumpeted of the Supreme Court in the Dred Scott case was pronounced by Judge Taney yesterday, having been held over from last year in order not too flagrantly to alarm and exasperate the Free States on the eve of an important Presidential election. Its cardinal points are reported as follows:

1. A negro, because of his color, is denied the rights of a citizen of the United States—even the right to sue in our Courts for the redress of the most flagrant wrongs.

2. A slave, being taken by his master into a Free State and thence returning under his master's sway, is not therefore entitled to his freedom.

3. *Congress has no rightful power to prohibit Slavery in the Territories*: hence the Missouri Restriction was unconstitutional. . . .

—This decision, we need hardly say, is entitled to just so much moral weight as would be the judgment of a majority of those congregated in any Washington bar-room. It is a *dictum* prescribed by the stump to the bench—the Bowie-knife sticking in the stump ready for instant use if needed. It is of a piece with the votes of Benton, Dix and Bagby for the Annexation of Texas with the boundary of the Rio Grande.[1]

This judgment annihilates all Compromises and brings us face to face with the great issue in the right shape. Slavery implies slave laws—that is, laws sustaining and enforcing the claim of one man to own and sell another. In the absence of such laws, Slavery cannot exist; and a Republican ascendancy in the nation, insuring Republican rule over the

---

[1]Democratic senators Thomas Hart Benton of Missouri, John Adams Dix of New York, and Arthur Pendleton Bagby of Alabama supported the annexation of Texas and the Mexican War. When the United States annexed Texas, Americans, Mexicans, and Texans did not agree on the boundary of the new state. Texans claimed it was at the Rio Grande, while Mexico claimed it was farther north. By claiming land all the way to the Rio Grande, the United States set the stage for the war with Mexico in 1846.

Territories, will prove a shield against the enactment of any such laws. Under any other rule, all our Territories are henceforth Slave Territories, on the way to be ripened into Slave States. . . .

18

DAILY TIMES (NEW YORK)

The Slavery Question —
The Decision of the Supreme Court

March 9, 1857

. . . The decision of the Supreme Court in the case of Dred Scott completes the nationalization of Slavery. Slavery is no longer a local institution, — the creature of local law, — dependent for its existence and protection upon State sovereignty and State legislation. It is incorporated into the Constitution of the United States. Its tenure is the tenure of all property, and the Constitution protects and preserves it, to the same extent and upon the same principles, as it protects any other property of any kind whatever. This is the fundamental position which the Supreme Court has just asserted, and upon which all its decisions in this case rest. Congress cannot exclude Slavery from Federal territory, because the *right* to slaves is the right to *property*, and cannot be divested. For the same reason the people of the Territory cannot exclude Slavery from their own domain: — and when the time for the next step comes, we shall have it in the logical sequence, that *no State Government has a right to deprive any citizen of property, which the Constitution of the United States protects him in holding.*

It is not too much to say that this decision revolutionizes the Federal Government, and changes entirely the relation which Slavery has hitherto held towards it. Slavery is no longer local: it is national. The Federal Government is no longer held aloof from it, as a thing wholly and exclusively out of its jurisdiction: — it is brought directly within its sphere and put immediately under its protection. The doctrine of State Rights, so long its friend, is now its foe.

That this decision is to produce the most profound impression upon the public judgment is certain. Its first effect will be to paralyze and astound the public mind. Familiar as our people have become to the advancement of Slavery towards supremacy in our Government, they have not believed that it could obtain so absolute a seat in the supreme council of the Republic at so early a day. The decision will be accepted and obeyed as law. There will be no wide or loud protest against it. The public peace will not be disturbed,—the public ear will not be vexed,—by clamorous outcries or noisy denunciation of the Court and its decree. But the doctrine it has promulgated will sink deep into the public heart, and germinate there as the seed of discontent and contest and disaster hereafter. They mistake the temper of the men of this Republic, who believe that they will ever accept Slavery as the fixed and permanent law of the American Union. They have trusted to time,—to the progress of civilization, to the melioration of legal codes,—to eliminate, to population, to established metes and bounds, to old covenants and compacts and the advancement of Christian principle, for ultimate deliverance. They will strive still to cling to such of these as violence and wrong have left untouched. But this last decision leaves little to hope and everything to fear. And the people will begin to ask why, if Slavery is *national*, the nation should not assume the custody and control of it:—why it should be constitutional for the Federal Government to protect, and not to remove, it:—why, if its extension is synonymous with its existence, both should not be ended together.

Apparent peace will follow the action of the Supreme Court. The partisans of its conduct and its doctrine will proclaim it to be the end of controversy upon this subject, and the immediate result will seem to confirm their hopes. But it has laid the only solid foundation which has ever yet existed for an Abolition party; and it will do more to stimulate the growth, to build up the power and consolidate the action of such a party, than has been done by any other event since the Declaration of Independence.

19

EVENING POST (NEW YORK)

The Supreme Court of the United States
March 7, 1857

The dangers apprehended from the organic tendencies of the Supreme Court to engross the legislative power of the federal government, which Jefferson foresaw and so often warned his countrymen against, are no longer imaginary. They are upon us. The decision rendered by that body yesterday, in the case of a Missouri negro who had appealed to it for assistance in asserting his right to share the promises of the Declaration of Independence, has struck at the very roots of the past legislative policy of this country in reference to slavery. It has changed the very blood of the constitution, from which we derive our political existence, and has given to our government a direction and a purpose as novel as it is barbarous and humiliating.

In the first place, it has annihilated at a single blow the citizenship of the entire colored population of the country, and with it all laws and constitutional provisions of the different states for the protection of those rights.

In the next place, it has stripped Congress of a power to exclude slavery from the territories, which has been exercised by every President of the United States from Washington down to Fillmore, and which has had an effect in shaping the political and domestic institutions of more than half the territory of the United States. The [Northwest] ordinance of 1787, with the passage or defence of which the names of the most eminent American statesman have been imperishably associated, is not only pronounced unconstitutional, but the power to enact any laws which contemplates a restriction upon the right to buy, hold and sell slaves in our territories is distinctly denied.

Nor is this all. The doctrine which has been recognized wherever the common law prevails, since the days of Lord Mansfield,[1] that when a slave is taken by his master into the jurisdiction of a state which prohibits slavery, he is from that moment free, is not only set aside, but the power is denied to the states of this Union to prohibit masters bringing slaves within their jurisdiction, provided that they do not enter it with the intention of establishing a permanent residence there.

All of these positions are new in the juridical history of the country; the law in reference to all of them was settled by a long line of judicial decisions by the highest tribunals of the several states, and until within the last twelve years was regarded as much beyond the reach of controversy as the right of the people of the United States to a republican form of government. If precedent, usage, public acquiescence could hallow any doctrines of constitutional interpretation, then were those doctrines hallowed which have been ruthlessly subverted by the Supreme Court.

---

[1]In the English case *Somerset v. Stewart* (1772), Lord Chief Justice Mansfield held that a slave brought into England could not be forcibly reenslaved or forcibly removed to a slaveholding colony. Before Dred Scott's case, the Missouri Supreme Court followed the *Somerset* precedent, holding that slaves brought to free states became free. Had the U.S. Supreme Court followed *Somerset*, Dred Scott would have gained his freedom.

. . . A conspiracy has been entered into of the most treasonable character; the justices of the Supreme Court and the leading members of the new administration are parties to it. One who runs may read the evidence of it in every revelation from the capital.

Of course the moment this conviction takes possession of the public mind, there is an end of the Supreme Court; for a judicial tribunal, which is not rooted in the confidence of the people, will soon either be disregarded as an authority or overturned. . . .

20

INDEPENDENT (NEW YORK)

Wickedness of the Decision in the Supreme Court against the African Race

March 19, 1857

To present the wickedness of this decision, and of the grounds on which it was based, without prejudice and without exaggeration, we must quote a portion of it. "It is difficult at this day," says Judge Taney, "to realize the state of public opinion respecting that unfortunate class, with the civilized and enlightened portion of the world, at the time of the Declaration of Independence and adoption of the Constitution; but history shows they have for more than a century been regarded as beings of an inferior order, and unfit associates for the white race, either socially or politically, and had no rights which white men were bound to respect; and the black man might be reduced to slavery, bought and sold, and treated as an ordinary . . . article of merchandise. This opinion at that time was fixed and universal with the civilized portion of the white race. It was regarded as an axiom in morals, which no one thought of disputing, and every one habitually acted upon it, without doubting for a moment the correctness of the opinion. . . ."

In this horrible hand-book of tyranny it is asserted, 1st. That according to the past century of opinion, adopted as law in the Constitution, black men have no rights which white men ought to respect, but may be reduced to slavery, bought and sold, and treated as an ordinary article of merchandise; 2d. That the negro race are excluded by the Constitution from the possibility of being citizens, and from having any personal rights or benefits: 3d. They are all articles of merchandise, all the negro race; 4th. Their being free makes no difference, for the Constitution treats and considers them as mere property and gives the government power over them as such.

These assertions the Judge attempts to sustain by a deliberate falsification of the Constitution and of history. If they were true, then the Constitution would be a document reprobated by the Almighty, and entitled only to the curses of mankind. It is [a] matter of thankfulness that if such infamous propositions were to be made under the solemn authority of a court of American justice, the Judge propounding them should have been a member of the Papal church, so that it is not Protestant Christianity that has given such a verdict, however Protestant ministers may possibly be found to sustain it. It is of a piece with that religion which has always been accustomed to anathematize races by the wholesale, that religion and church which consigns all heretics to perdition, and in time past declared that they have no rights which the infallible reigning church ought to respect. This habit of persecution has come to a personification in our Supreme Court of Justice.

The annals of the world cannot show a more astounding avowal of wrong as the justified principle of action. . . . The Declaration of Independence must be asserted to be a lie must be interpreted as such, as not meaning what it declares, because the authors of it were honorable men, and cannot be supposed to have professed any knowledge of right and wrong beyond the customary principles of morality in their day, nor any rule of freedom, nor any preference of freedom above slavery, higher than the world around them acknowledged and obeyed. They must be supposed to have uttered what they knew to be a lie, when they said that all men were entitled to life, liberty, and the pursuit of happiness, or else they must be supposed and insisted to have held the opinion that a negro is not a man, but a mere thing to be trampled on, a piece of property without rights, without a man's personality. They must be supposed to have themselves supposed that negroes were not entitled to life, liberty, and the pursuit of happiness, because they cannot be supposed themselves to have possessed any more enlarged ideas of liberty, and of the claims of all men to it, than the ages of darkness that preceded them or the century of darkness in the midst of which they were thrown. As honorable men, they cannot be supposed to have said what they did not believe, and they cannot be supposed to have believed in any other ideas than that the negro race were mere property and not men; and therefore, when they aver that all men are endowed by their Creator with certain inalienable rights, among which are life, liberty, and the pursuit of happiness, they must have meant to exclude the African race, they could not have regarded that race as a portion of all men, because that race had been from time immemorial deprived of the rights of men and treated as property; and the Declaration of Independence must, therefore, be interpreted to mean only white men, to mean that only white men had any of the inalienable rights of men, and that no black man, negro, or of the African race, could be born equal to white men, or endowed by the Creator with any right to liberty and the pursuit of happiness.

Such is the interpretation forced by a grave judicial court, the highest court in the most enlightened country in the world, a court of justice, a court called Supreme, and almost invested, according to the doctrines of many, with the attributes of Jehovah himself; such is the interpretation assumed and forced upon the grandest, most comprehensive, most unmistakable, most exalted preamble to the justest, freest, noblest constitution in the world! Such is the assumption of a court of justice, such the position against a down-trodden man and human family pleading justice, the assumption beforehand against the victim of injustice he never was born for any other purpose than to be deprived of all the rights of man, the position that by his very nature as the subject of a colored skin, he cannot appear in court as a man, cannot be possessed of any of the rights of humanity, cannot have any claim to justice under the Constitution, cannot be admitted to plead as a citizen. These are the positions taken by a court of justice! . . .

Now we fearlessly declare that there never was, under the whole heaven, a more atrocious, wholesale wickedness perpetrated upon the bench of justice than this. For not only is it exasperated beyond conception by issuing from the tribunal of a professedly Christian nation, but it is a perpetration by principle, and of widening reach and accumulating power to all time. It takes, moreover, not a man, nor a few men merely, nor a province to lay waste, . . . but a whole nation, nor even a nation merely, but a whole race by the throat, and strangles it, and flings forth the lifeless corpse, lifeless in law as to all possibility of rights; but with the living capacity of injury and insult, flings forth the strangled race by the roadside of the family of man, for all human beasts of prey to fatten on. . . .

The wickedness of such gross and horrible outlawry of a downtrodden class, is immeasurably more wicked in a period of advanced and enlarged philanthropy, than it ever was before; more inexcusable and intolerable, under the full light of the Gospel, and after the Declaration of Independence, than it could have been in any preceding age. But to think of springing back from this present point of light into that thick darkness, to think of a pack of judges deliberately returning like a pack of wolves to the dead carrion of immorality and injustice, cast out as offal for a hundred years! To think of their taking up the cast-off gaberdines of judges that have died long ago in the wilderness of this world, with the pestilence of this moral rot upon them, and putting on those leprosy-fretted garments for their robes of justice, and advancing those doctrines abhorred and reprobated of society for whole generations! To think of such justice and such judgment, the very dregs of the cup of past judicial corruption and depravity, chosen and adopted as the principle and life of constitutional law by the Supreme Judicial Court of the United States of America, in the middle of the nineteenth century! . . .

21

REGISTER (SALEM)

The U.S. Supreme Court
March 12, 1857

The recent extraordinary decision of the Supreme Court of the United States will be better understood and appreciated, when the thoroughly partisan character which it has been gradually made to assume is regarded. The veneration which that august tribunal secured for itself when its decisions were made and its judgments pronounced by such Justices as Jay, Rutledge, Ellsworth, Marshall, Story, and others — men whose ability, disinterestedness and patriotism were universally confided in, no matter from what section of the country they came — . . . has received a signal shock. . . .

The truth is, the Court has been wholly revolutionized. The sleepless vigilance of the Slave Power has been constantly watching its opportunity to invade the temple of justice, from time to time insisting upon the appointment of advocates of its most obnoxious doctrines, until now the tribunal is apparently its own, ready to sustain the most ultra Southern ground.

Lincoln's Paper Responds

The Chicago Tribune *was a leading Republican paper, and the short editorials printed here illustrate its sharp disagreement with Taney as well as the importance the Republicans placed on the McLean and Curtis dissents. That the* Tribune *reprinted the dissents in full suggests the strong public interest in the case.*

In 1860 the Chicago Tribune *would lead the supporters of Abraham Lincoln, helping set the stage for his nomination as the Republican presidential candidate.*

22

TRIBUNE (CHICAGO)

Who Are Negroes?

March 12, 1857

Chief Justice Taney decides, in the Dred Scott case, that *negroes* are not citizens of the United States. He defines a negro to be a person "whose ancestors were imported, and sold as slaves." And upon this definition he proceeded to build his decision. But are persons who are part *white*—mulattoes, for instance—not citizens? How is it with those, one of whose ancestors emigrated to this country from Europe? And how is it with that large class in whose veins the blood of the white preponderates? How much white blood is necessary to make a native born American a citizen? Will Chief Justice Taney settle the question? There are tens of thousands of men more than half white, many of whose sires belong to the real F. F. V.s,[1] and nearly all of their fathers claim to belong to the chivalry. It is important to settle the *status* of these people. They are very numerous, and, in the Slave States, rapidly multiplying.

[1] First Families of Virginia, the slaveholding elite of Virginia.

TRIBUNE (CHICAGO)

The Dred Scott *Case*

March 17, 1857

We publish this morning the opinion delivered by Chief Justice Taney on the Dred Scott case, on the 6th of March. The law of Illinois, as laid down by the Supreme Court of this State is, that if a slave be brought into this State by his master he becomes a free man.

. . . The case was carried to Washington, before the full bench. It was met at the threshold of the Court by a decision of the Chief Justice and his four Slave-holding associates, that a negro cannot sue in the United States Courts; that he is not a citizen of the United States. Of course this should have been the end of the case. The Court had no occasion, had no right to go a step further. But as a part of the grand conspiracy against Freedom, they proceeded to pronounce on extra judicial opinion, covering other points, and involving more important questions than it has ever before passed upon. We will not stop here to review the opinion of Judge Taney, but will leave that for Judges McLean and Curtis,—the reply of the former will be given tomorrow.

A War for Public Opinion: The Washington *Union* and the New York *Tribune*

The following editorials, from the Washington Union *and the New York* Tribune, *illustrate the "newspaper war" over the* Dred Scott *decision. The* Union *was the unofficial voice of the Buchanan administration, while the* Tribune *was one of the most important Republican papers in the North, edited by Horace Greeley, the long-time ally of Senator William H. Seward of New York. The* Union *quotes at length from the* Tribune *to attack the Republican paper. Similarly, the* Tribune *quotes from the* Union *and from the New York* Journal of Commerce *to attack those papers. The* Tribune *also attacks the legitimacy of the Court itself, arguing that the proslavery Justices were essentially political hacks.*

UNION (WASHINGTON, D.C.)

Unreasonable Complaints

March 21, 1857

The New York Tribune, referring to the late decision of the Supreme Judicial Court, says:

It is no longer in Congress or on the plains of Kansas that we are assailed. Now the slaveholders' majority in the Supreme Court of the United States have stepped into the arena.

Similar language, on the same subject, is employed along the entire line of the black-republican press, and, under such influence, there are some men at the North, we doubt not, who regard the Supreme Court as having made a gross and wicked attack upon their individual rights. If these men will take the trouble to think calmly and dispassionately upon the probabilities of the case, they, will readily admit that such an attack is hardly among them and that a tribunal, constituted as the Supreme Court is, is not likely to violate wilfully its duty and its judgment in order to make war upon any section or any citizen of our common country. Why should it do so? Why should Chief Justice Taney, for example, be governed in his official action by any other considerations than those of impartial justice and honest patriotism? Venerable in years, as well as in wisdom, he has earned, during a long life, those plaudits which, among all right-minded men, are freely bestowed upon private worth and public virtue and eminent ability. His home is in one of those central States of the Union, where the waves of public opinion meet and modify each other both from the North and from the South, and where excessive opinions on the subject of slavery are not generally understood to prevail. He must be insensible, also, to every consideration of personal ambition, because, of course, he has no political future, and he retains his present position by virtue of the constitution. If such a man, after twenty years of judicial service, is not surrounded with all the presumptions in favor of right action that can give confidence anywhere, it is difficult to imagine a position where such presumptions can exist. We mention the Chief Justice by way of example, but not to exclude presumptions of a similar character in favor of the other members of the court. Why should Judge Catron, or Judge Wayne, or Judge Nelson, or Judge Grier, be held any less reliable in character or patriotism, than Judge McLean or Judge Curtis, neither of whom do we think it decorous to attack for a mere expression of judicial opinion? Surely, if a southern judge is to be charged with southern prejudice, a northern judge may with equal propriety be charged with northern prejudice, or a western judge be distrusted for alleged partiality to the West, and thus the whole moral power of an institution, whose independence and wisdom and impartiality the country has been accustomed to respect, will be frittered away by local and sectional prejudices. We respectfully submit to any northern reader who holds the opinions of the New York Tribune whether he himself is not quite as likely to be the victim of local or partisan prejudice as any member of the court? Is he quite sure that on subjects connected with the slavery question he does not occupy a standpoint which renders his judgment almost necessarily a partial one? Does he place himself in the position of those who framed the constitution, when the States were all slave States, and from that position does he look out upon the great work of our fathers, and inquire, honestly and dispassionately, what its true meaning is? Or does he not rather come to the subject, if he thinks it worthy even of investigation, with his whole nature imbued with abolition theories and crude notions of abstract right, which, had they existed and had full sway in the convention of '87, would have rendered the constitution, impossible, as they now interfere dangerously with its practical workings? What the constitution *ought to be*, in the judgment of a modern theorist, is one thing; but what the constitution really *is*, is another and a very different thing. Upon this latter point, the determination of the Supreme Court of the United States, constituted as we have described it to be, is surely quite as respectable and authoritative as that of an abolition editor, or an infidel convention. Each of the judges, we have already said, is worthy of the public confidence; but it is a striking fact that Judge McLean was prominently before the Philadelphia convention of 1856, in competition with Col. [John C.] Frémont,[1] for its nomination, and it is equally to be remembered that, when Judge Curtis was appointed to his present place, the black-republican papers which now regard him favorably were loud in their denunciations of his subserviency to the South. Is it not better to believe that he was equally honest then and now, and to credit both him and his associates with upright dispositions, whether we agree with them or not in all their opinions? . . .

But what, after all, is there in the decision of the Dred Scott case, so far as it is either known or conjectured, which can justify, in the slightest degree, the assertions which we have copied, in the beginning of

---

[1]John C. Frémont, a hero of western exploration, was the Republican candidate for president in 1856. He was nominated at a convention in Philadelphia.

this article, from the New York Tribune? The Tribune describes itself as "assailed no longer in Congress or on the plains of Kansas," but "in the Supreme Court of the United States." If this language means anything, it must mean that the editor of the Tribune is deprived of some right which he ought to enjoy in common with other citizens, and that a northern man is degraded by the Supreme Court into an inequality, somehow or other, with a southern man. Yet, is there any foundation in fact for such a statement as this? Is not Horace Greeley [the editor of the New York *Tribune*] possessed of the same rights precisely under the law of the Scott case and every other case, as any other free citizen of the Union? Is there a single right or privilege asserted in the judgment referred to in favor of a southern man, that is not also asserted in favor of a northern man? If so, we should be glad to have it pointed out to us; but if not, with what show of reason or justice or common sense, do the Tribune and its kindred prints declaim constantly about the degradation of the North? How is the North or the South degraded when they enjoy equal political rights? How can a man lash himself into a fury about tyrannical assaults upon his liberty, when he enjoys precisely as much freedom as any one of his fellow-citizens? The writers and orators of the Garrison and Parker[2] school revel constantly in a perfect prodigality of license. They preach abolition and infidelity in their own way and to their hearts' content. They are not molested themselves, and they heap anathemas upon others. If anybody, on the face of this earth, enjoys greater liberty than they do, we confess that we cannot imagine where that person resides. And yet, to hear them talk or to read their writings, one would think they were suffering under greater oppression than any which ever induced a crushed and desperate people to fly to arms! Here they are, living under the best government in the world, with social enjoyments all around them, plenty on every side, secure in their persons and in their property, schools provided for their children, and church-bells proclaiming, from time to time, the safety and quiet and religious culture of their homes; and yet, instead of devoutly thanking God that their lines have thus fallen to them in pleasant places, they fill the air with complaints, they assail the structure of society, and they make war upon the government which protects them! We appeal to all good citizens to discountenance the agitations of such men, and to think calmly and dispassionately for themselves upon this whole subject of slavery and the constitution. The opinions of the

---

[2]William Lloyd Garrison was the most famous abolitionist in the nation; Rev. Theodore Parker was an activist abolitionist minister in Boston. Both opposed political action, believing that the Constitution was immorally proslavery.

majority of the Supreme Judicial Court, in the *Dred Scott* case, will soon be published, and will then be entitled to receive the candid consideration of the American people. If they shall make their way, at last, to public approval, notwithstanding the censure they have received in advance, they will only repeat the lesson of a previous judicial decision, which deserves now to be remembered. The judgment of the Supreme Court in the case of Prigg *vs.* Pennsylvania,[3] on the subject of returning fugitive slaves, was also assailed in the beginning with denunciation and ridicule, but was afterwards acquiesced in by the people and by the courts. It may be that the decision in the Scott case may receive an equally general assent, but it will, at all events, be practically respected, and the people will examine with care the reasonings upon which it is founded. Until these reasonings are published, it is the part of wisdom, even for those whose impressions are against the decision, to suspend their judgments.

[3]In *Prigg v. Pennsylvania*, 41 U.S. (16 Peters) 539 (1842), Justice Joseph Story of Massachusetts wrote a proslavery majority opinion striking down all northern laws aimed at giving alleged fugitive slaves due process protection. Many northerners were shocked by this opinion, especially because it was written by a northern justice.

25

TRIBUNE (NEW YORK)

Judge Taney's Opinion
March 21, 1857

The decision of the Supreme Court is hailed with delight by the "Court Organ" of Mr. Buchanan [the *Washington Union*]. It says "there was but one thing needed to give to the result in the Presidential contest the force of an absolute and final settlement of the sectional issue. That thing was the judgment of the Supreme Court in confirmation of democratic doctrines which had received the popular endorsement. The decision in the Dred Scott case has furnished the closing and clinching confirmation needed, and henceforth sectional fanaticism cannot maintain its warfare without arraying itself distinctly against the Constitution. The people have decided that sectional agitation must cease, and the highest judicial authority has declared that the people have decided in accordance with the Constitution. We feel, therefore, that the danger is for the present over, that sectionalism is virtually dead—that it has been crushed out by the popular verdict in the Presidential election; and that the decision of the Supreme Court has left nothing vital in republicanism, and has placed the democratic party beyond and above all competition as the constitutional, national, Union party . . . of the country. Mr. Buchanan takes the helm under these suspicion circumstances, and his acts thus far give token of a successful and prosperous administration."

Sectionalism dead? It was the most intense, bitter, overshadowing sectionalism that forced this decree from the Supreme Court. It was the political department of the government controlling the judicial. Had a [Chief Justice John] Marshall been upon the bench this decision never could have been obtained. Southern man as he was, he belonged to the purer and better days of the Republic, when all united in proclaiming that "liberty," and not "slavery," was national.

If the "Court Organ" thinks that the spirit of freedom at the North is to be "crushed out" by this political and sectional opinion of the Supreme Court, it labors under a great mistake. It will but condense and intensify the opposition to the encroachments of the slave power. It will melt the mass of the people into one great irresistible party of freedom, which will sweep everything before it.

The encroachment upon State rights and State sovereignty is not confined alone to the Supreme Court; but the District Judges, catching the spirit of federalism which pervades the dominant party, are attempting to do their part in this business. We understand that the Judge of this District—and probably those of the others have done the same—has issued orders to the Marshal, &c, to pay no regard to any writs issued by the State Courts—thus leaving the citizen without remedy, save that which the District Court may, in its graciousness, grant. These things call for State action to an extent that will let the federal judiciary know that the States are sovereign on their own soil, and that the federal officers exercise their functions within their jurisdiction only by sufferance.

26

TRIBUNE (NEW YORK)

Editorial

March 21, 1857

Whatever *The Journal of Commerce* may think of it, "more virulent expressions of abuse," whether directed against a Court or an individual, are not likely to make any very deep or permanent impression on the public mind. The serious danger which threatens the Supreme Court of the United States at this moment, and with the reality of which we are as much impressed as that journal is, comes much less from without than from within. Nor on the other hand will mere superstitious worship or fulsome flattery avail to sustain a Court or to hold up a decision which have not inherent strength enough to sustain themselves.

Had the opinion delivered by Chief Justice Taney in the Dred Scott case possessed the essential requisites of a weighty judicial decision, had it rested on grounds and reasons the existence and the force of which it was impossible to deny, however unpalatable might have been the result arrived at, the judgment of the Court would not have failed to tell even upon those minds to which its conclusions might have been most distasteful. The existing difficulty is much more serious, and one which all the efforts of *The Journal of Commerce* to dry or wet nurse the untimely, not to say monstrous, fruit of the Court's labor to vitality, cannot obviate. It is in vain to talk about the elevation of the "Court and its members above the intrigues of party politics and the influences of party passion," when we have before us an opinion every line and sentence of which is thoroughly infused with that spirit of political intrigue and that insanity of party passion in which the Kansas-Nebraska bill had its origin, and from which the Border-Ruffian brutalities of Kansas have drawn encouragement and support. It is absurd to tell us about the appointment of the Judges for life, for the express purpose of securing their independence and placing them beyond the reach of temptation, when the very course of reasoning to which they resort, and the basis of deliberate and studied misrepresentation on which . . . they have rested their decision, show these precautions to have entirely failed, and the Judges to be just as much the exponents of the popular passions of those sections of the country from which a majority of them came, as if liable to be turned out of office at any time by a popular vote. Independence, *The Journal of Commerce* ought to understand, is a quality of mind which, however certain positions may favor it, requires also a certain natural cast of character, without which it cannot exist. This is a point altogether too important to be left out of the account. Whatever precautions the framers of the Constitution may have taken, or may have thought they were taking, in the nature of office and otherwise, to invest the Judges with titles to public confidence and respect, unfortunately the sort of persons selected to fill those positions and the sort of grounds upon which those appointments have been made have by no means corresponded thereto.

Which of the Pro-Slavery Judges, we should like to know, owes his appointment exclusively or in any considerable degree to his eminence as a jurist or to his character as a man? Was Chief Justice Taney raised to his present position merely as an acknowledgment of his learning and talents and judicial virtues, or did he get his place as a reward for partisan services zealously and unscrupulously rendered at a time of high party excitement? As it is with the Chief, so it is with his associates. They, like him, owe their places to political considerations, not to a superiority over hundreds of other lawyers in any of the qualities calculated to inspire public respect.

It is in vain, by any terms of fulsome panegyric and eulogy, by dwelling upon the alleged legal lore, unsullied character, advanced age and life-tenure of the Judges, to make up for inherent falseness, weakness and emptiness in the allegations and arguments which they put forth. *The Journal of Commerce* may howl itself hoarse in shouting over the Dred Scott decision as "authoritative" and "irreversible"; that decision will carry the weight with the public mind, and will do nothing toward settling the interpretation of the Constitution, except so far as the reasons on which it is founded shall stand the test of sharp criticism and rigorous examination. If *The Journal of Commerce* can urge anything satisfactory by way of answer to the various exceptions taken to the assumptions and arguments of Chief Justice Taney's opinion, it will do the Court much more service and itself much more credit than by attempting to induce the public to swallow that decision with eyes shut and mouth open, asking no questions, venturing no doubts, and trusting exclusively to the authority of the Court and the indorsement of *The Journal of Commerce*.

27

TRIBUNE (NEW YORK)

Editorial

March 25, 1857

The Union desires to know what right or liberty of *ours* is assailed or endangered by the late Supreme Court decision in the Dred Scott case. We answer—That decision not merely assails but denies those rights which the Continental Congress of 1774 solemnly declared that our Revolutionary fathers had combined to maintain—"The rights of Human Nature." And when the Southern colonists were urged not to rush into rebellion because of a quarrel betwixt the British crown and the mob of Boston, they nobly answered that the liberties assailed by the Boston Port bill were *their* liberties—that the exercise of ungranted, despotic power which to-day destroyed the business and took away the livelihood of the people of Boston might tomorrow assail *their* dearest rights likewise. So they went to war for a preamble—risked their all in a contest which did not immediately concern them, because the *principle* involved was that which impelled every struggle between Freedom and Tyranny, Justice and Wrong.

It is true that Dred Scott is descended from Africans and is black, while we are descended from Europeans and are white; but "the rights of Human Nature" know no distinction founded on this difference of origin and color. If a black man commits a crime, he is punished for it just as though he were a white man; he ought therefore to have a voice in prescribing and modifying the penalties of crime. If he has property, that property is taxed for the support of our Federal, State and Municipal Governments; he ought therefore to have a voice in determining the objects and extent of expenditure for the support of those Governments. (Can it be possible that a *Democrat* needs to be reminded of these elementary truths?) We rest for the security of our rights, then, not on the fallible and fickle breath of any casual majority, whether embodied in a constitution or not, but on the firm basis of Eternal Justice; and we realize that whatever assails or defies that basis renders all rights unstable, our own included. The Golden Rule does enjoin us to "do unto white men (only) as we would have them do to us"; the Good Samaritan was not commended for humanity to one of his own kith and kin, but for cherishing a wronged fellow being of a despised and detested race. "A false balance is an abomination," says the Good Book; and what can be more abhorrent to any true idea of equity than a judgment that the outcast and downtrodden, by reason of their wrongs, shall be denied a hearing in our Courts of Justice! Whose rights are secure when such justice is dealt out from the bench of our very highest tribunal? Will *The Union* explain?

28

UNION (WASHINGTON, D.C.)

The Supreme Court and the New York Tribune

March 28, 1857

In reply to the assaults of the New York Tribune upon the late decision of the Supreme Court of the United States in the case of Dred Scott, we inquired of that journal what right or liberty of its editor had been taken away by that decision, and in what respect the court had given any superiority of rights to a southern man over a northern man. The Tribune answers, not by mentioning any right or liberty which it has lost, or pointing out any partiality shown by the court to the South over the North, but by declaring, in general terms, that the decision is an attack upon those "rights of human nature" for which our fathers fought in the revolution. This is begging the whole question. Its reasoning is in a circle. First, it makes the decision an outrage because it attacks certain rights, and then it declares that it has assailed these rights because it is an outrage! It is very easy to write general homilies upon humanity and the higher law, and to mourn over the tyranny of our government in not giving equal rights to men and women, black and white, minors and adults, but such general homilies are no sufficient reply to specific inquiries such as we propounded to the Tribune. If that journal means to say that our fathers fought for "human nature" in the sense of giving emancipation to the slaves, its proposition is directly in the teeth of all our history. Did Jefferson regard the Declaration of Independence as a declaration of freedom to his negro servants? Did Washington understand that all the slaves he owned were made free by the treaty of '83? Did Patrick Henry, when he cried "Give me liberty or give me death!" mean to say give me liberty for every Virginia negro, or give me death for myself? If these things were so, and these questions can be truthfully answered in the affirmative, how happened it that slavery was not immediately abolished by the success of our revolutionary struggle? How happened it that it continued on in all the States, and was recognised in the constitution? How happens it to exist now in fifteen States of the Union, and that in those States it is held to be beyond the political interference of anybody except the people of the States where it exists? What meant the fugitive-slave law, signed by Washington? How were new slave States admitted into the Union? Where was the need of a Missouri Compromise, allowing slavery on one side of an arbitrary line, and forbidding it on the other? Why was there any question in the case of this very Dred Scott, and why, instead of claiming his freedom under the act of 1820, did he not seek it under the Declaration of Independence, and by virtue of the "rights of human nature?" The Tribune utterly falls to meet the case we put to it. We regard it as admitting distinctly that no right of its own has been taken away by the decision referred to, and that no southern man has any superiority by that decision over any northern man; and we renew our wonder that, under such circumstances, it should assail the court as having made war upon northern rights or promulgated a "slaveholder's decision!" The truth is, the court was called to determine certain points of constitutional law, and the question before it was *not* what some fanatical theorist might regard as the "rights of human nature," or what a sober thinker even might regard as the rights of a white man, but what was the true meaning of the constitution and the law in reference to Dred Scott, who was a negro. "It is true that Dred Scott (says the Tribune) is descended from Africans and is black, while we are descended from Europeans and are white; but the 'rights of human nature' know no distinction founded on this difference of origin and color." We congratulate the Tribune upon its full appreciation of its own color; but whether "the rights of human nature" recognise any distinction founded on color was not, it ought to remember, the question before the court. The question before the court was, whether any such distinction was recognised by the constitution and laws of this Union; and if the editor of the Tribune ever gets before the court on a question like that, we advise him to stick fast to his own color, and not presume too much upon "the rights of human nature."

3

Political Debate in the North

In the South the response to the *Dred Scott* decision was universally supportive. The editorials from southern newspapers in Chapter 2 give us the flavor of southern opinion. In the North, however, opinion was much more divided. The selections in this chapter reveal the range of political debate in the North over the decision.

The first selection in this chapter is an excerpt from the inaugural address of President James Buchanan. *Dred Scott* was argued in December 1856, after the presidential election. Most of the debates in the election had been over the status of slavery in the territories. While preparing his inaugural address, President-elect Buchanan exchanged letters with Justices Catron and Grier about the case. In a highly inappropriate set of communications, the justices told Buchanan how the case would be decided, and Buchanan actually lobbied Justice Grier (who, like Buchanan, was from Pennsylvania) to concur with Chief Justice Taney's "Opinion of the Court." In the address reprinted here, Buchanan declared that the status of slavery in the territories was a judicial issue and that he would abide by whatever the Court decided. No one knew at the time that Buchanan actually knew in advance what the Court would decide. In his "House Divided" speech (also reprinted in this chapter), Lincoln accused Buchanan of being part of a conspiracy to nationalize slavery, and as an example of this, he pointed to Buchanan's endorsement of the Taney decision *before* it was announced.

The second selection was part of a speech (later published as a pamphlet) by the great black abolitionist Frederick Douglass, the most prominent black in America at the time. At first glance many Americans do not think about blacks participating in the political system in the mid-1800s. However, it is worth recalling that part of Justice Curtis's dissent focused on the fact that blacks had voted in a number of states at the time of the adoption of the Constitution. By 1857 blacks had lost the right of suffrage in New Jersey, Pennsylvania, and North Carolina, as well as the new state of Tennessee, where they had gained suffrage when that state was admitted to the Union in 1796. However, by this time they had also gained suffrage in Rhode Island and the new states of Vermont and Maine. Thus, at the time of the *Dred Scott* decision African Americans had equal suffrage in all of the New England states except Connecticut. Black males who owned some property could vote in New York. In Michigan, African Americans could vote in school board elections, and in some places in the state they sometimes voted in general elections, despite the state's ban on black suffrage. In Ohio, men who were of mixed ancestry but more than half white could vote. Moreover, blacks had held public office in Massachusetts and Ohio. In addition to voting in some places, African Americans actively participated in the debates over political issues. Frederick Douglass's speech, reprinted here, is an example of how blacks commented on political and legal issues.

In his quest for a U.S. Senate seat, Republican Abraham Lincoln challenged the incumbent, Democrat Stephen A. Douglas, to a series of debates. The central issue in these debates was the place of slavery in the nation and the legitimacy of the *Dred Scott* decision. Lincoln thought the decision was illegitimate and that Taney's comments on black citizenship were *dicta* and had no legal force. Douglas embraced the opinion, in part because if accepted by the nation it would end forever the debate over slavery in the territories, which threatened his party's success in the North.

The debate over placing a statue of Chief Justice Roger B. Taney in the Capitol illustrates the mixed emotions Americans had for the author of the *Dred Scott* decision. For a dedicated abolitionist like Senator Charles Sumner of Massachusetts, Taney was evil incarnate, and his memory was to be "hooted down the page of history." Others thought more highly of the chief justice. Some tried to excuse his *Dred Scott* opinion as an aberration in an otherwise impressive career. Others claimed that in *Dred Scott* Taney had the right motives—to preserve the Union by ending the debate over slavery—even if his approach did not work. Even in death Taney was at the center of a political debate about the nature of slavery, race, the Constitution, and his own opinion in *Dred Scott.*

29

PRESIDENT JAMES BUCHANAN

Inaugural Address

March 4, 1857

James Buchanan ran for president endorsing the Kansas-Nebraska Act and the idea of popular sovereignty, which would allow the settlers of the western territories to decide for themselves if they would adopt slavery. The new Republican Party ran against both issues, and the election can be seen as a referendum on slavery in the territories. Between the election in November and the inauguration in March, the Supreme Court heard rearguments in Dred Scott. *During this period Buchanan secretly corresponded with two members of the Court, and he lobbied one of them, Justice Robert C. Grier of Pennsylvania, to support Chief Justice Taney's majority opinion. In this address Buchanan endorsed the outcome of* Dred Scott *even though the case had not yet been decided. However, by the time of his inauguration, the president-elect knew exactly how the case would turn out.*

Fellow citizens, I appear before you this day to take the solemn oath "that I will faithfully execute the office of President of the United States and will to the best of my ability preserve, protect, and defend the Constitution of the United States."

* * *

We have recently passed through a Presidential contest in which the passions of our fellow-citizens were excited to the highest degree by questions of deep and vital importance; but when the people proclaimed their will the tempest at once subsided and all was calm.

The voice of the majority, speaking in the manner prescribed by the Constitution, was heard, and instant submission followed. Our own

---

James Buchanan, "Inaugural Address," March 4, 1857, in James D. Richardson, *A Compilation of the Messages and Papers of the Presidents* (New York: Bureau of National Literature, 1897), 5:2961–62.

country could alone have exhibited so grand and striking a spectacle of the capacity of man for self-government.

What a happy conception, then, was it for Congress to apply this simple rule, that the will of the majority shall govern, to the settlement of the question of domestic slavery in the Territories. Congress is neither "to legislate slavery into any Territory or State nor to exclude it therefrom, but to leave the people thereof perfectly free to form and regulate their domestic institutions in their own way, subject only to the Constitution of the United States."

As a natural consequence, Congress has also prescribed that when the Territory of Kansas shall be admitted as a State it "shall be received into the Union with or without slavery, as their constitution may prescribe at the time of their admission."

A difference of opinion has arisen in regard to the point of time when the people of a Territory shall decide this question for themselves.

This is, happily, a matter of but little practical importance. Besides, it is a judicial question, which legitimately belongs to the Supreme Court of the United States, before whom it is now pending, and will, it is understood, be speedily and finally settled. To their decision, in common with all good citizens, I shall cheerfully submit, whatever this may be, though it has ever been my individual opinion that under the Nebraska-Kansas act the appropriate period will be when the number of actual residents in the Territory shall justify the formation of a constitution with a view to its admission as a State into the Union. But be this as it may, it is the imperative and indispensable duty of the Government of the United States to secure to every resident inhabitant the free and independent expression of his opinion by his vote. This sacred right of each individual must be preserved. That being accomplished, nothing can be fairer than to leave the people of a Territory free from all foreign interference to decide their own destiny for themselves, subject only to the Constitution of the United States.

The whole Territorial question being thus settled upon the principle of popular sovereignty—a principle as ancient as free government itself—everything of a practical nature has been decided. No other question remains for adjustment, because all agree that under the Constitution slavery in the States is beyond the reach of any human power except that of the respective States themselves wherein it exists. May we not, then, hope that the long agitation on this subject is approaching its end, and that the geographical parties to which it has given birth, so much dreaded by the Father of his Country, will speedily become extinct? Most happy will it be for the country when the public mind shall be diverted from this question to others of more pressing and practical importance. Throughout the whole progress of this agitation, which has scarcely known any intermission for more than twenty years, whilst it has been productive of no positive good to any human being it has been the prolific source of great evils to the master, to the slave, and to the whole country. It has alienated and estranged the people of the sister States from each other, and has even seriously endangered the very existence of the Union. Nor has the danger yet entirely ceased. Under our system there is a remedy for all mere political evils in the sound sense and sober judgment of the people. Time is a great corrective. Political subjects which but a few years ago excited and exasperated the public mind have passed away and are now nearly forgotten. But this question of domestic slavery is of far graver importance than any mere political question, because should the agitation continue it may eventually endanger the personal safety of a large portion of our countrymen where the institution exists. In that event no form of government, however admirable in itself and however productive of material benefits, can compensate for the loss of peace and domestic security around the family altar. Let every Union-loving man, therefore, exert his best influence to suppress this agitation, which since the recent legislation of Congress is without any legitimate object.

It is an evil omen of the times that men have undertaken to calculate the mere material value of the Union. Reasoned estimates have been presented of the pecuniary profits and local advantages which would result to different States and sections from its dissolution and of the comparative injuries which such an event would inflict on other States and sections. Even descending to this low and narrow view of the mighty question, all such calculations are at fault. The bare reference to a single consideration will be conclusive on this point. We at present enjoy a free trade throughout our extensive and expanding country such as the world has never witnessed. This trade is conducted on railroads and canals, on noble rivers and arms of the sea, which bind together the North and the South, the East and the West, of our Confederacy. Annihilate this trade, arrest its free progress by the geographical lines of jealous and hostile States, and you destroy the prosperity and onward march of the whole and every part and involve all in one common ruin. But such considerations, important as they are in themselves, sink into insignificance when we reflect on the terrific evils which would result from disunion to every portion of the Confederacy—to the North, not more than to the South, to the East not more than to the West. These I shall not attempt to portray, because I feel an humble confidence that the kind Providence which inspired our fathers with wisdom to frame the most perfect form of government and union ever devised by man will not suffer it to perish until it shall have been peacefully instrumental by its example in the extension of civil and religious liberty throughout the world.

30

FREDERICK DOUGLASS

The Dred Scott *Decision: Speech at New York, on the Occasion of the Anniversary of the American Abolition Society*

May 11, 1857

Frederick Douglass was the most famous black abolitionist in the antebellum United States. Born a slave in Maryland in 1818, Douglass escaped to Massachusetts in 1838. He initially worked in the shipbuilding industry but later made his way to Boston, where he quickly became involved in the antislavery movement. He soon became an abolitionist speaker, a writer, and eventually a newspaper publisher.

Initially Douglass associated with William Lloyd Garrison, the abolitionist editor of the Liberator *and the founder of the American Anti-Slavery Society. Garrison believed that the Constitution was thoroughly proslavery—he called it a "covenant with death and an agreement with hell." Under the slogan "No Union with Slaveholders" Garrison argued that abolitionists should withdraw from politics and agitate for an end to the Union. Furthermore, because of the proslavery nature of the Constitution, Garrison believed that withdrawal from the Union was the only morally correct position for opponents of slavery. The Garrisonians were convinced that the legal protection of slavery in the Constitution made political activity futile, while support for the Constitution merely strengthened the stranglehold slavery had on America. Garrison also believed*

Two Speeches, by Frederick Douglass; One on West India Emancipation. Delivered at Canandaigua, Aug. 4th, and the Other on the Dred Scott *Decision. Delivered in New York, on the Occasion of the Anniversary of the American Abolition Society, May, 1857* (Rochester: C. P. Dewey, 1857).

*that if the North seceded from the United States, slavery in the South
would collapse.*

Douglass was initially a Garrisonian, but by the time of the Dred
Scott *decision he had rejected Garrison's constitutional views and had
aligned himself with the political abolitionists, like Senators William H.
Seward of New York and Salmon P. Chase of Ohio. Chase in particular
argued that the Constitution could be used to fight slavery.*

*The speech Douglass gave to the American Anti-Slavery Society on
May 11, 1857, was subsequently published in an edited and revised pamphlet version, which is reprinted here. In addition to attacking Taney, the
Supreme Court, and the* Dred Scott *decision, Douglass also takes issue
with those who claim that the Constitution is proslavery. This argument
is partially aimed at the Garrisonian abolitionists but is also attack on
Taney and the southern nationalists, who believed that the Constitution
protected slavery.*

While four millions of our fellow countrymen are in chains—while men,
women, and children are bought and sold on the auction-block with
horses, sheep, and swine—while the remorseless slave-whip draws the
warm blood of our common humanity—. . . we assemble . . . and lift up
our hearts and voices in earnest denunciation of the vile and shocking
abomination. It is not for us to be governed by our hopes or our fears in
this great work; yet it is natural on occasions like this, to survey the position of the great struggle which is going on between slavery and freedom,
and to dwell upon such signs of encouragement as may have been lately
developed, and the state of feeling these signs or events have occasioned
in us and among the people generally. It is a fitting time to take an obser-
vation to ascertain where we are, and what our prospects are.

To many, the prospects of the struggle against slavery seem from
cheering. Eminent men, North and South, in Church and State, tell us
that the omens are all against us. Emancipation, they tell us, is a wild,
delusive idea; the price of human flesh was never higher than now; slavery was never more closely entwined about the hearts and affections of
the southern people than now; that whatever of conscientious scruple,
religious conviction, or public policy, which opposed the system of slavery forty or fifty years ago, has subsided; and that slavery never reposed
upon a firmer basis than now. . . .

. . . [S]laveholders are in earnest, and mean to cling to their slaves as
long as they can, and to the bitter end. They show no sign of a wish to

quit their iron grasp upon the sable throats of their victims. Their motto is, "a firmer hold and a tighter grip" for every new effort that is made to break their cruel power. The case is one of life or death with them, and they will give up only when they must do that or do worse.

In one view slaveholders have a decided advantage over all opposition. It is well to notice this advantage—the advantage of complete organization. They are organized; and yet were not at the pains of creating their organizations. The State governments, where the system of slavery exists, are complete slavery organizations. The church organizations in those States are equally at the service of slavery; while the Federal Government, with its army and navy, from the chief magistracy in Washington, to the Supreme Court, and thence to the chief marshalship at New York, is pledged to support, defend, and propagate the crying curse of human bondage. The pen, the purse, and the sword, are united against the simple truth, preached by humble men in obscure places.

This is one view. It is, thank God, only one view; there is another, and a brighter view. David, you know, looked small and insignificant when going to meet Goliath, but looked larger when he had slain his foe. The Malakoff[1] was, to the eye of the world, impregnable, till the hour it fell before the shot and shell of the allied army. Thus hath it ever been. Oppression, organized as ours is, will appear invincible up to the very hour of its fall. Sir, let us look at the other side, and see if there are not some things to cheer our heart and nerve us up anew in the good work of emancipation.

Take this fact—for it is a fact—the antislavery movement has, from first to last, suffered no abatement. It has gone forth in all directions, and is now felt in the remotest extremities of the Republic. . . .

Those who have undertaken to suppress and crush out this agitation for Liberty and humanity, have been most woefully disappointed. Many who have engaged to put it down, have found themselves put down. The agitation has pursued them in all their meanderings, broken in upon their seclusion, and, at the very moment of fancied security, it has settled down upon them like a mantle of unquenchable fire. Clay, Calhoun, and Webster[2] each tried his hand at suppressing the agitation; and they went to their graves disappointed and defeated.

---

[1]A fortification erected by the Russians at Sevastopol and captured by the French in 1855.

[2]Henry Clay (1777–1852) of Kentucky, John C. Calhoun (1782–1850) of South Carolina, and Daniel Webster (1782–1852) of Massachusetts. Clay and Webster were Whigs who served as secretary of state in various administrations; Calhoun was vice president from 1825 until his resignation in 1832. All three had distinguished careers in Congress.

Loud and exultingly have we been told that the slavery question is settled, and settled forever. You remember it was settled thirty-seven years ago, when Missouri was admitted into the Union with a slaveholding constitution, and slavery prohibited in all territory north of thirty-six degrees of north latitude. Just fifteen years afterwards, it was settled again by voting down the right of petition, and gagging down free discussion in Congress.[3] Ten years after this it was settled again by the annexation of Texas, and with it the war with Mexico. In 1850 it was again settled.[4] This was called a final settlement. By it slavery was virtually declared to be the equal of Liberty, and should come into the Union on the same terms. By it the right and the power to hunt down men, women, and children, in every part of this country, was conceded to our southern brethren, in order to keep them in the Union.[5] Four years after this settlement, the whole question was once more settled, and settled by a settlement which unsettled all the former settlements.[6]

The fact is, the more the question has been settled, the more it has needed settling. The space between the different settlements has been strikingly on the decrease. The first stood longer than any of its successors.

There is a lesson in these decreasing spaces. The first stood fifteen years—the second, ten years—the third, five years—the fourth stood four years—and the fifth has stood the brief space of two years.

This last settlement must be called the Taney settlement. We are now told, in tones of lofty exultation, that the day is lost—all lost—and that we might as well give up the struggle. The highest authority has spoken.

Clay helped push the Missouri Compromise through Congress in 1820. He authored, and Webster supported, the Compromise of 1850, while Calhoun opposed it. The reference here is to their many attempts to compromise on the issue of slavery in order to promote national and sectional harmony.

[3]In the 1830s and early 1840s the House of Representatives annually adopted a "gag rule" that prohibited the reading of antislavery petitions. Many northerners believed that this rule violated the First Amendment's guarantee that Congress could "make no law . . . abridging . . . the right of the people . . . to petition the government for a redress of grievances." The best discussion of the gag rule is in Gilbert Hobbes Barnes, *The Antislavery Impulse, 1830–1844* (New York: Appleton-Century, 1933).

[4]Douglass refers to the Compromise of 1850, which sought to balance sectional interests. Under the compromise California entered the Union as a free state but slavery was allowed in the other territories ceded to the United States after the Mexican-American War. The compromise banned the public sale of slaves in Washington, D.C., but also provided for a stronger and more unfair fugitive slave law—the infamous Fugitive Slave Law of 1850.

[5]This is a reference to the Fugitive Slave Law of 1850, passed as part of the Compromise of 1850.

[6]The Kansas-Nebraska Act of 1854 allowed slavery in the Kansas and Nebraska Territories, thus repealing part of the Missouri Compromise. Hostility to this law led to the formation of the Republican Party.

The voice of the Supreme Court has gone out over the troubled waves of the National Conscience, saying peace, be still.

This infamous decision of the Slaveholding wing of the Supreme Court maintains that slaves are, within the contemplation of the Constitution of the United States, property; that slaves are property in the same sense that horses, sheep, and swine are property; that the old doctrine that slavery is a creature of local law is false; that the right of the slaveholder to his slave does not depend upon the local law, but is secured wherever the Constitution of the United States extends; that Congress has no right to prohibit slavery anywhere; that slavery may go in safety anywhere under the star-spangled banner; that colored persons of African descent have no rights that white men are bound to respect; that colored men of African descent are not and cannot be citizens of the United States.

You will readily ask me how I am affected by this devilish decision— this judicial incarnation of wolfishness! My answer is, and no thanks to the slaveholding wing of the Supreme Court, my hopes were never brighter than now.

I have no fear that the National Conscience will be put to sleep by such an open, glaring, and scandalous tissue of lies as that decision is, and has been, over and over, shown to be.

The Supreme Court of the United States is not the only power in this world. It is very great, but the Supreme Court of the Almighty is greater. Judge Taney can do many things, but he cannot perform impossibilities. He cannot bale out the ocean, annihilate this firm old earth, or pluck the silvery star of liberty from our Northern sky. He may decide, and decide again; but he cannot reverse the decision of the Most High. He cannot change the essential nature of things—making evil good, and good, evil.

Happily for the whole human family, their rights have been defined, declared, and decided in a court higher than the Supreme Court. . . .

Your fathers have said that man's right to liberty is self-evident.[7] There is no need of argument to make it clear. The voices of nature, of conscience, of reason, and of revelation, proclaim it as the right of all rights, the foundation of all trust, and of all responsibility. Man was born with it. It was his before he comprehended it. The *deed* conveying it to him is written in the centre of his soul, and is recorded in Heaven. The sun in the sky is not more palpable to the sight than man's right to liberty

---

[7]This is a reference to the Declaration of Independence: "We hold these Truths to be self-evident, That all Men are created equal, that they are endowed by their Creator with certain unalienable Rights, that among these are Life, Liberty, and the Pursuit of Happiness."

FREDERICK DOUGLASS **171**

is to the moral vision. To decide against this right in the person of Dred Scott, or the humblest and most whip-scarred bondman in the land, is to decide against God. It is an open rebellion against God's government. It is an attempt to undo what God [has] done, to blot out the broad distinction instituted by the *Allwise* between men and things, and to change the image and superscription of the everliving God into a speechless piece of merchandise.

Such a decision cannot stand. God will be true though every man be a liar. We can appeal from this hell-black judgment of the Supreme Court, to the court of common sense and common humanity. We can appeal from man to God. If there is no justice on earth, there is yet justice in heaven. You may close your Supreme Court against the black man's cry for justice, but you cannot, thank God, close against him the ear of a sympathising world, nor shut up the Court of Heaven. All that is merciful and just, on earth and in Heaven, will execrate and despise this edict of Taney. . . .

In one point of view, we, the abolitionists and colored people, should meet this decision, unlooked for and monstrous as it appears, in a cheerful spirit. This very attempt to blot out forever the hopes of an enslaved people may be one necessary link in the chain of events preparatory to the downfall and complete overthrow of the whole slave system.

The whole history of the anti-slavery movement is studded with proof that all measures devised and executed with a view to allay and diminish the anti-slavery agitation, have only served to increase, intensify, and embolden that agitation. This wisdom of the crafty has been confounded, and the counsels of the ungodly brought to nought. It was so with the Fugitive Slave Bill. It was so with the Kansas-Nebraska Bill; and it will be so with this last and most shocking of all pro-slavery devices, this Taney decision. . . .

Step by step we have seen the slave power advancing; poisoning, corrupting, and perverting the institutions of the country; growing more and more haughty, imperious, and exacting. The white man's liberty has been marked out for the same grave with the black man's.

The ballot box is desecrated, God's law set at nought, armed legislators stalk the halls of Congress, freedom of speech is beaten down in the Senate. The rivers and highways are infested by border ruffians, and white men are made to feel the iron heel of slavery. This ought arouse us to kill off the hateful thing. They are solemn warnings to which the white people, as well as the black people, should take heed.

If these shall fail, judgment, more fierce or terrible, may come. The lightning, whirlwind, and earthquake may come. Jefferson said that he trembled for his country when he reflected that God is just, and his justice cannot sleep forever.[8] The time may come when even the crushed worm may turn under the tyrant's feet. Goaded by cruelty, stung by a burning sense of wrong, in an awful moment of depression and desperation, the bondman and bondwoman at the south may rush to one wild and deadly struggle for freedom. Already slaveholders go to bed with bowie knives, and apprehend death at their dinners. Those who enslave, rob, and torment their cooks, may well expect to find death in their dinner-pots.

The world is full of violence and fraud, and it would be strange if the slave, the constant victim of both fraud and violence, should escape the contagion. He, too, may learn to fight the devil with fire and for one, I am in no frame of mind to pray that this may be long deferred. . . .

Come what will, I hold it to be morally certain that, sooner or later, by fair means or foul means, in quiet or in tumult, in peace or in blood, in judgment or in mercy, slavery is doomed to cease out of this otherwise goodly land, and liberty is destined to become the settled law of this Republic.

I base my sense of the certain overthrow of slavery, in part, upon the nature of the American Government, the Constitution, the tendencies of the age, and the character of the American people; and this notwithstanding the important decision of Judge Taney.

I know of no soil better adapted to the growth of reform than American soil. I know of no country where the conditions for affecting great changes in the settled order of things, for the development of right ideas of liberty and humanity, are more favorable than here in these United States.

The very groundwork of this government is a good repository of Christian civilization. The Constitution, as well as the Declaration of Independence, and the sentiments of the founders of the Republic, give us a platform broad enough, and strong enough, to support the most comprehensive plans for the freedom and elevation of all the people of this country, without regard to color, class, or clime.

There is nothing in the present aspect of the anti-slavery question which should drive us into the extravagance and nonsense of advocating

---

[8]Jefferson wrote in chapter 18 of *Notes on the State of Virginia*: "Indeed I tremble for my country when I reflect that God is just: that his justice cannot sleep for ever: that considering numbers, nature and natural means only, a revolution of the wheel of fortune, an exchange in situation, is among possible events: that it may become probable by supernatural interference!" However, on Jefferson's dubious antislavery credentials, see Paul Finkelman, *Slavery and the Founders: Race and Liberty in the Age of Jefferson*, 3rd ed. (New York: Routledge, 2014), 193–280.

a dissolution of the American Union as a means of overthrowing slavery, or freeing the North from the malign influence of slavery, or freeing the North from the malign influence of slavery upon the morals of the Northern people. While the press is at liberty, and speech is free and the ballot-box is open to the people of the sixteen free States; while the slaveholders are but four hundred thousand in number and we are fourteen millions; while we are really the strong and they are the weak, it would look worse than cowardly to retreat from the Union. . . .

The dissolution of the Union would not give the North one single additional advantage over slavery to the people of the North, but would manifestly take from them many which they now certainly possess.

Within the Union we have a firm basis of anti-slavery operation. National welfare, national prosperity, national reputation and honor, and national scrutiny; common rights, common duties, and common country, are so many bridges over which we can march to the destruction of slavery. To fling away these advantages because James Buchanan is President, or Judge Taney gives a lying decision in favor of slavery, does not enter into my notion of common sense.

Mr. Garrison and his friends have been telling us that, while in the Union, we are responsible for slavery; and in so telling us, he and they have told us the truth.[9] But in telling us that we shall cease to be responsible for slavery by dissolving the Union, he and they have not told us the truth.

There now, clearly, is no freedom from responsibility for slavery, but in the Abolition of slavery. We have gone too far in this business now to sum up our whole duty in the cant phrase of "no Union with slaveholders." . . .

. . . I have a quarrel with those who fling the Supreme Law of this land between the slave and freedom. It is a serious matter to fling the weight of the Constitution against the cause of human liberty, and those who do it, take upon them a heavy responsibility. Nothing but absolute necessity, shall, or ought to drive me to such a concession to slavery.

When I admit that slavery is constitutional, I must see slavery recognized in the Constitution. I must see that it is there plainly stated that one man of a certain description has a right of property in the body and soul of another man of a certain description. There must be no room for a doubt. In a matter so important as the loss of liberty, everything must be proved beyond all reasonable doubt. . . .

---

[9]For more on Garrison and the proslavery aspects of the Constitution, see Finkelman, *Slavery and the Founders*, 1–33.

How is the constitutionality of slavery made out, or attempted to be made out?

First, by discrediting and casting away as worthless the most benefi-cent rules of legal interpretation; by disregarding the plain and common sense reading of the instrument itself; by showing that the Constitution does not mean what it says, and says what it does not mean, by assum-ing that the WRITTEN Constitution is to be interpreted in the light of a SECRET and UNWRITTEN understanding of its framers, which understand-ing is declared to be in favor of slavery. It is in this mean, contemptible, underhand method that the Constitution is pressed into the service of slavery.

They do not point us to the Constitution itself, for the reason that there is nothing sufficiently explicit for their purpose; but they delight in supposed intentions — intentions no where expressed in the Constitu-tion, and every where contradicted in the Constitution.

Judge Taney lays down this system of interpreting in this wise:

"The general words above quoted would seem to embrace the whole human family, and, if they were used in a similar instrument at this day, would be so understood. But it is too clear for dispute that the enslaved African race were not intended to be included, and formed no part of the people who framed and adopted this declaration; for if the language, as understood in that day, would embrace them, the conduct of the distinguished men who framed the Declaration of Independence would have been utterly and flagrantly inconsistent with the principles they asserted; and instead of the sympathy of mankind, to which they appealed, they would have deserved and received universal rebuke and reprobation.

"It is difficult, at this day, to realize the state of public opinion respect-ing that unfortunate class with the civilized and enlightened portion of the world at the time of the Declaration of Independence and the adop-tion of the Constitution; but history shows they had, for more than a cen-tury, been regarded as beings of an inferior order, and unfit associates for the white race, either socially or politically, and had no rights which white men are bound to respect; and the black man might be reduced to slavery, bought and sold, and treated as an ordinary article of merchan-dise. This opinion, at that time, was fixed and universal with the civilized portion of the white race. It was regarded as an axiom of morals, which no one thought of disputing, and every one habitually acted upon it, without doubting, for a moment, the correctness of the opinion. And in no nation was this opinion more fixed, and generally acted upon, than in England; the subjects of which government not only seized them on the coast of Africa, but took them, as ordinary merchandise, to where they could make a profit on them. The opinion, thus entertained, was universally maintained on the colonies this side of the Atlantic; accordingly, negroes of the African race were regarded by them as property, and held and bought and sold as such in every one of the thirteen colonies which united in the Declaration of Independence, and afterwards formed the Constitution."

The argument here is, that the Constitution comes down to us from a slaveholding period and a slaveholding people; and that, therefore, we are bound to suppose that the Constitution recognizes colored persons of African descent, the victims of slavery at that time, as debarred forever from all participation in the benefit of the Constitution and the Declaration of Independence, although the plain reading of both includes them in their beneficent range.

As a man, an American, a citizen, a colored man of both Anglo-Saxon and African descent, I denounce this representation as a most scandalous and devilish perversion of the Constitution, and a brazen misstatement of the facts of history.

But I will not content myself with mere denunciation; I invite attention to the facts.

It is a fact, a great historic fact, that at the time of the adoption of the Constitution, the leading religious denominations in this land were antislavery, and were laboring for the emancipation of the colored people of African descent. . . .

I might quote, at length, from the sayings of the Baptist Church and the sayings of eminent divines at this early period, showing that Judge Taney has grossly falsified history, but [I] will not detain you with these quotations.

The testimony of the church, and the testimony of the founders of this Republic, from the declaration downward, prove Judge Taney false; as false to history as he is to law.

Washington and Jefferson, and Adams, and Jay, and Franklin, and Rush, and Hamilton,[10] and a host of others, held no such degrading

[10]George Washington, Thomas Jefferson, John Adams, John Jay, Benjamin Franklin, Dr. Benjamin Rush, and Alexander Hamilton. Jay (1745–1829), a Revolutionary leader, diplomat, coauthor (with James Madison and Alexander Hamilton) of the *Federalist Papers*, and first chief justice of the Supreme Court, was president of the New York Manumission Society. Rush (1745–1813), a Philadelphia physician, signer of the Declaration of Independence, and treasurer of the U.S. Mint, was president of the Pennsylvania Abolition Society. Hamilton, a military aide-de-camp to George Washington during the Revolution, a coauthor of the *Federalist Papers*, and the first secretary of the treasury, was also a member of the New York Manumission Society. Benjamin Franklin was

views on the subject as are imputed by Judge Taney to the Fathers of the Republic.

All, at that time, looked for the gradual but certain abolition of slavery, and shaped the constitution with a view to this grand result.

George Washington can never be claimed as a fanatic, or as the representative of fanatics. The slaveholders impudently use his name for the base purpose of giving respectability to slavery. Yet, in a letter to Robert Morris,[11] Washington uses this language—language which, at this day, would make him a terror of the slaveholders, and the natural representative of the Republican party.

"There is not a man living, who wishes more sincerely than I do, to see some plan adopted for the abolition of slavery; but there is only one proper and effectual mode by which it can be accomplished, and that is by Legislative authority; and this, as far as my suffrage will go, shall not be wanting."

Washington only spoke the sentiment of his times. There were, at that time, Abolition societies in the slave States—Abolition societies in Virginia, in North Carolina, in Maryland, in Pennsylvania, and in Georgia—all slaveholding States. Slavery was so weak, and liberty so strong, that free speech could attack the monster to its teeth. Men were not mobbed and driven out of the presence of slavery, merely because they condemned the slave system. The system was then on its knees imploring to be spared, until it could get itself decently out of the world.

In the light of these facts, the Constitution was framed, and framed in conformity to it.

It may, however, be asked, if the Constitution were so framed that the rights of all the people were naturally protected by it, how happens it that a large part of the people have been held in slavery ever since its adoption? Have the people mistaken the requirements of their own Constitution?

The answer is ready. The Constitution is one thing, its administration is another, and, in this instance, a very different and opposite thing. I am here to vindicate the law, not the administration of the law. It is the written Constitution, not the unwritten Constitution, that is now before us.

---

president of the Pennsylvania Abolition Society. Washington opposed slavery and freed all his slaves in his will. Adams also opposed slavery. The record on Jefferson is far more ambiguous. He freed only three slaves during his lifetime and only five at his death. His views on the abilities of blacks and their right to citizenship were probably far closer to Taney's than Douglass knew or was willing to admit. On Jefferson's racism, see Finkelman, *Slavery and the Founders*, 193–280.

[11]Robert Morris (1734–1806) was a leading political figure during the Revolution and Confederation period and a delegate to the Constitutional Convention from Pennsylvania.

If, in the whole range of the Constitution, you can find no warrant for slavery, then we may properly claim it for liberty.

Good and wholesome laws are often found dead on the statute book. We may condemn the practice under them and against them, but never the law itself. To condemn the good law with the wicked practice, is to weaken, not to strengthen our testimony.

It is no evidence that the Bible is a bad book, because those who profess to believe the Bible are bad. The slaveholders of the South, and many of their wicked allies at the North, claim the Bible for slavery; shall we, therefore, fling the Bible away as a pro-slavery book? It would be as reasonable to do so as it would be to fling away the Constitution. . . .

The American people have made void our Constitution by just such traditions as Judge Taney and Mr. Garrison have been giving to world of late, as the true light in which to view the Constitution of the United States. I shall follow neither. It is not what Moses allowed for the hardness of heart, but what God requires, [which] ought to be the rule.

It may be said that it is quite true that the Constitution was designed to secure the blessings of liberty and justice to the people who made it, and to the posterity of the people who made it, but was never designed to do any such thing for the colored people of African descent.

This is Judge Taney's argument, and it is Mr. Garrison's argument, but it is not the argument of the Constitution. The Constitution imposes no such mean and satanic limitations upon its own beneficent operation. And, if the Constitution makes none, I beg to know what right has any body, outside of the Constitution, for the special accommodation of slave-holding villainy, to impose such a construction upon the Constitution?

The Constitution knows all the human inhabitants of this country as "the people." It makes, as I have said before, no discrimination in favor of, or against, any class of the people, but is fitted to protect and preserve the rights of all, without reference to color, size, or any physical peculiarities. Besides, it has been shown by William Goodell and others, that in eleven out of the old thirteen States, colored men were legal voters at the time of the adoption of the Constitution.[12]

In conclusion, let me say, all I ask of the American people is, that they live up to the Constitution, adopt its principles, imbibe its spirit and enforce its provisions.

---

[12]William Goodell (1792–1878) was a leading antislavery legal theorist and an activist in various antislavery political parties. Goodell opposed the Garrisonians, arguing that the Constitution could be used to combat slavery; see his book *Views of American Constitutional Law: In Its Bearing upon American Slavery* (Utica, N.Y.: Lawson and Chaplin, 1845).

When this is done, the wounds of my bleeding people will be healed, the chain will no longer rust on their ankles, their backs will no longer be torn by the bloody lash, and liberty, the glorious birthright of our common humanity, will become the inheritance of all the inhabitants of this highly favored country.

Lincoln-Douglas Debates and the *Dred Scott* Decision

The Lincoln-Douglas Debates are the best-known head-to-head political confrontations in American history. In 1858 the Illinois Republican Party chose Abraham Lincoln, an Illinois lawyer with modest political experience, to challenge the incumbent Democratic U.S. senator Stephen A. Douglas. At the beginning of the campaign Lincoln shadowed Douglas, giving speeches in Chicago, Springfield, and other Illinois cities immediately after Douglas gave speeches in those places. Thus from early July until mid-August the candidates debated without actually answering each other face to face. Eventually, however, Douglas accepted Lincoln's challenge to a series of face-to-face debates. Douglas agreed to joint appearances in seven of the state's nine congressional districts but refused to debate Lincoln in Chicago and Springfield because both had spoken in those places separately.

Like the United States, Illinois was divided politically along a deep geographic cleavage. Southern Illinois was heavily Democratic and clearly Douglas country; northern Illinois was hostile to slavery, solidly Republican, and Lincoln's stronghold.

Rarely have two candidates been so different. Lincoln was born to poverty in Kentucky, a slave state. He was largely self-educated and never very cultured. He was tall, lean, and gawky and never seemed quite to fit into his clothing. Lincoln had a high-pitched voice, a Kentucky twang, and an unimpressive presence. Douglas was born in Vermont, a state where blacks had full legal equality with whites and where antislavery sentiment was almost universal. His family was somewhat better off than Lincoln's, and he had more formal education. He rose quickly from a lawyer to a judge, a congressman, and a U.S. senator. Short and pudgy, but also very dignified, he was the "Little Giant" of Illinois politics. He was a superb speaker and a brilliant debater. Surely the candidates were an odd pair. One journalist, Henry Villard, offered this description of the two men as they faced off their first debate, in Ottawa, Illinois:

The Democratic spokesman commanded a strong, sonorous voice, a rapid vigorous utterance, a telling play of countenance, impressive gestures, and all the other arts of the practiced speaker. As far as all external conditions were concerned, there was nothing in favor of Lincoln. He had a lean, lank, indescribably gawky figure, an odd-featured, wrinkled, inexpressive, and altogether uncomely face. He used singularly awkward, almost absurd, up-and-down and sidewise movements of his body to give emphasis to his arguments. His voice was naturally good but he frequently raised it to an unnatural pitch.[1]

Despite his lack of "external" advantages, Lincoln was quick on his feet and had a brilliant sense of humor. Douglas, known for his lack of humor, admitted that Lincoln's "droll ways and dry jokes" made him "the best stump speaker . . . in the West."[2]

Their politics by this time were as different as their physical appearance and speaking styles. By 1857 Douglas had emerged as the most prominent northern Democrat and the odds-on favorite for the presidential nom-ination in 1860. Lincoln was virtually unknown. He had served only one term in Congress and a handful in the Illinois legislature. Before Dred Scott, *Douglas had always tolerated slavery, while Lincoln had emerged as a candidate in the nation's first serious antislavery party.*

Ironically, Douglas's own legislative success had led to the creation of Lincoln's new party. In 1854 Senator Douglas introduced the bill that became the Kansas-Nebraska Act, which allowed for the organization of the territories west and northwest of Missouri and Iowa without regard to slavery. Douglas argued that the territories should be settled on the basis of popular sovereignty, with the settlers deciding for themselves if they wanted slavery. This was a partial repeal of the Missouri Compro-mise, which had flatly prohibited slavery in this area for thirty-four years. In engineering the Kansas-Nebraska Act, Douglas gained enormous support in the South while seemingly not losing his Democratic base in the North.

Many northerners, however, shocked by the idea of allowing slavery in what had been previously free territories, organized the Republican Party as a response to this law. The Republicans attracted most of the old Whig Party as well as many antislavery Democrats. In the 1856 presidential election, the party carried most of the North, although James Buchanan,

---

[1]Henry Villard, *Memoirs of Henry Villard, Journalist and Financier, 1835–1900*, 2 vols. (Boston: Houghton Mifflin, 1904), 1:92–93, quoted in Harold Holzer, *The Lincoln-Douglas Debates: The First Unexpurgated Text* (New York: HarperCollins, 1993), 19.

[2]Douglas quoted in Holzer, *Lincoln-Douglas Debates*, 16.

a Pennsylvania Democrat, won the presidency. The most important plank of the Republican platform was the party's unswerving opposition to the addition of any more slave states or allowing slavery in the territories. Following the election and Buchanan's inauguration, the Supreme Court announced its opinion in Dred Scott. *By holding that Congress had no power to prohibit slavery in the territories, Chief Justice Taney, in essence, held that the main goal of the Republican Party was not constitutionally possible.*

The proslavery victory in Dred Scott *led southerners to demand that a new slave state be brought into the Union. In 1857, to placate the South, where the Democratic Party was strongest, President Buchanan tried to force Congress to admit Kansas into the Union as a slave state. The basis of this admission was a constitution written in Lecompton, Kansas, by an unrepresentative convention and approved in a fraudulent referendum. Buchanan and the southern majority in the Democratic Party made support for the Lecompton constitution a matter of party loyalty. Douglas was not opposed to the admission of new slave states, but he objected to the admission of Kansas because he argued, correctly, that the Lecompton constitution was not truly the result of popular sovereignty. This made Douglas an outcast in his own party. Indeed, in 1858 President Buchanan tried to get Illinois Democrats to support someone else for the U.S. Senate. Nevertheless, Douglas was their candidate.*

During the 1858 senatorial campaign, Douglas continued to support popular sovereignty and to defend the Dred Scott *decision. Lincoln argued that Douglas was part of a conspiracy to make slavery legal everywhere in the country. According to Lincoln, this conspiracy included Douglas, President Buchanan, former President Franklin Pierce, and Chief Justice Taney.*

The debates made Lincoln a national political figure and set the stage for his presidential nomination and election in 1860. His chief opponent in that election would be Stephen A. Douglas. In the senatorial election of 1858, however, Douglas was the victorious candidate.[3]

The following excerpts from the campaign speeches and direct debates of the 1858 contest illustrate the way Dred Scott *had become a major political issue. Various newspapers reported the speeches and debates, often working from transcripts or notes provided by the candidates.*

---

[3]Had senators been elected directly by the people, as they are today, it is likely that Lincoln would have won in 1858. But at that time (and until the adoption of the Seventeenth Amendment in 1913), the state legislatures chose U.S. senators. In the general election of 1858 Illinois Democrats won the most seats in the state legislature, in part because the apportionment of the legislature favored the less populous and heavily democratic southern part of the state.

Lincoln collected newspaper clippings, which served as the basis for a published version of the debates in 1860. Since then the texts have often been reprinted.[4]

---

[4]The most comprehensive collection remains Paul M. Angle, *Created Equal? The Complete Lincoln-Douglas Debates of 1858* (1958; Chicago: University of Chicago Press, 1990). Holzer, in *Lincoln-Douglas Debates*, presents a somewhat different version of the debates themselves but does not include any of the speeches leading up to the debates.

31

ABRAHAM LINCOLN

The "House Divided" Speech at Springfield, Illinois

June 16, 1858

Lincoln began his campaign with a speech to the Illinois Republican convention in Springfield. In what became known as the "House Divided" speech, Lincoln outlined his view that Douglas was part of a conspiracy to nationalize slavery. To modern eyes, Lincoln's fears seem fantastic. But suppose Douglas or some other Democrat had won the presidency in 1860. Would the "next Dred Scott *decision" have declared that masters had a right to travel in the North with their slaves, as Dr. Emerson had done with Dred Scott? Such a case,* Lemmon v. The People, *was in fact making its way through the New York courts. In 1852 the Lemmons had gone from Virginia to New York City, where they hoped to catch a steamboat directly to New Orleans. They brought eight slaves with them. A New York court freed those slaves, on the ground that there could be no slavery in New York.* Had there been no Civil War, it seems likely that the* Lemmon

---

*The initial case was *The People, ex rel. Lewis Napoleon v. Lemmon*, 5 Sandford (N.Y.) 681 (1852). In 1857 a New York appeals court upheld that result in *Lemmon v. The People*, 26 Barbour (N.Y.) 270 (1857). Lincoln knew about this case at the time he wrote the "House Divided" speech. In 1860 New York's highest court affirmed the result in *Lemmon v. The People*, 20 N.Y. 562 (1860). The *Lemmon* case is discussed in Paul Finkelman, *An Imperfect Union: Slavery, Federalism, and Comity* (Chapel Hill: University of North Carolina Press, 1981), 296–332.

Illinois State Journal, June 18, 1858, reprinted in Paul M. Angle, *Created Equal? The Complete Lincoln-Douglas Debates of 1858* (Chicago: University of Chicago Press, 1958), 1–9.

case would have reached the Supreme Court in 1861 or 1862. Lincoln believed that the Court would have forced New York, and by extension all other free states, to allow masters to bring their slaves into the North.

Is Lincoln's theory of a conspiracy far-fetched? Was the Supreme Court planning to nationalize slavery? Recall the end of Justice Nelson's concurring opinion in Dred Scott *suggesting that in a future opinion the Court would support the right of a master to travel in the free states with his slaves. If the* Lemmon *case had reached the Supreme Court, would slavery have been nationalized?*

Mr. President and Gentlemen of the Convention: If we could first know *where* we are, and *whither* we are tending, we could then better judge *what* to do, and *how* to do it.[1]

We are now far into the *fifth* year, since a policy was initiated, with the *avowed* object, and *confident* promise, of putting an end to slavery agitation.[2]

Under the operation of that policy, that agitation has not only, *not ceased*, but has *constantly augmented.*

In *my* opinion, it *will* not cease, until a *crisis* shall have been reached, and passed.

"A house divided against itself cannot stand."[3]

I believe this government cannot endure, permanently half *slave* and half *free.*

I do not expect the Union to be *dissolved*—I do not expect the house to *fall*—but I *do* expect it will cease to be divided.

It will become *all* one thing, or *all* the other.

Either the *opponents* of slavery, will arrest the further spread of it, and place it where the public mind shall rest in the belief that it is in course of ultimate extinction; or its *advocates* will push it forward, till it shall become alike lawful in *all* the states, *old* as well as *new*—*North* as well as *South.*

---

[1]The italics used in the speeches and debates reflects the emphasis placed on particular words when Lincoln and Douglas spoke. Lincoln underlined most of the words on his own text before delivering the speech.

[2]In 1854 Stephen Douglas introduced what became the Kansas-Nebraska Act, which repealed the part of the Missouri Compromise that had prohibited slavery in the territory west of Missouri, Iowa, and Minnesota and allowed the settlers of a territory to decide if they wanted slavery in the area (popular sovereignty).

[3]Here Lincoln is paraphrasing Mark 3:25 (King James Version): "And if a house be divided against itself, that house cannot stand."

Have we no *tendency* to the latter condition?

Let any one who doubts, carefully contemplate that now almost complete legal combination—piece of *machinery* so to speak—compounded of the Nebraska doctrine, and the Dred Scott decision. Let him consider not only *what work* the machinery is adapted to do, and *how well* adapted; but also, let him study the *history* of its construction, and trace, if he can, or rather *fail*, if he can, to trace the evidences of design, and concert of action, among its chief bosses, from the beginning.

But, so far, *Congress* only, had acted; and an *indorsement* by the people, *real* or apparent, was indispensable, to *save* the point already gained, and give chance for more.

The new year of 1854 found slavery excluded from more than half the states by state constitutions, and from most of the national territory by congressional prohibition.

Four days later, commenced the struggle, which ended in repealing that congressional prohibition.

This opened all the national territory to slavery; and was the first point gained.

This necessity had not been overlooked; but had been provided for, as well as might be, in the notable argument of *"squatter sovereignty,"* otherwise called *"sacred right of self government,"* which latter phrase, though expressive of the only rightful basis of any government, was so perverted in this attempted use of it as to amount to just this: That if any *one* man, choose to enslave *another*, no *third* man shall be allowed to object.

That argument was incorporated into the Nebraska Bill itself, in the language which follows: *"It being the true intent and meaning of this act not to legislate slavery into any territory or state, nor exclude it therefrom; but to leave the people thereof perfectly free to form and regulate their domestic institutions in their own way, subject only to the Constitution of the United States."*

Then opened the roar of loose declamation in favor of "Squatter Sovereignty," and "Sacred right of self government."

"But," said opposition members, "let us be more *specific*—let us *amend* the bill so as to expressly declare that the people of the territory *may* exclude slavery." "Not we," said the friends of the measure; and down they voted the amendment.

While the Nebraska Bill was passing through Congress, a *law* case, involving the question of a negro's freedom, by reason of his owner having voluntarily taken him first into a free state and then a territory covered by the congressional prohibition, and held him as a slave, for a long time in each, was passing through the U.S. Circuit Court for the District of

Missouri; and both Nebraska Bill and law suit were brought to a decision in the same month of May, 1854. The negro's name was "Dred Scott," which name now designates the decision finally made in the case.

Before the *then* next presidential election,[4] the law case came *to*, and was argued *in* the Supreme Court of the United States; but the *decision* of it was deferred until *after* the election. Still, *before* the election, Senator Trumbull,[5] on the floor of the Senate, requests the leading advocate[6] of the Nebraska Bill to state *his opinion* whether the people of a territory can constitutionally exclude slavery from their limits; and the latter answers, "That is a question for the Supreme Court."

The election came. Mr. Buchanan was elected, and the *indorsement*, such as it was, secured. That was the *second* point gained. The indorsement, however, fell short of a clear popular majority by nearly four hundred thousand votes, and so, perhaps, was not overwhelmingly reliable and satisfactory.

The *outgoing* President,[7] in his last annual message, as impressively as possible *echoed back* upon the people the *weight* and *authority* of the indorsement.

The Supreme Court met again; *did not* announce their decision, but ordered a re-argument.

The presidential inauguration came, and still no decision of the court; but the *incoming* President, in his inaugural address, fervently exhorted the people to abide by the forthcoming decision, *whatever it might be.*

Then, in a few days, came the decision.

The reputed author of the Nebraska Bill[8] finds an early occasion to make a speech at this capitol indorsing the *Dred Scott* decision, and vehemently denouncing all opposition to it.

The new President,[9] too, seizes the early occasion of the Silliman letter[10] to *indorse* and strongly *construe* that decision, and to express his *astonishment* that any different view had ever been entertained.

---

[4]The 1856 election.

[5]Lyman Trumbull was the other U.S. senator from Illinois. Trumbull opposed slavery and was an early member of the Republican Party. In 1865 he would draft the Thirteenth Amendment, which abolished slavery in the United States.

[6]Stephen A. Douglas, Lincoln's opponent in the 1858 election and these debates, was the "leading advocate" of the Kansas-Nebraska Act.

[7]Franklin Pierce of New Hampshire was president in 1854 when the Kansas-Nebraska Act was passed. Pierce was a "doughface" Democrat—a northerner with southern principles—who consistently supported slavery and the South on such matters as the Fugitive Slave Law and the settlement of the territories.

[8]Stephen A. Douglas.

[9]James Buchanan, who, like Pierce, was a "doughface" Democrat.

[10]In July 1857 Robert J. Walker, the governor of the Kansas Territory, ordered troops to Lawrence to intimidate proponents of an antislavery government in the territory.

At length a squabble springs up between the President and the author of the Nebraska Bill, on the *mere* question of *fact,* whether the Lecompton constitution was or was not, in any just sense, made by the people of Kansas;[11] and in that squabble the latter declares that all he wants is a fair vote for the people, and that he *cares* not whether slavery be voted *down* or voted *up.* I do not understand his declaration that he cares not whether slavery be voted down or voted up, to be intended by him other than as an *apt definition* of the *policy* he would impress upon the public mind—the *principle* for which he declares he has suffered much, and is ready to suffer to the end.

And well may he cling to that principle. If he has any parental feeling, well may he cling to it. That principle, is the only *shred* left of his original Nebraska doctrine. Under the Dred Scott decision, "squatter sovereignty" squatted out of existence, tumbled down like temporary scaffolding—like the mould at the foundry served through one blast and fell back into loose sand—helped to carry an election, and then was kicked to the winds. His late *joint* struggle with the Republicans, against the Lecompton constitution, involves nothing of the original Nebraska doctrine. That struggle was made on a point, the right of a people to make their own constitution, upon which he and the Republicans have never differed.

The several points of the Dred Scott decision, in connection with Senator Douglas' "care not" policy, constitute the piece of machinery, in its *present* state of advancement. This was the third point gained.

The *working* points of that machinery are:

Benjamin Douglas Silliman, a distinguished chemistry professor at Yale, and forty-two other citizens of Connecticut wrote to President Buchanan, protesting Walker's unnecessary and rather foolish use of military force. In a long answer to Silliman's letter, published in the Washington *Union*, Buchanan argued that under the *Dred Scott* decision slavery had always been legal in Kansas. The Silliman letter became a code word for Buchanan's proslavery policies in the 1857 and 1858 elections.

[11]The "Lecompton constitution" was written by a proslavery constitutional convention called in Kansas by the Buchanan administration. The convention did not represent the majority of the settlers in Kansas, who were opposed to slavery. Nevertheless, the Buchanan administration recognized the convention and the referendum it supported. That referendum had not allowed voters to reject either the whole constitution or the clause allowing slavery in Kansas. Thus free-state settlers in Kansas boycotted the referendum. About six thousand people voted for the constitution, although many lived in the slave state of Missouri and simply crossed into Kansas to bolster support for slavery. In a subsequent election, organized by antislavery people in Kansas, about ten thousand residents of the territory endorsed a constitution that prohibited slavery. Despite the irregularity of the constitution-making process in Kansas, President Buchanan brought the issue of Kansas statehood to Congress. Senator Stephen A. Douglas opposed Kansas admission, not because he objected to the admission of a new slave state but solely because the process in Kansas had not been a fair implementation of popular sovereignty.

First, that no negro slave, imported as such from Africa, and no descendant of such slave can ever be a *citizen* of any state, in the sense of that term as used in the Constitution of the United States.

This point is made in order to deprive the negro, in every possible event, of the benefit of this provision of the United States Constitution, which declares that—

"The citizens of each state shall be entitled to all privileges and immunities of citizens in the several states."

Secondly, that "subject to the Constitution of the United States," neither *Congress* nor a *territorial legislature* can exclude slavery from any United States territory.

This point is made in order that individual men may *fill up* the territories with slaves, without danger of losing them as property, and thus to enhance the chances of *permanency* to the institution through all the future.

Thirdly, that whether the holding a negro in actual slavery in a free state, makes him free, as against the holder, the United States courts will not decide, but will leave to be decided by the courts of any slave state the negro may be forced into by the master.

This point is made, not to be pressed *immediately*; but, if acquiesced in for a while, and apparently *indorsed* by the people at an election, *then* to sustain the logical conclusion that what Dred Scott's master might lawfully do with Dred Scott, in the free state of Illinois, every other master may lawfully do with any other *one*, or one *thousand* slaves, in Illinois, or in any other free state.

Auxiliary to all this, and working hand in hand with it, the Nebraska doctrine, or what is left of it, is to *educate* and *mould* public opinion, at least *Northern* public opinion, to not *care* whether slavery is voted *down* or voted *up*.

This shows exactly where we now *are*; and *partially* also, whither we are tending.

It will throw additional light on the latter, to go back, and run the mind over the string of historical facts already stated. Several things will *now* appear less *dark* and *mysterious* than they did *when* they were transpiring. The people were to be left "perfectly free" "subject only to the Constitution." What the *Constitution* had to do with it, outsiders could not *then* see. Plainly enough *now*, it was an exactly fitted *niche*, for the Dred Scott decision to afterwards come in, and declare the *perfect freedom* of the people, to be just no freedom at all.

Why was the amendment, expressly declaring the right of the people to exclude slavery, voted down? Plainly enough *now*, the adoption of it, would have spoiled the niche for the Dred Scott decision.

Why was the court decision held up? Why, even a Senator's individual opinion withheld, till *after* the presidential election? Plainly enough *now*, the speaking out *then* would have damaged the "*perfectly free*" argument upon which the election was to be carried.

Why the *outgoing* President's felicitation on the indorsement? Why the delay of a reargument? Why the incoming President's *advance* exhortation in favor of the decision?

These things *look* like the cautious *patting* and *petting* a spirited horse, preparatory to mounting him, when it is dreaded that he may give the rider a fall.

And why the hasty after-indorsements of the decision by the President and others?

We can not absolutely *know* that all these exact adaptations are the result of preconcert. But when we see a lot of framed timbers, different portions of which we know have been gotten out at different times and places and by different workmen—Stephen, Franklin, Roger and James,[12] for instance—and when we see these timbers joined together, and see they exactly make the frame of a house or a mill, all the tenons and mortices exactly fitting, and all the lengths and proportions of the different pieces exactly adapted to their respective places, and not a piece too many or too few—not omitting even scaffolding—or, if a single piece be lacking, we can see the place in the frame exactly fitted and prepared to yet bring such piece in—in *such* a case, we find it impossible to not *believe* that Stephen and Franklin and Roger and James all understood one another from the beginning, and all worked upon a common *plan* or *draft* drawn up before the first lick was struck.

It should not be overlooked that, by the Nebraska Bill, the people of a *state* as well as *territory*, were to be left "*perfectly free*" "*subject only to the Constitution.*"

Why mention a *state*? They were legislating for *territories*, and not *for* or *about* states. Certainly the people of a state *are* and *ought to be* subject to the Constitution of the United States; but why is mention of this *lugged* into this merely *territorial* law? Why are the people of a *territory* and the people of a *state* therein *lumped* together, and their relation to the Constitution therein treated as being *precisely* the same?

While the opinion of the *Court*, by Chief Justice Taney, in the Dred Scott case, and the separate opinions of all the concurring judges, expressly declare that the Constitution of the United States neither permits Congress nor a territorial legislature to exclude slavery from any

[12]Senator Stephen A. Douglas, President Franklin Pierce, Chief Justice Roger B. Taney, and President James Buchanan.

United States territory, they all *omit* to declare whether or not the same constitution permits a *state*, or the people of a state, to exclude it.

Possibly, this was a mere *omission*; but who can be *quite* sure, if McLean or Curtis[13] had sought to get into the opinion a declaration of unlimited power in the people of a *state* to exclude slavery from their limits, just as Chase and Macy[14] sought to get such declaration, in behalf of the people of a territory, into the Nebraska Bill—I ask, who can be quite *sure* that it would not have been voted down, in the one case, as it had been in the other.

The nearest approach to the point of declaring the power of a state over slavery, is made by Judge Nelson.[15] He approaches it more than once, using the precise idea, and *almost* the language too, of the Nebraska Act. On one occasion his exact language is, "except in cases where the power is restrained by the Constitution of the United States, the law of the state is supreme over the subject of slavery within its jurisdiction."

In what *cases* the power of the *states is* so restrained by the U.S. Constitution, is left an *open* question, precisely as the same question, as to the restraint on the power of the *territories* was left open in the Nebraska Act. Put *that* and *that* together, and we have another nice little niche, which we may, ere long, see filled with another Supreme Court decision, declaring that the Constitution of the United States does not permit a *state* to exclude slavery from its limits.

And this may especially be expected if the doctrine of "care not whether slavery be voted *down* or voted *up*," shall gain upon the public mind sufficiently to give promise that such a decision can be maintained when made.

Such a decision is all that slavery now lacks of being alike lawful in all the states.

Welcome or unwelcome, such decision *is* probably coming, and will soon be upon us, unless the power of the present political dynasty shall be met and overthrown.

We shall *lie down* pleasantly dreaming that the people of *Missouri* are on the verge of making their state *free*; and we shall *awake* to the *reality*, instead, that the *Supreme* Court has made *Illinois* a *slave* state.

To meet and overthrow the power of that dynasty, is the work now before all those who would prevent that consummation.

---

[13]Justices John McLean of Ohio and Benjamin Robbins Curtis of Massachusetts, the two dissenters in *Dred Scott*; see Documents 8 and 9.

[14]Senator Salmon P. Chase of Ohio and Representative Daniel May of Indiana. In 1864 Lincoln would appoint Chase to be chief justice of the United States, to succeed Taney.

[15]Justice Samuel Nelson of New York, who concurred in *Dred Scott*; see Document 3.

That is *what* we have to do.

But *how* can we best do it?

There are those who denounce us *openly* to their *own* friends, and yet whisper *us softly*, that *Senator Douglas* is the *aptest* instrument there is, with which to effect that object. *They* do *not* tell us, nor has *he* told us, that he *wishes* any such object to be effected. They wish us to *infer* all, from the facts, that he now has a little quarrel with the present head of the dynasty; and that he has regularly voted with us, on a single point, upon which, he and we, have never differed.

They remind us that *he* is a very *great man*, and that the largest of *us* are very small ones. Let this be granted. But "a *living dog* is better than a *dead lion*."[16] Judge Douglas,[17] if not a *dead* lion *for this work*, is at least a *caged* and *toothless* one. How can he oppose the advances of slavery? He don't *care* anything about it. His avowed *mission is impressing* the "public heart" to *care* nothing about it.

A leading Douglas Democratic newspaper thinks Douglas' superior talent will be needed to resist the revival of the African slave trade.

Does Douglas believe an effort to revive that trade is approaching? He has not said so. Does he *really* think so? But if it is, how can he resist it? For years he has labored to prove it a *sacred right* of white men to take negro slaves into the new territories. Can he possibly show that it is *less* a sacred right to *buy* them where they can be bought cheapest? And, unquestionably they can be bought *cheaper in Africa* than in *Virginia*.

He has done all in his power to reduce the whole question of slavery to one of a mere *right of property*; and as such, how can *he* oppose the foreign slave trade—how can he refuse that trade in that "property" shall be "perfectly free"—unless he does it as *a protection* to the home production? And as the home *producers* will probably not *ask* the protection, he will be wholly without a ground of opposition.

Senator Douglas holds, we know, that a man may rightfully be *wiser to-day* than he was *yesterday*—that he may rightfully *change* when he finds himself wrong.

But, can we for that reason, run ahead, and *infer* that he *will* make any particular change, of which he, himself, has given no intimation? Can we *safely* base *our* action upon any such *vague* inference?

---

[16]See Eccles. 9:4: "For to him that is joined to all the living there is hope: for a living dog is better than a dead lion."

[17]Throughout the debates Lincoln refers to his opponent as "Judge Douglas." Douglas had served on the Illinois Supreme Court, which was considered to be a higher office than senator.

Now, as ever, I wish to not *misrepresent* Judge Douglas' *position*, question his *motives*, or do ought that can be personally offensive to him.

Whenever, *if ever*, he and we can come together on *principle* so that *our great cause* may have assistance from *his great ability*, I hope to have interposed no adventitious obstacle.

But clearly, he is not *now* with us—he does not *pretend* to be—he does not *promise* to *ever* be.

Our cause, then, must be intrusted to, and conducted by its own undoubted friends—those whose hands are free, whose hearts are in the work—who *do care* for the result.

Two years ago the Republicans of the nation mustered over thirteen hundred thousand strong.[18]

We did this under the single impulse of resistance to a common danger, with every external circumstance against us.

Of *strange, discordant*, and even, *hostile* elements, we gathered from the four winds, and *formed* and fought the battle through, under the constant hot fire of a disciplined, proud, and pampered enemy.

Did we brave all *then*, to *falter* now?—*now*—when that same enemy is *wavering*, dissevered and belligerent?

The result is not doubtful. We shall not fail—if we stand firm, we shall not fail.

Wise councils may *accelerate* or *mistakes delay* it, but, sooner or later the victory is *sure* to come.

[18]Lincoln is referring to the popular vote for the 1856 Republican presidential candidate, John C. Frémont. In that election, Frémont won 1,341,000 votes.

32

STEPHEN A. DOUGLAS

Speech at Chicago, Illinois

July 9, 1858

On the evening of July 9 Douglas responded to Lincoln's "House Divided" speech with a speech in Chicago. Douglas first laid out his own political agenda. Then, in the part of the speech reprinted here, he turned to Lincoln's assertions that the Dred Scott *decision was part of a conspiracy to nationalize slavery. Lincoln was in the audience for this speech, and Douglas invited him to sit on the podium. Lincoln was sitting behind Douglas as the "Little Giant" gave his speech, setting the stage for their subsequent formal debates. Note Douglas defends states' rights in arguing that states are free to discriminate against blacks, while at the same time supporting the Supreme Court's decision in* Dred Scott. *Also note Douglas's blatantly racist appeals and his assertions that blacks and Indians are members of "an inferior race."*

. . . I have observed from the public prints that but a few days ago the Republican party of the state of Illinois assembled in convention at Springfield, and not only laid down their platform, but nominated a candidate for the United States Senate as my successor. I take great pleasure in saying that I have known, personally and intimately, for about a quarter of a century, the worthy gentleman who has been nominated for my place, and I will say that I regard him as a kind, amiable, and intelligent gentleman, a good citizen and an honorable opponent; and whatever issue I may have with him will be of principle, and not involving personalities. — Mr. Lincoln made a speech before that Republican Convention which unanimously nominated him for the Senate — a speech evidently well prepared and carefully written — in which he states the basis upon which he proposes to carry on the campaign during this summer. In it he lays down two distinct propositions which I shall notice, and upon which I shall take a direct and bold issue with him.

Chicago Times, July 11, 1858, reprinted in Paul M. Angle, *Created Equal? The Complete Lincoln-Douglas Debates of 1858* (Chicago: University of Chicago Press, 1958), 17–24.

His first and main proposition I will give in his own language, scripture quotations and all, I give his exact language—"'A house divided against itself cannot stand.' I believe this government cannot endure, permanently, half *slave* and half *free*. I do not expect the Union to be *dissolved*. I do not expect the house to *fall*; but I do expect it to cease to be divided. It will become *all* one thing or *all* the other."

In other words, Mr. Lincoln asserts as a fundamental principle of this government, that there must be uniformity in the local laws and domestic institutions of each and all the states of the Union; and he therefore invites all the non-slaveholding states to band together, organize as one body, and make war upon slavery in Kentucky, upon slavery in Virginia, upon the Carolinas, upon slavery in all of the slave-holding states in this Union, and to persevere in that war until it shall be exterminated. He then notifies the slaveholding states to stand together as a unit and make an aggressive war upon the free states of this Union with a view of establishing slavery in them all; of forcing it upon Illinois, of forcing it upon New York, upon New England, and upon every other free state, and that they shall keep up the warfare until it has been formally established in them all. In other words, Mr. Lincoln advocates boldly and clearly a war of sections, a war of the North against the South, of the free states against the slave states—a war of extermination—to be continued relentlessly until the one or the other shall be subdued and all the states shall either become free or become slave.

Now, my friends, I must say to you frankly, that I take bold, unqualified issue with him upon that principle. I assert that it is neither desirable nor possible that there should be uniformity in the local institutions and domestic regulations of the different states of this Union. The framers of our government never contemplated uniformity in its internal concerns. The fathers of the Revolution, and the sages who made the Constitution well understood that the laws and domestic institutions which would suit the granite hills of New Hampshire would be totally unfit for the rice plantations of South Carolina; they well understood that the laws which would suit the agricultural districts of Pennsylvania and New York would be totally unfit for the large mining regions of the Pacific, or the lumber regions of Maine. They well understood that the great varieties of soil, of production and of interests, in a republic as large as this, require different local and domestic regulations in each locality, adapted to the wants and interests of each separate state, and for that reason it was provided in the federal Constitution that the thirteen original states should remain sovereign and supreme within their own limits in regard to all that was local, and internal, and domestic, while the federal government should have certain specified powers which were general and national, and could be exercised only by the federal authority.

The framers of the Constitution well understood that each locality, having separate and distinct interests, required separate and distinct laws, domestic institutions, and police regulations adapted to its own wants and its own condition; and they acted on the presumption, also, that these laws and institutions would be as diversified and as dissimilar as the states would be numerous, and that no two would be precisely alike, because the interests of the two would [not] be precisely the same. Hence, I assert, that the great fundamental principle which underlies our complex system of state and federal governments, contemplated diversity and dissimilarity in the local institutions and domestic affairs of each and every state then in the Union, or thereafter to be admitted into the confederacy. I therefore conceive that my friend, Mr. Lincoln, has totally misapprehended the great principles upon which our government rests. Uniformity in local and domestic affairs would be destructive of state rights, of state sovereignty, of personal liberty and personal freedom. Uniformity is the parent of despotism the world over, not only in politics, but in religion. Wherever the doctrine of uniformity is proclaimed, that all the states must be free or all slave, that all labor must be white or all black, that all the citizens of the different states must have the same privileges or be governed by the same regulations, you have destroyed the greatest safeguard which our institutions have thrown around the rights of the citizen.

How could this uniformity be accomplished, if it was desirable and possible? There is but one mode in which it could be obtained, and that must be by abolishing the state legislatures, blotting out state sovereignty, merging the rights and sovereignty of the states in one consolidated empire, and vesting Congress with the plenary power to make all the police regulations, domestic and local laws, uniform throughout the limits of the Republic. When you shall have done this you will have uniformity. Then the states will all be slave or all be free; then negroes will vote everywhere or nowhere; then you will have a Maine liquor law in every state or none; then you will have uniformity in all things local and domestic by the authority of the federal government. But when you attain that uniformity, you will have converted these thirty-two sovereign, independent states, into one consolidated empire, with the uniformity of despotism reigning triumphant throughout the length and breadth of the land.

From this view of the case, my friends, I am driven irresistibly to the conclusion that diversity, dissimilarity, variety in all our local and domestic institutions, is the great safeguard of our liberties; and that the framers of our institutions were wise, sagacious, and patriotic when they made this government a confederation of sovereign states with a legislature for each, and conferred upon each legislature the power to make all local and domestic institutions to suit the people it represented, without interference from any other state or from the general Congress of the Union. If we expect to maintain our liberties we must preserve the rights and sovereignty of the states, we must maintain and carry out that great principle of self-government incorporated in the compromise measures of 1850 . . . [and] emphatically embodied and carried out in the Kansas-Nebraska Bill. . . .

The other proposition discussed by Mr. Lincoln in his speech consists in a crusade against the Supreme Court of the United States on account of the *Dred Scott* decision. On this question, also, I desire to say to you unequivocally, that I take direct and distinct issue with him. I have no warfare to make on the Supreme Court of the United States, either on account of that or any other decision which they have pronounced from that bench. The Constitution of the United States has provided that the powers of government (and the constitution of each state has the same provision) shall be divided into three departments, executive, legislative, and judicial. The right and the province of expounding the Constitution, and construing the law, is vested in the judiciary established by the Constitution. — As a lawyer, I feel at liberty to appear before the Court and controvert any principle of law while the question is pending before the tribunal; but when the decision is made, my private opinion, your opinion, all other opinions must yield to the majesty of that authoritative adjudication. I wish you to bear in mind that this involves a great principle, upon which our rights, our liberty and our property all depend. What security have you for your property, for your reputation, and for your personal rights, if the courts are not upheld, and their decisions respected when once firmly rendered by the highest tribunal known to the Constitution? I do not choose, therefore, to go into any argument with Mr. Lincoln in reviewing the various decisions which the Supreme Court has made, either upon the Dred Scott case, or any other. I have no idea of appealing from the decision of the Supreme Court upon a constitutional question to the decisions of a tumultuous town meeting. I am aware that once an eminent lawyer of this city, now no more, said that the state of Illinois had the most perfect judicial system in the world, subject to but one exception, which could be cured by a slight amendment, and that amendment was to so change the law as to allow an appeal from the decisions of the Supreme Court of Illinois, on all constitutional questions, to [a] Justice of the Peace. . . .

. . . I am opposed to this doctrine of Mr. Lincoln, by which he proposes to take an appeal from the decision of the Supreme Court of the United States, upon this high constitutional question to a Republican caucus sitting in the country. Yes, or any other caucus or town meeting, whether it be Republican, American, or Democratic. I respect the decisions of that august tribunal; I shall always bow in deference to them. I am a law-abiding man. I will sustain the Constitution of my country as our fathers have made it. I will yield obedience to the laws, whether I like them or not, as I find them on the statute book. I will sustain the judicial tribunals and constituted authorities in all matters within the pale of their jurisdiction as defined by the Constitution.

But I am equally free to say that the reason assigned by Mr. Lincoln for resisting the decision of the Supreme Court in the Dred Scott case does not in itself meet my approbation. He objects to it because that decision declared that a negro descended from African parents who were brought here and sold as slaves is not, and cannot be a citizen of the United States. He says it is wrong, because it deprives the negro of the benefits of that clause of the Constitution which says that citizens of one state shall enjoy all the privileges and immunities of citizens of the several states; in other words, he thinks it wrong because it deprives the negro of the privileges, immunities, and rights of citizenship, which pertain, according to that decision, only to the white man. I am free to say to you that in my opinion this government of ours is founded on the white basis. It was made by the white man, for the benefit of the white man, to be administered by white man, in such manner as they should determine. It is also true that a negro, an Indian, or any other man of an inferior race to a white man, should be permitted to enjoy, and humanity requires that he should have all the rights, privileges and immunities which he is capable of exercising consistent with the safety of society. I would give him every right and every privilege which his capacity would enable him to enjoy, consistent with the good of the society in which he lived. But you may ask me what are these rights and these privileges. My answer is that each state must decide for itself the nature and extent of these rights. Illinois has decided for herself. We have decided that the negro shall not be a slave, and we have at the same time decided that he shall not vote, or serve on juries, or enjoy political privileges. I am content with that system of policy which we have adopted for ourselves. I deny the right of any other State to complain of our policy in that respect, or to interfere with it, or to attempt to change it. On the other hand, the state of Maine has decided that in that state a negro man may vote on an equality with the white man. The sovereign power of Maine had the right to prescribe that rule for herself. Illinois has no right to complain of Maine for conferring the right of negro suffrage, nor has Maine any right to interfere with, or complain of Illinois because she has denied negro suffrage.

The state of New York has decided by her constitution that a negro may vote, provided that he own $250 worth of property, but not otherwise. The rich negro can vote, but the poor one cannot. Although that distinction does not commend itself to my judgment, yet I assert that the sovereign power of New York had a right to prescribe that form of the elective franchise. Kentucky, Virginia, and other states have provided that negroes, or a certain class of them in those states, shall be slaves, having neither civil or political rights. Without endorsing the wisdom of that decision, I assert that Virginia has the same power by virtue of her sovereignty to protect slavery within her limits, as Illinois has to banish it forever from our own borders. I assert the right of each state to decide for itself on all these questions and I do not subscribe to the doctrine of my friend, Mr. Lincoln, that uniformity is either desirable or possible. I do not acknowledge that the states must all be free or must all be slave.

I do not acknowledge that the negro must have civil and political rights everywhere or nowhere. I do not acknowledge that the Chinese must have the same rights in California that we would confer upon him here. I do not acknowledge that the cooley imported into this country must necessarily be put upon an equality with the white race. I do not acknowledge any of these doctrines of uniformity in the local and domestic regulations in the different states.

Thus you see, my fellow-citizens, that the issues between Mr. Lincoln and myself, as respective candidates for the U.S. Senate, as made up, are direct, unequivocal, and irreconcilable. He goes for uniformity in our domestic institutions, for a war of sections, until one or the other shall be subdued. I go for the great principle of the Kansas-Nebraska Bill, the right of the people to decide for themselves.

On the other point, Mr. Lincoln goes for a warfare upon the Supreme Court of the United States, because of their judicial decision in the Dred Scott case. I yield obedience to the decisions of that Court—to the final determination of the highest judicial tribunal known to our Constitution. He objects to the Dred Scott decision because it does not put the negro in the possession of the rights of citizenship on an equality with the white man. I am opposed to negro equality. I repeat that this nation is a white people—a people composed of European descendants—a people that have established this government for themselves and their posterity, and I am in favor of preserving not only the purity of the blood, but the purity of the government from any mixture or amalgamation with inferior races. I have seen the effects of this mixture of superior and inferior races—this amalgamation of white men and Indians and negroes; we have seen it in Mexico, in Central America, in South America, and in all the Spanish-American states, and its result has been degeneration, demoralization, and degradation below the capacity for self-government.

I am opposed to taking any step that recognizes the negro man or the Indian as the equal of the white man. I am opposed to giving him a voice in the administration of the government. I would extend to the negro, and the Indian, and to all dependent races every right, every privilege, and every immunity consistent with the safety and welfare of the white races; but equality they never should have, either political or social, or in any other respect whatever. . . .

33

ABRAHAM LINCOLN

Speech at Chicago, Illinois

July 10, 1858

The day after Douglas's Chicago speech, Lincoln addressed a large crowd in Chicago. He quickly focused on Dred Scott. *Note Lincoln's sarcasm, as he talks about the "sacredness" of the Court's decision. Here he also refers to Andrew Jackson's veto of the recharter of the Second Bank of the United States. This was a shrewd and intellectually solid strategy on Lincoln's part. Jackson was the most significant figure in the antebellum Democratic Party. He was the only president elected for two terms between James Monroe (1816 and 1820) and Abraham Lincoln (1860 and 1864). Jackson was a hero to Douglas and all other Democrats. In* McCulloch v. Maryland *(1819) the Supreme Court had upheld the constitutionality of the Bank of the United States. However, in 1832 President Jackson vetoed a bill for the recharter of the bank, claiming that the*

Chicago Daily Democrat, July 13, 1856, as corrected by Lincoln, reprinted in Paul M. Angle, *Created Equal? The Complete Lincoln-Douglas Debates of 1858* (Chicago: University of Chicago Press, 1958), 26, 36–38.

bank bill was unconstitutional. Lincoln's point, in this speech, is that the
Supreme Court is not the only arbiter of constitutionality. Is he right? Do
the president and Congress have a role in deciding what is constitutional?

My Fellow Citizens:

On yesterday evening, upon the occasion of the reception given to Senator Douglas, I was furnished with a seat very convenient for hearing him, and was otherwise very courteously treated by him and his friends, and for which I thank him and them. During the course of his remarks my name was mentioned in such a way, as I suppose renders it at least not improper that I should make some sort of reply to him. I shall not attempt to follow him in the precise order in which he addressed the assembled multitude upon that occasion, though I shall perhaps do so in the main. . . .

A little now on the other point — the *Dred Scott* decision. Another one of the issues he says that is to be made with me, is upon his devotion to the Dred Scott decision, and my opposition to it.

I have expressed heretofore, and I now repeat, my opposition to the Dred Scott decision, but I should be allowed to state the nature of that opposition, and I ask your indulgence while I do so. What is fairly implied by the term Judge Douglas has used "resistance to the decision?" I do not resist it. If I wanted to take Dred Scott from his master, I would be interfering with property, and that terrible difficulty that Judge Douglas speaks of, of interfering with property, would arise. But I am doing no such thing as that, but all that I am doing is refusing to obey it as a political rule. If I were in Congress, and a vote should come up on a question whether slavery should be prohibited in a new territory, in spite of that Dred Scott decision, I would vote that it should.

That is what I would do. Judge Douglas said last night, that before the decision he might advance his opinion, and it might be contrary to the decision when it was made; but after it was made he would abide by it until it was reversed. Just so! We let this property abide by the decision, but we will try to reverse that decision. We will try to put it where Judge Douglas would not object, for he says he will obey it until it is reversed. Somebody has to reverse that decision, since it is made, and we mean to reverse it, and we mean to do it peaceably.

What are the uses of decisions of courts? They have two uses. As rules of property they have two uses. First — they decide upon the question before the court. They decide in this case that Dred Scott is a slave.

Nobody resists that. Not only that, but they say to everybody else, that persons standing just as Dred Scott stands is as he is. That is, they say that when a question comes up upon another person it will be so decided again, unless the court decides in another way, unless the court overrules its decision. Well, we mean to do what we can to have the court decide the other way. That is one thing we mean to try to do.

The sacredness that Judge Douglas throws around this decision, is a degree of sacredness that has never been before thrown around any other decision. I have never heard of such a thing. Why, decisions apparently contrary to that decision, or that good lawyers thought were contrary to that decision, have been made by that very court before. It is the first of its kind; it is an astonisher in legal history. It is a new wonder of the world. It is based upon falsehood in the main as to the facts—allegations of facts upon which it stands are not facts at all in many instances, and no decision made on any question—the first instance of a decision made under so many unfavorable circumstances—thus placed has ever been held by the profession as law, and it has always needed confirmation before the lawyers regarded it as settled law. But Judge Douglas will have it that all hands must take this extraordinary decision, made under these extraordinary circumstances, and give their vote in Congress in accordance with it, yield to it and obey it in every possible sense. Circumstances alter cases. Do not gentlemen here remember the case of that same Supreme Court, some twenty-five or thirty years ago, deciding that a national bank was constitutional? I ask, if somebody does not remember that a national bank was declared to be constitutional? Such is the truth, whether it be remembered or not. The bank charter ran out, and a recharter was granted by Congress. That re-charter was laid before General Jackson. It was urged upon him, when he denied the constitutionality of the bank, that the Supreme Court had decided that it was constitutional; and that General Jackson then said that the Supreme Court had no right to lay down a rule to govern a co-ordinate branch of the government, the members of which had sworn to support the Constitution—that each member had sworn to support that Constitution as he understood it. I will venture here to say, that I have heard Judge Douglas say that he approved of General Jackson for that act. What has now become of all his tirade about "resistance to the Supreme Court?"

34

STEPHEN A. DOUGLAS

Speech at Springfield, Illinois

July 17, 1858

A week after Lincoln's Chicago speech, Douglas spoke at Springfield (the site of Lincoln's "House Divided" speech). Here Douglas directly confronts Lincoln's opposition to the Dred Scott *decision, mocking Lincoln and at the same time arguing that a Supreme Court decision is not subject to political debate. Furthermore, Douglas argues against a "litmus test" for Supreme Court justices. Is Douglas right on these issues? Is there room to criticize and even oppose a Supreme Court decision within our constitutional framework? Is it reasonable for presidents to ask potential judges how they might decide certain cases? Finally, Douglas argues that the Declaration of Independence was meant to apply only to white men. Is Douglas right? In thinking about this, recall that Jefferson owned more than 150 slaves when he wrote the Declaration of Independence.*

. . . Mr. Lincoln makes another point upon me. . . . [H]e will wage a warfare upon the Supreme Court of the United States because of the Dred Scott decision. He takes occasion, in his speech made before the Republican convention, in my absence, to arraign me, not only for having expressed my acquiescence in that decision, but to charge me with being a conspirator with that court in devising that decision three years before Dred Scott ever thought of commencing a suit for his freedom. The object of his speech was to convey the idea to the people that the court could not be trusted, that the late President could not be trusted, that the present one could not be trusted, and that Mr. Douglas could not be trusted; that they were all conspirators in bringing about that corrupt decision, to which Mr. Lincoln is determined he will never yield a willing obedience.

He makes two points upon the Dred Scott decision. The first is that he objects to it because the court decided that negroes descended of

Illinois State Register, July 19, 1858, reprinted in Paul M. Angle, *Created Equal? The Complete Lincoln-Douglas Debates of 1858* (Chicago: University of Chicago Press, 1958), 55–65.

slave parents are not citizens of the United States; and secondly, because they have decided that the act of Congress, passed 8th of March, 1820, prohibiting slavery in all of the territories north of 36°30′, was unconstitutional and void, and hence did not have effect in emancipating a slave brought into that territory. And he will not submit to that decision. He says that he will not fight the judges or the United States marshals in order to liberate Dred Scott, but that he will not respect that decision, as a rule of law binding on this country in the future. Why not? Because, he says, it is unjust. How is he going to remedy it? Why, he says he is going to reverse it. How? He is going to take an appeal. To whom is he going to appeal? The Constitution of the United States provides that the Supreme Court is the ultimate tribunal on earth, and Mr. Lincoln is going appeal from that. To whom? I know he appealed to the Republican State Convention of Illinois, and I believe that convention reversed the decision, but I am not aware that they have yet carried it into effect. How are they going to make that reversal effectual? Why, Mr. Lincoln tells us in his late Chicago speech. He explains it as clear as light. He says to the people Illinois that if you elect him to the senate he will introduce a bill to re-enact the law which the court pronounced unconstitutional. Yes, he is going to spot the law.[1] The court pronounces that law, prohibiting slavery, unconstitutional and void, and Mr. Lincoln is going to pass on act reversing that decision and making valid. I never heard before of an appeal being taken from the Supreme Court to the Congress of the United States to reverse its decision. I have heard of appeals being taken from Congress to the Supreme Court to declare a statute void. That has been done from the earliest days of Chief Justice Marshall, down to the present time.

The supreme court of Illinois do not hesitate to pronounce an act the legislature void, as being repugnant to the constitution, and the Supreme Court of the United States is vested by the Constitution with that very power. The Constitution says that the judicial power of the United States shall be vested in the Supreme Court, and such inferior courts as Congress shall, from time to time, ordain and establish Hence it is the province

[1]During his only term in Congress (1847–1849), Lincoln had opposed the Mexican-American War. President James K. Polk asked for a declaration of war with Mexico on the grounds that American blood had been shed on American soil. Lincoln presented a resolution to determine "whether the spot of soil on which the blood of our *citizens* was so shed, was, or was not *our own soil*, at that time." "'Spot's Resolutions in the United States House of Representatives," December 22, 1847, in *The Collected Works of Abraham Lincoln*, ed. Roy P. Basler (New Brunswick, N.J.: Rutgers University Press, 1953), 1:421. After this speech Lincoln's opponents sometimes called him "spotty Lincoln," and here Douglas is making a reference to that speech, known as "The Spot Speech."

and duty of the Supreme Court to pronounce judgment on the validity and constitutionality of an act of Congress. In this case they have done so, and Mr. Lincoln will not submit to it, and he is going to reverse it by another act of Congress of the same tenor. My opinion is that Mr. Lincoln ought to be on the supreme bench himself, when the Republicans get into power, if that kind of law knowledge qualifies a man for the bench. But Mr. Lincoln intimates that there is another mode by which he can reverse the Dred Scott decision. How is that? Why, he is going to appeal to the people to elect a President who will appoint judges who will reverse the Dred Scott decision. Well, let us see how that is going to be done. First, he has to carry on his sectional organization, a party confined to the free states, making war upon the slaveholding states until he gets a Republican President elected. I do not believe he ever will. But suppose he should; when that Republican President shall have taken his seat—Mr. Seward,[2] for instance—will he then proceed to appoint judges? No! he will have to wait until the present judges die before he can do that, and perhaps his four years would be out before a majority of these judges found it agreeable to die; and it very possible, too, that Mr. Lincoln's senatorial term would expire before these judges would be accommodating enough to die. If it should so happen I do not see a very great prospect for Mr. Lincoln to reverse the Dred Scott decision. But suppose they should die, then how are the new judges to be appointed? Why, the Republican President is to call up the candidates and catechise them, and ask them, "How will you decide this case if I appoint you judge?" Suppose, for instance, Mr. Lincoln to be a candidate for a vacancy on the supreme bench to fill Chief Justice Taney's place, and when he applied to Seward, the latter would say, "Mr. Lincoln, I cannot appoint you until I know how you will decide the Dred Scott case." Mr. Lincoln tells him, and then [Seward] asks him how he will decide Tom Jones' case, and Bill Wilson's case, and thus catechises the judge as to how he will decide any case which may arise before him. Suppose you get a Supreme Court composed of such judges, who have been appointed by a partisan President upon their giving pledges how they would decide a case before it arise, what confidence would you have in such a court?

Would not your court be prostituted beneath the contempt of all mankind! What man would feel that his liberties were safe; his right of person or property was secure if the supreme bench, that august tribunal,

[2]In 1858 Senator William Henry Seward of New York was the front-runner for the 1860 Republican nomination. Most people considered Seward more radical than Lincoln in his opposition to slavery.

the highest on earth, was brought down to that low, dirty pool wherein the judges are to give pledges in advance how they will decide all the questions which may be brought before them. It is a proposition to make that court the corrupt, unscrupulous tool of a political party. But Mr. Lincoln cannot conscientiously submit, he thinks, to the decision of a court composed of a majority of Democrats. If he cannot, how can he expect us to have confidence in a court composed of a majority of Republicans, selected for the purpose of deciding against the Democracy, and in favor of the Republicans? The very proposition carries with it the demoralization and degradation destructive of the judicial department of the federal government.

I say to you, fellow citizens, that I have no warfare to make upon the Supreme Court because of the Dred Scott decision. I have no complaints to make against that court, because of that decision. My private opinions on some points of the case may have been one way and on other points of the case another; in some things concurring with the court and in others dissenting, but what have my private opinions in a question of law to do with the decision after it has been pronounced by the highest judicial tribunal known to the Constitution? You, sir, [addressing the chairman], as an eminent lawyer, have a right to entertain your opinions on any question that comes before the court and to appear before the tribunal and maintain them boldly and with tenacity until the final decision shall have been pronounced, and then, sir, whether you are sustained or overruled your duty as a lawyer and a citizen is to bow in deference to that decision. I intend to yield obedience to the highest tribunals in the land in all cases whether their opinions are in conformity with my views as a lawyer or not. When we refuse to abide by judicial decisions what protection is there left for life and property? To whom shall you appeal? To mob law, to partisan caucuses, to town meetings, to revolution? Where is the remedy when you refuse obedience to the constituted authorities? I will not stop to inquire whether I agree or disagree with all the opinions expressed by Judge Taney or any other judge. It is enough for me to know that the decision has been made. It has been made by a tribunal appointed by the Constitution to make it; it was a point within their jurisdiction, and I am bound by it.

But, my friends, Mr. Lincoln says that this *Dred Scott* decision destroys the doctrine of popular sovereignty, for the reason that the court has decided that Congress had no power to prohibit slavery in the territories, and hence he infers that it would decide that the territorial legislatures could not prohibit slavery there. I will not stop to inquire whether the court will carry the decision that far or not. It would be interesting as a matter of theory, but of no importance in practice; for this reason, that if the people of a territory want slavery they will have it, and if they do not want it they will drive it out, and you cannot force it on them. Slavery cannot exist a day in the midst of an unfriendly people with unfriendly laws. There is truth and wisdom in a remark made to me by an eminent Southern Senator, when speaking of this technical right to take slaves into the territories. Said he:

> I do not care a fig which way the decision shall be, for it is of no particular consequence; slavery cannot exist a day or an hour in any territory or state unless it has affirmative laws sustaining and supporting it, furnishing police regulations and remedies, and an omission to furnish them would be as fatal as a constitutional prohibition. Without affirmative legislation in its favor slavery could not exist any longer than a new born infant could survive under the heat of the sun on a barren rock without protection. It would wilt and die for the want of support.

So it would be in the territories. See the illustration in Kansas. The Republicans have told you, during the whole history of that territory, down to last winter, that the pro-slavery party in the legislature had passed a pro-slavery code, establishing and sustaining slavery in Kansas, but that this pro-slavery legislature did not truly represent the people, but was imposed upon them by an invasion from Missouri, and hence the legislature were one way and the people another. Granting all this, and what has been the result? With laws supporting slavery, but the people against, there are not as many slaves in Kansas today as there were on the day the Nebraska Bill passed and the Missouri Compromise was repealed. Why? Simply because slave owners knew that if they took their slaves into Kansas, where a majority of the people were opposed to slavery, that it would soon be abolished, and that they would lose their right of property in consequence of taking them there. For that reason they would not take or keep them there. If there had been a majority of the people in favor of slavery and the climate had been favorable, they would have taken them there, but the climate not being suitable, the interest of the people being opposed to it, and a majority of them against it, the slave owner did not find it profitable to take his slaves there, and consequently there are not as many slaves there today as on the day the Missouri Compromise was repealed. This shows clearly that if the people do not want slavery they will keep it out and that if they do want it they will protect it. . . .

But Mr. Lincoln's main objection to the *Dred Scott* decision I have reserved for my conclusion. His principal objection to that decision is that it was intended to deprive the negro of the rights of citizenship in the different states of the Union. Well, suppose it was, and there is no doubt that that was its legal effect, what is his objection to it? Why, he thinks that a negro ought to be permitted to have the rights of citizenship. He is in favor of negro citizenship, and opposed to the *Dred Scott* decision, because it declares that a negro is not a citizen, and hence is not entitled to vote. Here I have a direct issue with Mr. Lincoln. I am not in favor of negro citizenship. I do not believe that a negro is a citizen or ought to be a citizen. I believe that this government of ours was founded, and wisely founded, upon the white basis. It was made by white men for the benefit of white men and their posterity, to be executed and managed by white men. I freely concede that humanity requires us to extend all the protection, all the privileges, all the immunities, to the Indian and the negro which they are capable of enjoying consistent with the safety of society. You may then ask me what are those rights, what is the nature and extent of the rights which a negro ought to have. My answer is that this is a question for each state and each territory to decide for itself. . . .

Hence, you find that Mr. Lincoln and myself come to a direct issue on this whole doctrine of slavery. He is going to wage a war against it everywhere, not only in Illinois but in his native state of Kentucky. And why? Because he says that the Declaration of Independence contains this language: "We hold these truths to be self-evident, that all men are created equal; that they are endowed by their Creator with certain inalienable rights; that among these are life, liberty and the pursuit of happiness," and he asks whether that instrument does not declare that all men are created equal. Mr. Lincoln then goes on to say that that clause of the Declaration of Independence includes negroes. Well, if you say not I do not think you will vote for Mr. Lincoln. Mr. Lincoln goes on to argue that the language "all men" included the negroes, Indians, and all inferior races.

In his Chicago speech he says in so many words that it includes the negroes, that they were endowed by the Almighty with the right of equality with the white man, and therefore that that right is divine—a right under the higher law; that the law of God makes them equal to the white man, and therefore that the law of the white man cannot deprive them of that right. This is Mr. Lincoln's argument. He is conscientious in his belief. I do not question his sincerity, I do not doubt that he, in his conscience, believes that the Almighty made the negro equal to the white man. He thinks that the negro is his brother. I do not think that the negro is any kin of mine at all. And here is the difference between us. I believe that the Declaration of Independence, in the words "all men are created equal," was intended to allude only to the people of the United States, to men of European birth or descent, being white men, that they were created equal, and hence that Great Britain had no right to deprive them of their political and religious privil[e]ges; but the signers of that paper did not intend to include the Indian or the negro in that declaration, for if they had would they not have been bound to abolish slavery in every state and colony from that day? Remember, too, that at the time the Declaration was put forth every one of the thirteen colonies were slaveholding colonies; everyman who signed the Declaration represented slaveholding constituents. Did those signers mean by that act to charge themselves all their constituents with having violated the law of God, in holding the negro in an inferior condition to the white man? And yet, if they included negroes in that term they were bound, as conscientious men, that day and that hour, not only to have abolishes slavery throughout the land, but to have conferred political rights and privileges on the negro, and elevated him to an equality with the white man. I know they not do it, and the very fact that they did not shows that they did not understand the language they used to include any but the white race. Did they mean to say that the Indian, on this continent, was created equal to the white man, and that he was endowed by the Almighty with inalienable rights—rights so sacred that they could not be taken away by any constitution or law that man could pass? Why, their whole action towards the Indian showed that they never dreamed that they were bound to put him on an equality. I am not only opposed to negro equality, but I am opposed to Indian equality. I am opposed to putting the coolies, now importing into this country, on an equality with us, or putting the Chinese or any other inferior race on an equality with us. I hold that the white race, the European race, I care not whether Irish, German, French, Scotch, English, or to what nation they belong, so [long as] they are the white race to be our equals, and I am for placing them, as our fathers did, on an equality with us. Emigrants from Europe and their descendants constitute the people of the U.S. The Declaration of Independence only included the white people of the U.S. The Constitution of the U.S. was framed by the white people. . . .

For that reason [Mr. Lincoln] wishes the Dred Scott decision reversed. He wishes to confer those privil[e]ges of citizenship on the negro. Let us see how he will do it. He will first be called upon to strike out of the constitution of Illinois that clause which prohibits free negroes and slaves from Kentucky or any other state coming into Illinois. When he blots out that clause, when he lets down the door or opens the gate for all the negro population to flow in and cover our prairies in mid-day they will look dark and black as night, when we shall have done this, his mission will yet be unfulfilled. Then it will be that he will apply his principles of negro equality, that is if he can get the Dred Scott decision reversed in the meantime. He will then change the constitution again, and allow negroes to vote and hold office, and will make them eligible to the legislature so that thereafter they can have the right men for U.S. Senators. He will allow them to vote to elect the legislature, the judges and the governor, and will make them eligible to the office of judge or governor, or to the legislature. He will put them on an equality with the white man. What then? Of course, after making them eligible to the judiciary, when he gets Cuffee[3] elevated to the bench, he certainly will not refuse his judge the privilege of marrying any woman he may select! I submit to you whether these are not the legitimate consequences of his doctrine. If it be true, as he says, that by the Declaration of Independence and by divine law, the negro is created the equal of the white man; if it be true that the Dred Scott decision is unjust and wrong, because it deprives the negro of citizenship and equality with the white man, then does it not follow that if he had the power he would make negroes citizens, and give them all the rights and privileges of citizenship on an equality with white men? I think that is the inevitable conclusion. I do not doubt Mr. Lincoln's conscientious conviction on the subject, and I do not doubt that he will carry out that doctrine if he ever has the power; but I resist it because I am utterly opposed to any political amalgamation or any other amalgamation on this continent. We are witnessing the result of giving civil and political rights to inferior races in Mexico, in Central America, in South America, and in the West India Islands. Those young men who went from here to Mexico to fight the battles of their country in the Mexican war, can tell you the fruits of negro equality with the white man. They will tell you that the result of that equality is social amalgamation, demoralization and degradation, below the capacity for self-government.

My friends, if we wish to preserve this government we must maintain it on the basis on which it was established, to wit: the white basis. We must preserve the purity of the race not only in our politics but in our domestic relations. We must then preserve the sovereignty of the states, and we must maintain the federal Union by preserving the federal constitution inviolate. Let us do that and our Union will not only be perpetual but may extend until it shall spread over the entire continent. . . .

[3]A derogatory term for blacks.

35

The Debate at Freeport: Lincoln's Questions and Douglas's Answer

August 27, 1858

Lincoln and Douglas argued about the meaning of Dred Scott *throughout their debates. The most famous exchange was in the debate at Freeport, Illinois. Here Lincoln asked Douglas a series of questions designed to embarrass the senator by driving a wedge between him and the southern wing of the Democratic Party. Although running for the Senate, in 1858 Douglas clearly had his eye on the Democratic presidential nomination for 1860. To win that nomination Douglas had to carry the southern wing of the party; to win the election he had to sweep the South. Before* Dred Scott *Douglas had a great deal of support in the South. But Douglas's failure to support the admission of Kansas into the Union as a slave state had cost him much of that support. Lincoln's questions at Freeport were shrewdly designed to further undermine Douglas's support in the South while at the same time getting him to admit that there were at least some ways of opposing the Supreme Court decision in* Dred Scott. *Alternatively, Lincoln hoped Douglas might support the South and the implications of* Dred Scott *and in the process lose votes in Illinois. Douglas's answers have been called the "Freeport Doctrine." His answers may have helped elect him in 1858 to the U.S. Senate, but they also permanently destroyed any chance of his regaining substantial southern support for the presidency.*

Lincoln

. . . I now proceed to pronounced to the Judge the interrogatories so far as I have framed them. . . .

Q. 2. Can the people of a United States territory, in any lawful way, against the wish of any citizen of the United States, exclude slavery from its limits prior to the formation of a state constitution?

Paul M. Angle, *Created Equal? The Complete Lincoln-Douglas Debates of 1858* (Chicago: University of Chicago Press, 1958), 143–44, 152, 154.

Q. 3. If the Supreme Court of the United States shall decide that states can not exclude slavery from their limits, are you in favor of acquiescing in, adopting and following such decision as a rule of political action?

Douglas

The next question propounded to me by Mr. Lincoln is, can the people of a territory in any lawful way against the wishes of any citizen of the United States; exclude slavery from their limits prior to the formation of a state constitution? I answer emphatically, as Mr. Lincoln has heard me answer a hundred times from every stump in Illinois that in my opinion the people of a territory can, by lawful means, exclude slavery from their limits prior to the formation of a state constitution. Mr. Lincoln knew that I had answered that question over and over again. He heard me argue the Nebraska Bill on that principle all over the state in 1854, in 1855 and in 1856, and he has no excuse for pretending to be in doubt as to my position on that question. It matters not what way the Supreme Court may hereafter decide as to the abstract question whether slavery may or may not go into a territory under the Constitution, the people have the lawful means to introduce it or exclude it as they please, for the reason that slavery cannot exist a day or an hour anywhere, unless it is supported by local police regulations. Those police regulations can only be established by the local legislature, and if the people are opposed to slavery they will elect representatives to that body who will by unfriendly legislation effectually prevent the introduction of it into their midst. If, on the contrary, they are for it, their legislation will favor its extension. Hence, no matter what the decision of the Supreme Court may be on that abstract question, still the right of the people to make a slave territory or a free territory is perfect and complete under the Nebraska Bill. I hope Mr. Lincoln deems my answer satisfactory on that point. . . .

The third question which Mr. Lincoln presented is, if the Supreme Court of the United States shall decide that a state of this Union cannot exclude slavery from its own limits will I submit to it? I am amazed that Lincoln should ask such a question. . . . Mr. Lincoln's object is to cast an imputation upon the Supreme Court. He knows that there never was but one man in America, claiming any degree of intelligence or decency, who ever for a moment pretended such is true that the Washington *Union*, in an article published on the 17th of last December, did put forth that doctrine, and I denounced the article on the floor of the Senate, in a speech which Mr. Lincoln now pretends was against the President. The *Union* had claimed that slavery had a right to go into the free states, and that any provision in the Constitution or laws of the free states to the contrary were null and void. I denounced it in the Senate, as I said before, and I was the first man who did. Lincoln's friends, Trumbull, and Seward, and Hale, and Wilson,[1] and the whole Black Republican side of the Senate were silent. They left it to me to denounce it. And what was the reply made to me on that occasion? Mr. Toombs,[2] of Georgia, got up and undertook to lecture me on the ground that I ought not to have deemed the article worthy of notice, and ought not to have replied to it; that there was not one man, woman or child south of the Potomac, in any slave state, who did not repudiate any such pretension. Mr. Lincoln knows that that reply was made on the spot, and yet now he asks this question. He might as well ask me, suppose Mr. Lincoln should steal a horse would I sanction it; and it would be as genteel in me to ask him, in the event he stole a horse, what ought to be done with him. He casts an imputation upon the Supreme Court of the United States by supposing that they would violate the Constitution of the United States. I tell him that such a thing is not possible. It would be an act of moral treason that no man on the bench could ever descend to. Mr. Lincoln himself would never in his partisan feelings so far forget what was right as to be guilty of such an act.

[1]Senators Lyman Trumbull of Illinois, William H. Seward of New York, John P. Hale of New Hampshire, and Henry Wilson of Massachusetts were among the most prominent Republican opponents of slavery. Seward would become secretary of state under Lincoln; Wilson would be elected vice president in 1872.

[2]Senator Robert Toombs of Georgia.

36

The Debate at Jonesboro

September 15, 1858

At Freeport, Douglas had to respond quickly to Lincoln's questions. At Jonesboro, Lincoln responded to Douglas's Freeport answers. Douglas in turn responded to Lincoln. This debate sets out their full views on Dred

Paul M. Angle, *Created Equal? The Complete Lincoln-Douglas Debates of 1858* (Chicago: University of Chicago Press, 1958), 215–20, 229–31.

Scott *and the ability of citizens or politicians to resist or reject a decision by the U.S. Supreme Court.*

Lincoln

At Freeport I answered several interrogatories that had been propounded to me by Judge Douglas at the Ottawa meeting.[1] . . . At the same time, I propounded four interrogatories to him. . . .

The second interrogatory that I propounded to him, was this:

Q. 2. Can the people of a United States territory, in any lawful way. against the wish of any citizen of the United States, exclude slavery from its limits prior to the formation of a state constitution?

To this Judge Douglas answered that they can lawfully exclude slavery from the territory prior to the formation of a constitution. He goes on to tell us how it can be done. As I understand him, he holds that it can be done by the territorial legislature refusing to make any enactments for the protection of slavery in the territory, and especially by adopting unfriendly legislation to it. For the sake of clearness I state it again; that they can exclude slavery from the territory, 1st, by withholding what he assumes to be an indispensable assistance to it the way of legislation; and 2d, by unfriendly legislation. If I rightly understand him, I wish to ask your attention for a while to his position.

In the first place, the Supreme Court of the United States has decided that any congressional prohibition of slavery in the territories is unconstitutional—that they have reached this proposition as a conclusion from their former proposition that the Constitution of the United States expressly recognizes property in slaves, and from that other constitutional provision that no person shall be deprived of property without due process of law. Hence they reach the conclusion that as the Constitution of the United States expressly recognizes property in slaves, and prohibits any person from being deprived of property without due process of law, to pass an act of Congress by which a man who owned a slave on one side of a line would be deprived of him if he took him on the other side, is depriving him of that property without due process of law. That I understand to be the decision of the Supreme Court. I understand also that Judge Douglas adheres most firmly to that decision; and the difficulty is, how is it possible for any power to exclude slavery from the territory unless in violation of that decision? That is the difficulty.

[1]The debate at Ottawa, Illinois, took place on August 21, 1858.

In the Senate of the United States, in 1856, Judge Trumbull[2] in a speech, substantially if not directly, put the same interrogatory to Judge Douglas, as to whether the people of a territory had the lawful power to exclude slavery prior to the formation of a constitution? Judge Douglas then answered at considerable length, and his answer will be found in the *Congressional Globe*, under date of June 9th, 1856. The Judge[3] said that whether the people could exclude slavery prior to the formation of a constitution or not *was a question to be decided by the Supreme Court*. He put that proposition, as will be seen by the *Congressional Globe*, in a variety of forms, all running to the same thing in substance—that it was a question for the Supreme Court. I maintain that when he says, after the Supreme Court have decided the question, that the people may yet exclude slavery by any means whatever, he does virtually say, that it is *not* a question for the Supreme Court. He shifts his ground. I appeal to you whether he did not say it was a question for the Supreme Court. Has not the Supreme Court decided that question? When he now says the people *may* exclude slavery, does he not make it a question for the people? Does he not virtually shift his ground and say that it is *not* a question for the Court, but for the people? This is a very simple proposition—a very plain and naked one. It seems to me that there is no difficulty in deciding it. In a variety of ways he said that it was a question for the Supreme Court. He did not stop then to tell us that whatever the Supreme Court decides the people can by withholding necessary "police regulations" keep slavery out. He did not make any such answer. I submit to you now, whether the new state of the case has not induced the Judge to sheer away from his original ground. Would not this be the impression of every fair-minded man?

I hold that the proposition that slavery cannot enter a new country without police regulations is historically false. It is not true at all. I hold that the history of this country shows that the institution of slavery was originally planted upon this continent *without* these "police regulations" which the Judge now thinks necessary for the actual establishment of it. Not only so, but is there not another fact—how came this *Dred Scott* decision to be made? It was made upon the case of a negro being taken and actually held in slavery in Minnesota Territory, claiming his freedom because the act of Congress prohibited his being so held there. *Will the Judge pretend that Dred Scott was not held there without police*

---

[2]Like Douglas, Senator Lyman Trumbull had served on the Illinois Supreme Court. Thus Lincoln refers to him as Judge Trumbull.

[3]"The Judge" throughout the rest of Lincoln's speech is Douglas.

regulations? There is at least one matter of record as to his having been held in slavery in the territory, not only without police regulations, but in the teeth of congressional legislation supposed to be valid at the time. This shows that there is vigor enough in slavery to plant itself in a new country even against unfriendly legislation. It takes not only law but the *enforcement* of law to keep it out. That is the history of this country upon the subject.

I wish to ask one other question. It being understood that the Constitution of the United States guarantees property in slaves in the territories, if there is any infringement of the right of that properly, would not the United States courts, organized for the government of the territory, apply such remedy as might be necessary in that case? It is a maxim held by the courts, that there is no wrong without its remedy; and the courts have a remedy for whatever is acknowledged and treated as a wrong.

Again: I will ask you my friends, if you were elected members of the legislature, what would be the first thing you would have to do before entering upon your duties? *Swear to support the Constitution of the United States.* Suppose you believe, as Judge Douglas does, that the Constitution of the United States guarantees to your neighbor the right to hold slaves in that territory—that they are his properly—how can you clear your oaths unless you give him such legislation as is necessary to enable him to enjoy that property? What do you understand by supporting the constitution of a state or of the United States? Is it not to give such constitutional helps to the rights established by that constitution as may be practically needed? Can you, if you swear to support the constitution, and believe that the constitution establishes a right, clear your oath, without giving it support? Do you support the constitution if, knowing or believing there is a right established under it which needs specific legislation, you withhold that legislation? Do you not violate and disregard your oath? I can conceive of nothing plainer in the world. There can be nothing in the words "support the constitution," if you may run counter to it by refusing support to any right established under the constitution. And what I say here will hold with still more force against the Judge's doctrine of "unfriendly legislation." How could you, having sworn to support the constitution, and believing it guaranteed the right to hold slaves in the territories, assist in legislation *intended* to defeat that right? That would be violating your own view of the constitution. Not only so, but if you were to do so, how long would it take the courts to hold your votes unconstitutional and void? Not a moment. . . .

At the end of what I have said here I propose to give the Judge my fifth interrogatory which he may take and answer at his leisure. My fifth interrogatory is this: If the slaveholding citizens of a United States territory should need and demand congressional legislation for the protection of their slave property in such territory, would you, as a member of Congress, vote for or against such legislation? . . .

Douglas

Mr. Lincoln has framed another question, propounded it to me, and desired my answer. . . . I will answer his question. It is as follows: "If the slaveholding citizens of a United States territory should need and demand congressional legislation for the protection of their slave property in such territory, would you, as a member of Congress, vote for or against such legislation?" . . .

. . . My doctrine is, that even taking Mr. Lincoln's view that the decision recognizes the right of a man to carry his slaves into the territories of the United States, if he pleases, yet after he gets there he needs affirmative law to make that right of any value. The same doctrine not only applies to slave property, but all other kinds of property. Chief Justice Taney places it upon the ground that slave property is on an equal footing with other property. Suppose one of your merchants should move to Kansas and open a liquor store; he has a right to take groceries and liquors there, but the mode of selling them, and the circumstances under which they shall be sold, and all the remedies must be prescribed by local legislation, and if that is unfriendly it will drive him out just as effectually as if there was a constitutional provision against the sale of liquor. So the absence of local legislation to encourage and support slave property in a territory excludes it practically just as effectually as if there was a positive constitutional provision against it. Hence, I assert that under the *Dred Scott* decision you cannot maintain slavery a day in a territory where there is an unwilling people and unfriendly legislation. If the people are opposed to it, our right is a barren, worthless, useless right, and if they are for it, they will support and encourage it. We come right back, therefore, to the practical question, if the people of a territory want slavery they will have it, and if they do not want it you cannot force it on them. And this is the practical question, the great principle upon which our institutions rest. I am willing to take the decision of the Supreme Court as it was pronounced by that august tribunal without stopping to inquire whether I would have decided that way or not. I have had many a decision made against me on questions of law which I did not like, but I was bound by them just as much as if I had had a hand in making them, and approved them. Did you ever see a lawyer or a client lose his case that he approved the decision of the court. They always think the decision unjust when it is given against them. In a government of laws like ours we must sustain the Constitution as our fathers made it, and maintain the rights of the states as they are guaranteed under the Constitution, and then we will have peace and harmony between the different states and sections of this glorious Union.

Congressional Debate

Chief Justice Roger B. Taney died on October 12, 1864. The Civil War was still raging, although the U.S. government was moving toward its ultimate victory that would preserve the nation. During the war Taney had written a number of decisions designed to impede the war effort.

On February 23, 1865, Senator Lyman Trumbull of Illinois offered a bill to appropriate money for a bust of Taney, to be placed in the Supreme Court chambers, which was located in the basement of the Senate. Trumbull was no fan of Taney or the Dred Scott *decision. As a lawyer in the 1840s Trumbull had argued on behalf of slaves in Illinois. He was an early Republican and the author of the Thirteenth Amendment, then pending before the states. That amendment, which the states ratified in December 1865, prohibited all slavery in the United States. But despite his opposition to slavery, Trumbull believed that Taney deserved the same honors accorded other deceased chief justices. Charles Sumner of Massachusetts, who was probably the most radically egalitarian member of the Senate, objected. He believed that Taney had dishonored his office and betrayed the Constitution. Sumner compared Taney to Lord Jeffreys, one of the most hated and tyrannical judges in English history. Sumner's objection led to a brief but intense debate over the merits of Chief Justice Taney. Supporting Taney was Senator Reverdy Johnson, a conservative, proslavery Democrat from Maryland who had argued the* Dred Scott *case in the Supreme Court. In portions of the debate not reprinted here, Senator John P. Hale of New Hampshire, a lifelong opponent of slavery, opposed erecting a bust for Taney because he believed that doing so would imply acceptance of the* Dred Scott *decision. Similarly, Benjamin F. Wade, a staunchly abolitionist senator, suggested that his Ohio constituents would "pay $2,000 to hang this man in effigy rather than $1,000 for a bust to commemorate his merits."*

Congress did not appropriate money for a bust of Taney in 1865. How-ever, after the death of his successor, Chief Justice Salmon P. Chase, Con-gress appropriated money for busts of both men.

37

CONGRESSIONAL GLOBE

Bust of Chief Justice Taney
February 23, 1865

Mr. Trumbull: I move now to proceed to the consideration of House bill No. 748.

Mr. Sumner: What is that?

Mr. Trumbull: A bill providing for a bust of the late Chief Justice Taney, to be placed in the Supreme Court Room of the United States.

Mr. Sumner: I object to that; that now an emancipated country should make a bust to the author of the Dred Scott decision. . . .

Mr. Trumbull: I trust the bill will be taken up; that a person who has presided over the Supreme Court of the United States for more than a quarter of a century, and has added reputation to the character of the judiciary of the United States throughout the world is not to be hooted down by an exclamation that the country is to be emancipated. Suppose he did make a wrong decision. No man is infallible. He was a great and learned and an able man. I trust the Senate will take up the bill, and not only take it up, but pass it.

Mr. Sumner: The Senator from Illinois says that this idea of a bust is not to be hooted down. Let me tell that Senator that the name of Taney is to be hooted down the page of history. Judgment is beginning now; and an emancipated country will fasten upon him the stigma which he deserves. The Senator says that he for twenty-five years administered justice. He administered justice at last wickedly, and degraded the judi-ciary of the country, and degraded the age.

Congressional Globe, February 23, 1865, 1012–17.

Mr. Johnson: I cannot fail to express my astonishment at the course of the honorable Senator from Massachusetts, which he thinks it, I suppose, his duty to pursue. Sir, if the times in which we are living are honestly and truly recorded by the historian, I think the honorable member from Massachusetts will be very happy if he stands as pure and as high upon the historic page as the learned judge who is now no more.

The honorable member seems to suppose that the decision in the *Dred Scott* case was a decision of the Chief Justice alone. It was not so. In that decision a majority of the court concurred. Whether that decision is right or not, permit me to say to the honorable member there are men belonging to the profession at least his equals, who think it to have been right; but whether right or wrong, those who knew the moral character of the Chief Justice as well as I did would blush to say that his name is to be execrated among men. Sir, the decisions of that learned jurist are now quoted with approbation everywhere, and there is not a judge upon the bench now, three or four of them having been selected by the present incumbent of the presidential office, who will not say at once that a brighter intellect never adorned the judicial station. But it is a matter of history. Every judge who has been at the head of that tribunal has his bust placed in that court-room. Does the honorable member wish to have it unknown in future times that there was such a Chief Justice? I suppose he does; I presume he does; and why? Because he differed with him. If so, to be consistent, he will be compelled to wish that two thirds of the profession in the United States, and two thirds of the country, should be forgotten in all after time, for I am sure I am not mistaken in supposing that at least that number will be found in opposition to the peculiar opinions of the honorable member from Massachusetts. . . .

Mr. Summer: . . . I know well the trivial apology which may be made for this proposition, and the Senator from Maryland [Mr. Johnson] has already shown something of the hardihood with which it may be defended. But in the performance of public duty I am indifferent to both.

The apology is too obvious. "Nothing but good of the dead." This is a familiar saying, which, to a certain extent, may be acknowledged. But it is entirely inapplicable when statues and busts are proposed in honor of the dead. Then, at least, truth must prevail.

If a man has done evil during life he must not be complimented in marble. And if indiscreetly it is proposed to decree such a signal honor, then the evil he has done must be exposed; nor shall any false delicacy seal my lips. It is not enough that he held high place, that he enjoyed worldly honors, or was endowed with intellectual gifts.

Who wickedly is wise, or madly brave,
Is but the more a fool, the more a knave.[1]

What is the office of Chief Justice, if it has been used to betray Human Rights? The crime is great according to the position of the criminal.

If you were asked, sir, to mention the incident of our history previous to the rebellion which was in all respects most worthy of condemnation, most calculated to cause the blush of shame, and most deadly in its consequences, I do not doubt that you would say the *Dred Scott* decision, and especially the wicked opinion of the Chief Justice on that occasion. I say this with pain. I do not seek this debate. But when a proposition is made to honor the author of this wickedness with a commemorative bust, at the expense of the country, I am obliged to speak plainly.

I am not aware that the English judges who decided contrary to Liberty in the case of ship-money, and thus sustained the king in those pretensions which ended in civil war, have ever been commemorated in marbled.[2] I am not aware that Jeffreys, Chief Justice and Chancellor of England, famous for his talents as for his crimes, has found any niche in Westminster Hall[.] No, sir. They have been left to the judgment of history, and there I insist that Taney shall be left in sympathetic companionship. Each was the tool of unjust power. But the Power which Taney served was none other than that Slave Power which has involved the country in war.

I speak what cannot be denied when I declare that the opinion of the Chief Justice in the case of Dred Scott was more thoroughly abominable than anything of the kind in the history of courts. Judicial baseness reached its lowest point on that occasion. You have not forgotten that terrible decision where a most unrighteous judgment was sustained by a falsification of history. Of course the Constitution of the United States and every principle of Liberty was falsified, but historical truth was falsified also. I have here the authentic report of the case, from which it

---

[1]Alexander Pope, "Essay on Man," in *Alexander Pope*, ed. Pat Rogers, Epistle IV, lines 231–32 (New York: Oxford University Press, 1993), 305.

[2]In 1634 and 1635 King Charles I issued writs to raise money for constructing ships for the British navy. Many Englishmen considered this tax illegal because it was raised without an act of Parliament. In 1636 John Hampden refused to pay the tax, but in *Hampden's Case, or the Case of the Ship Money*, 3 Howell's State Trials 825 (1637), an English court upheld the tax by a vote of seven to five. As one scholar has concluded, "The case of the ship-money finally wrecked the reputation of the bench, at least in this generation, and brought on their impeachment in the summer of 1641." J. P. Kenyon, *The Stuart Constitution, 1603–1688: Documents and Commentary*, 2nd ed. (Cambridge: Cambridge University Press, 1986), 90–91. The Long Parliament, which impeached the justices, reversed this decision, declaring the tax to have been illegal.

appears that the Chief Justice, while enforcing his unjust conclusion which was to blast a whole race, used the following language:

> It is difficult at this day to realize the state of public opinion in relation to that unfortunate race, which prevailed in the civilized and enlightened portions of the world *at the time of the Declaration of Independence, and when the Constitution of the United States was framed and adopted. But the public history of every European nation displays it in a manner too plain to be mistaken.*
>
> They had for more than a century before been regarded as beings of an inferior order and altogether unfit to associate with the white race, either in social or political relations; *and so far inferior that they had no rights which the white man was bound to respect,* and that the negro might justly and lawfully be reduced to slavery for his benefit.—19 *Howard's Reports,* 407.

In these words, solemnly and authoritatively uttered by the Chief Justice of the United States, humanity and truth were set at naught, and the whole country was humbled. "Then you and I and all of us fell down while bloody *slavery* flourished over us."

I quote his words fully so that there can be no mistake. Here then is his expressed assertion, that at the Declaration of Independence in 1776, and the adoption of the national Constitution in 1789, in Europe as well as in our own country, "colored men had no rights which white men were bound to respect." Now, sir, this is false—atrociously false. It is notorious that there were States of the Union where, at the adoption of the Constitution, colored persons were free, and even in the enjoyment of the electoral franchise, while in England the *Somersett* case[3] had already decided that there could be no distinction of persons on account of color, and Scotland, Holland, and France had all declared the same rule. On this point there can be no question. And yet this Chief Justice, whom you propose to honor with a marble bust, had the unblushing effrontery to declare that at that time, as well abroad as at home, "colored men had no rights which white men were bound to respect"; and this he said in order to justify a wicked interpretation of the Constitution. Search the judicial annals and you will find no perversion of truth more flagrant.

Sir, it is not fit, it is not decent, that such a person should be commemorated by a vote of Congress; especially at this time when liberty is at last recognized. If you have money to appropriate in this way, let it be

---

[3] *Somerset v. Stewart,* 1 Lofft (G.B.) 1 (1772).

in honor of the defenders of liberty now gathered to their fathers. There was John Quincy Adams. There also was Joshua R. Giddings.[4] Let their busts be placed in the court-room, if you please, where with marble lips they can plead always for human rights and teach judge and advocate the glory and the beauty of justice. Then will you do something not entirely unworthy of a regenerated land; something which will be an example for future times; something which will help to fix the standard of history.

I know that in the court-room there are busts of the other Chief Justices. Very well. So in the hall of the doges, at Venice, there are pictures of all who filled that high office in unbroken succession, with the exception of Marino Faliero, who, although as venerable from years as Taney, was deemed unworthy of a place in that lines.[5] Where his picture should have been there was a vacant space which testified always to the justice of the republic. Let such a vacant space in our courtroom testify to the justice of our Republic. Let it speak in warning to all who would betray liberty. . . .

Mr. Trumbull: . . . The Senator [Charles Sumner] talks about honoring Roger B. Taney. Sir, Roger B. Taney has passed beyond your assaults or your honors. He has gone where the feelings of hate and animosity or love and affection can reach him no more; and I for one am not for undertaking to follow a departed brother into that other world for the purpose of denouncing him. I agree that the decision in the *Dred Scott* case was wrong. I always thought so. The Senator has read from it, and he says that the late Chief Justice made a mistake as to the truth of history, that he made a statement in regard to the condition of the negro at the time of the Declaration of Independence which was not true. Suppose he did; what has that to do with the question of preserving in the Supreme Court of the United States busts of the Chief Justices of that court? Every man who has presided over that eminent tribunal from the foundation of the Government has had his bust preserved in marble. It

---

[4]John Quincy Adams (1767–1848) retired from politics after Andrew Jackson defeated him in the 1828 presidential election, but in 1831 he returned to the House of Representatives, where he remained until his death. In the House Adams became an unrelenting foe of slavery and the increasing demands of the South to protect its peculiar institution. The other leading antislavery voice in the House was Joshua Reed Giddings (1795–1864). In the 1830s and 1840s, mainstream politicians considered both congressmen dangerous troublemakers, but by the end of the Civil War most northerners saw them as prophets and visionaries who understood, long before the rest of the nation did, the dangers of slavery.

[5]Faliero was executed in 1355 for attempting to overthrow the Venetian Republic and make himself dictator. See Guido Ruggiero, *Violence in Early Renaissance Venice* (New Brunswick: Rutgers University Press, 1980), 3–5.

is proposed to continue that custom. Chief Justice Taney presided there for a long time; Marshall himself did not sit there much longer. I will not undertake to institute a comparison between Marshall and Taney. They were great men, both of them, great jurists, and each has shed luster upon the judicial tribunal over which he presided. Each was a man of great ability, of great learning, of great purity of character, and I am sorry that the Senator from Massachusetts should come in with this denunciation of a man against whom he can find no fault except that he made an erroneous decision. If the Senator from Massachusetts [Charles Sumner] had presided, or should ever preside over the Supreme Court of the United States for thirty years, he would be more than man if he did not make any erroneous decision.

4

Reversing *Dred Scott*:
Formal Constitutional Change

Chief Justice Taney's opinion was based on the premise that slavery was a specially protected form of private property and that blacks could never be considered American citizens or have rights under the Constitution. During the Civil War, Congress and the president completely ignored the Court's decision. Thus, in the First and Second Confiscation Acts, passed in 1861 and 1862, Congress empowered the Army to free slaves under certain conditions. In 1862 Congress ended slavery in the District of Columbia and in the federal territories, provided for the enlistment of black soldiers, and prohibited army officers from returning fugitive slaves. Similarly, in the summer of 1861 the War Department authorized U.S. military officers to emancipate slaves who escaped from Confederate masters, and on January 1, 1863, President Lincoln declared that all slaves in the Confederacy were free.

These statutes and executive branch acts undermined slavery and the *Dred Scott* decision but left open the possibility that a future Congress or president might reverse them or that the Supreme Court might find them unconstitutional. Between 1865 and 1870 Congress passed and the states ratified three new constitutional amendments to permanently end slavery and to undo the damage of *Dred Scott*.

38

The Thirteenth Amendment

1865

1: Neither slavery nor involuntary servitude, except as a punishment for crime whereof the party shall have been duly convicted, shall exist within the United States, or any place subject to their jurisdiction.

2: Congress shall have power to enforce this article by appropriate legislation.

U.S. Constitution, Amendment XIII, 1865.

39

The Fourteenth Amendment

1868

1: All persons born or naturalized in the United States, and subject to the jurisdiction thereof, are citizens of the United States and of the State wherein they reside. No State shall make or enforce any law which shall abridge the privileges or immunities of citizens of the United States; nor shall any State deprive any person of life, liberty, or property, without due process of law; nor deny to any person within its jurisdiction the equal protection of the laws.

2: Representatives shall be apportioned among the several States according to their respective numbers, counting the whole number of persons in each State, excluding Indians not taxed. But when the right to vote at any election for the choice of electors for President and Vice President of the United States, Representatives in Congress, the Executive and Judicial officers of a State, or the members of the Legislature thereof, is denied to any of the male inhabitants of such State, being

U.S. Constitution, Amendment XIV, 1868.

twenty-one years of age, and citizens of the United States, or in any way abridged, except for participation in rebellion, or other crime, the basis of representation therein shall be reduced in the proportion which the number of such male citizens shall bear to the whole number of male citizens twenty-one years of age in such State.

3: No person shall be a Senator or Representative in Congress, or elector of President and Vice President, or hold any office, civil or military, under the United States, or under any State, who, having previously taken an oath, as a member of Congress, or as an officer of the United States, or as a member of any State legislature, or as an executive or judicial officer of any State, to support the Constitution of the United States, shall have engaged in insurrection or rebellion against the same, or given aid or comfort to the enemies thereof. But Congress may by a vote of two-thirds of each House, remove such disability.

4: The validity of the public debt of the United States, authorized by law, including debts incurred for payment of pensions and bounties for services in suppressing insurrection or rebellion, shall not be questioned. But neither the United States nor any State shall assume or pay any debt or obligation incurred in aid of insurrection or rebellion against the United States, or any claim for the loss or emancipation of any slave; but all such debts, obligations and claims shall be held illegal and void.

5: The Congress shall have power to enforce, by appropriate legislation, the provisions of this article.

40

The Fifteenth Amendment

1870

1: The right of citizens of the United States to vote shall not be denied or abridged by the United States or by any State on account of race, color, or previous condition of servitude.

2: The Congress shall have power to enforce this article by appropriate legislation.

U.S. Constitution, Amendment XV, 1870.

A Chronology of Events
Related to *Dred Scott*
(1787–1876)

1787   The Northwest Ordinance prohibits slavery in the American territories north and west of the Ohio River. This includes Illinois and part of present-day Minnesota, where Scott would live for a time.

1795–
1801   Dred Scott born in Virginia sometime during this period.

1818   Illinois enters the Union as a free state.

Peter Blow moves from Virginia to Alabama, taking his slave Dred Scott with him.

1820   The Missouri Compromise prohibits slavery in the territories north and west of the state of Missouri. This territory includes the present-day state of Minnesota, where Dred Scott will live in the 1830s.

1824   In the case of *Winny v. Whitesides*, the Missouri Supreme Court declares that slaves become free by living in Illinois or any other free jurisdiction.

1830   Peter Blow moves to St. Louis, Missouri, taking his slave Dred Scott with him.

1831   *January*   The Boston abolitionist William Lloyd Garrison begins publishing the *Liberator*, signaling the beginning of a new and aggressive antislavery movement.

August   In Virginia the slave Nat Turner leads a bloody rebellion that terrifies much of the South.

1832   Peter Blow, Dred Scott's owner, dies.

1832
or
1833   Dr. John Emerson, an army surgeon, purchases Dred Scott from the estate of Peter Blow.

1833   Dr. Emerson is assigned to military duty at Fort Armstrong, Illinois, a free state. He takes Dred Scott with him.

1836   A Missouri court rules in *Rachael v. Walker* that the slave Rachael became free when her master took her to military bases in the North and to federal territories where slavery was prohibited.

April 20   Congress establishes the Wisconsin Territory, applying the slavery prohibition of the Northwest Ordinance to the new territory. The Wisconsin Territory includes the present-day state of Minnesota.

May   Dr. Emerson moves to his new assignment at Fort Snelling in the Wisconsin Territory, bringing Dred Scott with him.

The Texas revolution leads to the independent Republic of Texas, which immediately seeks admission into the Union as a slave state.

1836 or 1837   Dred Scott and Harriet Robinson are formally married at Fort Snelling.

1837   *October*   Dr. Emerson moves from Fort Snelling to St. Louis. He leaves the Scotts at Fort Snelling, where they are rented out.

November   Dr. Emerson transferred to Fort Jesup, Louisiana.

1838   *February*   Dr. Emerson marries Irene Sanford.
Dred Scott and his wife spend five months in Louisiana.

1838– 1840   Dr. Emerson reassigned to Fort Snelling. The Scotts go back to Fort Snelling on a Mississippi River steamboat. While on the boat north of the state of Missouri, with the free state of Illinois on one side and the free territory of Wisconsin on the other, Harriet Scott gives birth to her first child, Eliza.

1840   Dr. Emerson reassigned to Florida during the Second Seminole War. The Scotts sent to St. Louis.

1842   Dr. Emerson, discharged from the army, moves to the free territory of Iowa. The Scotts remain in St. Louis.

1843   *December*   Dr. Emerson dies. Irene Emerson becomes his heir and executrix.

1845   Texas admitted to the Union as a slave state.

1846– 1847   The Mexican-American War leads to the acquisition of new territories in the West and reignites the issue of slavery in the western territories. Congress debates but does not pass the Wilmot Proviso, which would have banned slavery in any of the newly acquired territories.

1846   Dred Scott files suit in a Missouri court to gain his freedom.

1847   Dred Scott loses in St. Louis Circuit Court on a technicality.

1848   The Missouri Supreme Court grants Scott the right to a new trial in the circuit court.

1850   In the retrial, a jury in the St. Louis Circuit Court declares Dred Scott to be free.

The Compromise of 1850 brings California into the Union as a free state but allows slavery in all of the other newly acquired western territories, including the present-day states of Utah, Nevada, New Mexico, Arizona, and Colorado. The compromise also includes a new Fugitive Slave Law, which provides federal support for the return of runaway slaves. This law increases tension in the nation over slavery, as many northerners protest the law and vow to oppose it.

1851   Mobs in Boston and Syracuse rescue fugitive slaves from custody; in Christiana, Pennsylvania, fugitive slaves resist capture, killing a slaveowner from Maryland.

1852   In *Scott v. Emerson* the Missouri Supreme Court declares Dred Scott still a slave, reversing nearly thirty years of Missouri precedents dating from *Winny v. Whitesides.*

1853   Dred Scott begins a new suit in the U.S. Circuit Court for Missouri, naming John F. A. Sanford as the defendant.

1854   Dred Scott is allowed to sue Sanford in federal court but loses when Judge Robert W. Wells directs the jury to find for Sanford.

The Kansas-Nebraska Act opens Kansas, Nebraska, and the Dakota Territories to slavery. The Republican Party emerges out of "anti-Nebraska" protest meetings throughout the North.

1855–
1856   Free-state and proslavery forces begin fighting in Kansas. A mini-civil war breaks out, known as *Bleeding Kansas.*

1856   James Buchanan elected president in a three-way race. Buchanan carries all but one southern state but wins in only five free states. The new Republican Party carries eleven free states. Buchanan is the first president elected since John Quincy Adams who does not win a majority of both the northern and the southern states.

1857   *March 4*   At his inauguration, Buchanan pledges to abide by the *Dred Scott* decision, which will be announced two days later.

March 6   Chief Justice Roger B. Taney announces the Supreme Court's 7–2 decision declaring that the ban on slavery in the territories was unconstitutional and that Dred Scott had no right to sue in federal court and was still a slave.

May 5   John Sanford dies.

May 26   Taylor Blow formally manumits Dred Scott and his family in St. Louis.

May 27   Lawyers for Calvin Chaffee claim all money that had accumulated from renting out the Scotts.

1858   *June 16*   In his "House Divided" speech, Abraham Lincoln alleges a conspiracy to force slavery on the whole nation. Lincoln asserts that the conspirators include his opponent for the U.S. Senate, Stephen A. Douglas; President James Buchanan and former President Franklin Pierce; and Chief Justice Roger B. Taney.

August–October   Abraham Lincoln debates Senator Stephen A. Douglas in Illinois during the 1858 senatorial campaign, constantly raising the *Dred Scott* case. Even though Lincoln loses the election, the campaign catapults him to the forefront of the Republican Party.

September 17   Dred Scott dies from tuberculosis.

October 16   John Brown, a northern opponent of slavery, raids the U.S. arsenal at Harpers Ferry, Virginia (now West Virginia).

1860   Abraham Lincoln elected president.

1861   The Civil War begins.

1862   Congress ends slavery in the District of Columbia and all federal territories and passes a law allowing the enlistment of black troops. In August the first black troops are mustered into the U.S. Army.

1863   Lincoln issues the Emancipation Proclamation, freeing all slaves in the Confederacy.

1864   Chief Justice Roger B. Taney dies.

1865   Senator Charles Sumner successfully opposes the placement of a bust of Taney in the Capitol.

The Thirteenth Amendment abolishes slavery, effectively mooting Chief Justice Taney's statements on the status of slavery under the Constitution.

1868   The Fourteenth Amendment gives citizenship to all people born in the United States, without regard to race. This effectively reverses Chief Justice Taney's ruling on black citizenship in *Dred Scott*.

1870   The Fifteenth Amendment prohibits discrimination in voting on the basis of race.

1876   Harriet Robinson Scott dies in St. Louis.

Questions for Consideration

1. How might Chief Justice Taney have decided the *Dred Scott* case in favor of Sanford without offending so many northerners?

2. In his "Opinion of the Court" Taney places great stress on the Declaration of Independence in interpreting the meaning of the Constitution. Is this legitimate? Is the Declaration a "legal" or "constitutional" document, or is it merely a political and polemical statement that should have no effect on our understanding of law?

3. Taney argues that, at the time of the founding, blacks had "no rights" and that they cannot be citizens of the United States. When thinking about this, consider the fact that the primary author of the Declaration of Independence, Thomas Jefferson, owned more than 150 slaves when he wrote that all people "are created equal" and "endowed by their Creator" with the rights of "Life, Liberty, and the Pursuit of Happiness." Could Jefferson and the other framers have meant to claim these rights for blacks while simultaneously enslaving them?

4. Consider the arguments of Justice Curtis that blacks voted in a number of states at the time of the founding. Does this show that the Declaration of Independence included free blacks among the "People" who were revolting against the king? If free blacks voted in some states at the time of the ratification of the Constitution, then is it plausible that they were not citizens within the meaning of the Constitution?

5. Is Abraham Lincoln correct that Taney's views on the Missouri Compromise are without any legal force because he had already determined that Dred Scott had no right to sue in a federal court? Or is Taney correct in arguing that the Court had to decide both the right of blacks to sue and the constitutionality of the Missouri Compromise?

6. James Buchanan's inaugural address may be the only time in history that a president endorsed a Supreme Court decision before it was announced. What were his motivations? Was this a wise tactic on his part?

7. In his speech on the *Dred Scott* decision, Frederick Douglass seems to welcome Taney's opinion, even though he denounces it and hates it. What is his tactic here? Does it work?

8. Is Lincoln right in the "House Divided" speech that Taney, Stephen A. Douglas, and Presidents Buchanan and Pierce were engaged in a conspiracy to nationalize slavery?

9. The *Dred Scott* case raises a very modern question about law. Should politicians ignore a Supreme Court decision if they do not agree with it? Is Lincoln arguing that Republicans should ignore Taney's decision or work to overturn it with new legislation and new appointments to the Supreme Court?

10. Many scholars consider *Dred Scott* to be the Supreme Court's "self-inflicted wound." Should the Court have risked this wound? Does the Court have an obligation to try to solve big national problems that cannot be settled by the political process?

11. The post–Civil War amendments were designed to protect black liberty after slavery and to give blacks access to the political process. These amendments formally reversed most of Chief Justice Taney's opinion. But by the early twentieth century, most southern blacks had lost the right to vote in the South, and the Supreme Court had upheld segregation. How might the amendments have been written to head off this outcome?

12. In *Dred Scott* Taney asserted that the Bill of Rights applied to the territories, which is why he ruled that it was unconstitutional to "take" Dred Scott from his owner through the Missouri Compromise. After the Spanish-American War, the Court ruled in a number of cases, known as "the Insular Cases," that the Constitution did not follow the flag to foreign territories. In the twenty-first century some scholars have argued that the Bill of Rights should apply to U.S. facilities overseas, especially the military prison at Guantánamo. Is *Dred Scott* a useful precedent for this argument?

Selected Bibliography

Allen, Austin. *Origins of the Dred Scott Case: Jacksonian Jurisprudence and the Supreme Court, 1837–1857.* Athens: University of Georgia Press, 2006.

Angle, Paul. *Created Equal? The Complete Lincoln-Douglas Debates of 1858.* Chicago: University of Chicago Press, 1958.

Bestor, Arthur. "State Sovereignty and Slavery: A Reinterpretation of Proslavery Constitutional Doctrine, 1846–1860." *Journal of the Illinois State Historical Society* 54 (1961): 117–80.

Bogen, David Skillen. "The Maryland Context of *Dred Scott*: The Decline in the Legal Status of Maryland Free Blacks, 1776–1810." *American Journal of Legal History* 34 (1990): 381–411.

Boman, Dennis K. *Lincoln's Resolute Unionist: Hamilton Gamble, Dred Scott Dissenter and Missouri's Civil War Governor.* Baton Rouge: Louisiana State University Press, 2006.

Ehrlich, Walter. *They Have No Rights: Dred Scott's Struggle for Freedom.* Westport, Conn.: Greenwood Press, 1979.

———. "Was the Dred Scott Case Valid?" *Journal of American History* 55 (1968): 256–65.

Fehrenbacher, Don E. *The Dred Scott Case: Its Significance in American Law and Politics.* New York: Oxford University Press, 1978.

———. *The Federal Government and Slavery.* Claremont, Calif.: Claremont Institute, 1984.

———. *Prelude to Greatness: Lincoln in the 1850s.* Stanford, Calif.: Stanford University Press, 1962.

Finkelman, Paul. *Defending Slavery: Proslavery Thought in the Old South.* Boston: Bedford/St. Martin's, 2003.

———. " 'Hooted Down the Page of History': Reconsidering the Greatness of Chief Justice Taney." *Journal of Supreme Court History* 1994 (1995): 83–102.

———. *An Imperfect Union: Slavery, Federalism, and Comity.* Chapel Hill: University of North Carolina Press, 1981.

———. *Slavery and the Founders: Race and Liberty in the Age of Jefferson.* 3rd ed. New York: Routledge, 2014.

———. "Was *Dred Scott* Correctly Decided? An 'Expert Report' for the Defendant." *Lewis & Clark Law Review* 12 (2008): 1219–52.

Finkelman, Paul, Jack M. Balkin, and Sandford Levinson, eds. "Symposium: 150th Anniversary of *Dred Scott.*" Special issue, *Chicago-Kent Law Review* 82, no. 1 (2006).

Finkelman, Paul, and Donald Kennon, eds. *Congress and the Crisis of the 1850's.* Athens: Ohio University Press, 2012.

Foner, Eric. *Free Soil, Free Labor, Free Men: The Ideology of the Republican Party before the Civil War.* New York: Oxford University Press, 1970.

Franklin, John Hope. *Racial Equality in America.* Chicago: University of Chicago Press, 1976.

Freehling, William W. *The Road to Disunion: Secessionists at Bay, 1776–1854.* New York: Oxford University Press, 1990.

Graber, Mark A. *Dred Scott and the Problem of Constitutional Evil.* New York: Cambridge University Press, 2006.

Huebner, Timothy S. "Roger B. Taney and the Slavery Issue: Looking beyond—and before—*Dred Scott.*" *Journal of American History* 97 (June 2010): 39–62.

———. *The Taney Court: Justices, Rulings, and Legacy.* Santa Barbara, Calif.: ABC-CLIO, 2003.

———. "The 'Unjust Judge': Roger Taney, the Slave Power, and the Meaning of Emancipation." *Journal of Supreme Court History* 40 (2015): 249–62.

Hyman, Harold M., and William M. Wiecek. *Equal Justice under Law: Constitutional Development, 1835–1875.* New York: Harper and Row, 1982.

Kaufman, Kenneth C. *Dred Scott's Advocate: A Biography of Roswell M. Field.* Columbia: University of Missouri Press, 1996.

Konig, David Thomas. "The Long Road to *Dred Scott*: Personhood and Rule of Law in the Trial Court Records of St. Louis Slave Freedom Suits." *University of Missouri, Kansas City Law Review* 75 (2006): 53–79.

Konig, David Thomas, Paul Finkelman, and Christopher Alan Bracey, eds. *The Dred Scott Case: Historical and Contemporary Perspectives on Race and Law.* Athens: Ohio University Press, 2010.

Potter, David M. *The Impending Crisis, 1848–1861.* New York: Harper and Row, 1976.

Sewell, Richard. *Ballots for Freedom: Antislavery Politics in the United States, 1837–1860.* New York: Oxford University Press, 1976.

Stampp, Kenneth. *America in 1857: A Nation on the Brink.* New York: Oxford University Press, 1990.

Swisher, Carl B. *The Taney Period, 1836–1864.* Vol. 5 of *History of the Supreme Court of the United States.* New York: Macmillan, 1974.

Vandervelde, Lea. *Mrs. Dred Scott: A Life on Slavery's Frontier.* New York: Oxford University Press, 2009.

Wiecek, William M. "Slavery and Abolition before the United States Supreme Court, 1820–1860." *Journal of American History* 65 (1978–1979): 34–59.

———. *The Sources of Antislavery Constitutionalism in America, 1760–1848.* Ithaca, N.Y.: Cornell University Press, 1977.

Winn, Kenneth H., ed. *Missouri Law and the American Conscience: Historical Rights and Wrongs.* Columbia: University of Missouri Press, 2016.

Index

abolitionist movement, 36, 129–30, 135, 143, 166–67, 171, 176
Adams, John, 175–76n10
Adams, John Quincy, 23, 220, 220n4
Adams, Samuel, 92, 92n3, 93
African Americans. *See* blacks
American Anti-Slavery Society, 166
American Revolution, 93n4
Angle, Paul M., 181n4
antislavery movement, 22–24, 135, 225
Articles of Confederation, 8

Bank of the United States, 56, 197, 199
Bickel, Alexander, 4
binding precedents, 51n35
Black, Hugo, 5
blacks. *See also* rights for free blacks; slaves
citizenship of, 48
property ownership by, 161–62
as soldiers in Civil War, 222, 228
Taney's opinion on the status of, 2, 7
Wells's determination of citizenship for, 21
Blair, Montgomery, 22–23
Bleeding Kansas, 227
Blow, Peter, 12, 17, 45, 46, 225
sons of, 2, 20, 22, 45
Blow, Taylor, 46–47, 227
Brennan, William, 5, 49n10
Brown, John, 228
Buchanan, James, 24, 42, 173, 179–80, 184, 227
Dred Scott decision and, 40–41, 84, 132, 161–62, 184–85n10
inaugural address, 39, 40–41, 163–66
Lecompton constitution and, 185n11
slavery in the territories and, 39–40, 180
Washington *Union* and, 44, 125, 150, 154, 155
Burns, Anthony, 107

Calhoun, John C., 168, 168–69n2
Campbell, John A.
background of, 24, 27, 90–91
opinion of, excerpt from, 91–94
Catron, John, 151
background of, 24, 27, 94–95
consults with president-elect Buchanan on forthcoming *Dred Scott* decision, 41
opinion of, excerpt from, 95–98
Chaffee, Calvin C., 18–19, 33, 46–47, 227

Chaffee, Irene. *See* Emerson, Irene
Charleston *Daily Courier*, 44
Charleston *Mercury*, 125, 126, 129n1, 132
responses to the *Dred Scott* decision in, 129–30
Chase, Jeremiah, 56
Chase, Salmon P., 23, 42, 52n47, 52n50, 127, 167, 216
Chicago *Tribune*, 40, 149
responses to the *Dred Scott* decision in, 149–50
Christianity, 146, 172
citizenship. *See also* Fourteenth Amendment
Civil Rights Act on, 48
Dred Scott briefs and oral arguments concerning, 23
Fourteenth Amendment on, 45
jurisdictional issues in *Dred Scott* case and, 25, 29–30
opinions of *Dred Scott* judges on, 86
Taney as attorney general on, 26
Taney's opinion on, 1, 4, 7, 29, 30–33, 58, 59, 61–63, 68–69
Wells's determination of, in *Dred Scott* case, 21
Civil Rights Act of 1866, 48
Civil War, 76, 127, 222, 228
Dred Scott case and coming of, 2, 4
Clay, Henry, 168, 168–69n2
Clinton, George, 91, 92, 92n3
Compromise of 1850, 10, 38, 169n4, 226–27
Confiscation Acts of 1861 and 1862, 222
Congress
citizenship rights and, 60
Dred Scott briefs and oral arguments on power to prohibit slavery, 23
Dred Scott case, attack of, 47–48
Dred Scott case and 1858 elections, 7, 10, 24, 41, 43
elections of 1858, 7, 10, 24, 41, 43, 178, 180n3
gag rule of, 169, 169n3
Missouri Compromise and, 9, 13
Northwest Ordinance passage by, 8
slavery in territories and, 8–12, 36
Taney's opinion on power to prohibit slavery, 1, 2, 4, 7, 36, 38, 53n71
territories clause of Constitution on power over territories, 34–35, 72
Wilmot Proviso in, 39

233